ЈА

CEVDET BAYBURTLUOĞLU

Suna & İnan Kıraç
Research Institute on Mediterranean Civilizations

ISBN 975-7078-20-4

Suna & İnan Kıraç Research Institute on Mediterranean Civilizations
Travel Guide Series: 1

Lycia
Cevdet Bayburtluoğlu

Translation by
Yaprak Erdem Georgescu

Photographs by
Cevdet Bayburtluoğlu ve AKMED arşivi.

Prepared by
Homer Kitabevi

Book Design by
Sinan Turan

Color Separation
Dört Renk Ltd. Şti.

Printed by
Barış Matbaa

First Published 2004

Suna & İnan Kıraç Research Institute On Mediterranean Civilizations
Barbaros Mah. Kocatepe Sok. No: 25 Kaleiçi 07100 - Antalya
Tel: +90 242 243 42 74
Fax: +90 242 243 80 13
e-mail: akmed@akmed.org.tr • www.akmed.org.tr

Distributed by
Homer Kitabevi ve Yayıncılık Ltd. Şti.
Yeni Çarşı Caddesi, No: 28/A, 34433, Galatasaray - İstanbul

Tel: +90 242 249 59 02 • +90 242 292 42 79
Fax: +90 242 251 39 62
e-mail: homer@homerbooks.com

Telmessos, Tomb of Amyntas ▶

My commitment to and fascination with Lycia began with my appointment to the excavations in Xanthos in 1971 a whole five decades ago, and continued with two other excavation projects; the Arykanda project, which is still underway, and the Phaselis project (1981 - 1985) that hardly even got started due to certain legal and financial constraints. I have had the chance to share with fellow travellers and readers my findings and experiences gathered from many surveys and explorations in the Lycia region in another publication: the "Lycia" guidebook printed in 1981. But, at the point where we stand today, it is my clear responsibility to write a new book, from the rich pile of notes I have kept from my visits to the area, that will also aim to cover the less well-known and less visited parts of the region. Not forgetting however, there are other reasons that make the writing of this book a must for me: The extensive new findings and the growing number of surveys in the region; the ever-increasing popular interest in Lycia backed by important recent improvements in the accommodation and transportation and the development of new and different styles of travelling.

I was searching around for a publisher while, at the same time, adding the final touches to the reports of the Arykanda excavation and I had the good luck to wonder if my new publisher could be the Suna & İnan Kıraç Research Institute on Mediterranean Civilizations (AKMED) - an outstanding institute of the Vehbi Koç Foundation, which allocates a great amount of precious time to the archaeology of the region as well as so many other cultural aspects of the area. They accepted my offer and also offered to help me out in the printing of any other books that I might have to hand at the time. This is how the institute came to publish this book that you are now holding in your hands. I would like very much to take this chance to congratulate Suna and İnan Kıraç, to whom I owe the printing of "Lycia", not only for the sake of my own publication, but also for their priceless contribution to the archaeology of the region and our country in general with all the cultural activities that the Institute - a very good example for all to follow - has so generously organized over the years.

I cannot mention all the names of those who helped me so vigorously in the typing of this book, the drawings contained and the selection of photographic media. I am grateful to each and every one of the people that helped me. If this book has pleased you at all, the pride should not go only to the author but also to Homer Publishing House and their co-workers. More gratitude is owed to Dilek Yaprak Erdem-Georgescu, the translator of this book, who, at times of severe health problems in her dear family, took all the trouble to complete the translation project. I would also like to thank John Moorcroft for his assistance in the translation.

Last but not least, I must thank Kayhan Dörtlük, Director of AKMED, for all his support and interest in the publication of this book.

Take good care of your health and do not ever forget to travel and see a lot!

Sincerely,
Cevdet Bayburtluoğlu

Arykanda, theatre

How It All Started: My Lycian Adventure And My Passion For Lycia

Myra, rock tombs

◀ *Kandyba, store*

Lycia

*A*fter days of correspondence, it was around the end of August 1954 that I finally received an invitation to participate in the excavation of the city of Xanthos (Kınık) following the excavation of the city of Phokaia.

Antiphellos, sarcophagus

On August 26, my friends who had worked with me in Phokaia, handed me a box of pastries before I waved them good-bye from aboard the "Erzurum" which was waiting at the port of Alsancak and we set out, as the 'Express Mail' service as it was, then, called. (A vessel that could make a maximum of 8 nautical miles an hour when it ran on full power and when blessed with a following wind), The Erzurum was full of emigrants headed for Israel.

Not being able to arrange a cabin, I slept outside, on the deck, on a folding bed that I had brought with me. There we were heading for the Mediterranean Sea. After two nights and three days under very difficult conditions, I landed in Antalya (although we had stopped in Fethiye) believing that it would be easier to get to the ruins of Xanthos in the village of Kınık in Kaş from here. Only after arriving in Kınık, would I find out that the most convenient means of getting to Xanthos would have been catching a bus -which rarely ran- or taking a tractor from Fethiye.

I am trying to make a major point here by telling this real life story because this is a story that young people especially should hear. Besides, I do believe that it will help both local people and visitors to get a better glimpse of the development that Turkey has achieved over the years.

Now, I will take up the story from the port of Antalya. The vessel moored offshore since it was impossible to tie up at the

Engraving of the Granary at Andriake

port, and boats carried us from the ship to the shore. It would
have been most unfeasible for me to carry the saddlebag with
the camp bed and the rest of my luggage to the city from the
old port, which happens to be the Marina today. And it sure
was rare to find a cab at that time in Antalya. Therefore, I hired
a horse and cart to take me to the bus station, which took 45
minutes. Today, you can find buses going all over the city at any
time from this very station. But then, there were only a couple
of trucks. I asked the people around about getting to Kaş only
to find out that it would be really very difficult, that the only
way was via Korkuteli-Elmalı-Gömbe to Kaş, that it would be
even harder to get to Kınık from Kaş and that I would be lucky
to catch a motorboat from Kaş to Kalkan. I was also told that a
truck was about to set out for Korkuteli. Inevitably, I got on the
truck. I suppose the road took us 5 - 6 hours for a distance which
you can cover in an hour today. Night was falling and the truck
driver stopped in front of a building and left me right there
saying that it was a good place to stay and was close to the bus
station. The receptionist studied me carefully and told me that
before going up I should take my shoes off, take up my luggage
only and leave the saddlebag downstairs as nothing would
happen to it. He, then, stowed my luggage in a corner of the

The next day, my efforts to set out for Kaş and Kınık turned fruitful as I happened to hear that a shared taxi driver, informally called "the Guy from Ankara" would leave for Gömbe in the morning and from there, perhaps, I could find a jeep for Kaş.

living room and asked me to follow him to show me the bathroom where he suggested I should have a shower to clean myself off all the dust. He added that I should find some soap in the bathroom. Only after the shower, did I understand why the receptionist was being so particular: I found the cleanest bed, which wouldn't be common even in the biggest cities of the day. The two-storey, adobe "Gül Hotel" in Korkuteli and a bed with spotless, starched linen. Astonishing!

It took me another day and a truck-ride to arrive in Elmalı from Korkuteli (45 kilometers), where I only just managed to find myself a bed at a multi-storey, adobe hotel, near the station today. I was covered in white dust from the daylong ride on a truck. After taking a shower, I tried to find something to eat and sniffed through the town to discover a plethora of meatball shops, all under a heavy cloud of barbecue smoke. I still remember Elmalı with its delicious meatballs and piyaz (a cold dish with dried beans).

The next day, my efforts to set out for Kaş and Kınık turned fruitful as I happened to hear that a shared taxi driver, informally called "the Guy from Ankara" would leave for Gömbe in the morning and from there, perhaps, I could find a jeep for Kaş. Indeed, somewhat later in the morning this shared taxi set out for Gömbe with two passengers - me being one and the other a Mr. Lami whom I would later find out to be the owner of the Plain of Kınık. It was an ancient taxi and since there were no constructed roads but only open fields, when we arrived in Gömbe, I got out a man of white hair and eyebrows. Mr. Lami was ready for the conditions on the road and was knowledgable enough to sit on the seat next to the driver where he would get the least dust. As if this was not precaution enough, he also placed his luggage on the seat right behind him to block the dust. Not only he did not allow me to sit next to him but he also denied all my requests to move his luggage one seat behind. This trip lasted until the afternoon and was heavily marked with discussions about the seating plan. At the time, Mr. Lami was

How It All Started: My Lycian Adventure And My Passion For Lycia

Bay of Antalya

in his 50's and I was quite a well-built young man in my 20's and I had all the power in my arms to squeeze Mr. Lami to his bones. It turned out quite fortunate that I did not seek to do so: When we did not focus on this duel on the seating plan, we did get a chance to talk as ordinary people do and I found out in utter astonishment that this peasant (albeit a landlord) could speak three foreign languages: Greek, Italian and English. Eventually, we got out of the taxi in Gömbe in front of an inn, which I had seen pictured in some old books, and we began to wait for a jeep. One of the peasants came up to me to see where I was trying to get to and told me that if this Mr. Lami wanted to, he could get me on the jeep even if it turned up to be all full with other passengers. This was the moment that I was grateful to God for not resorting to brute force against this man.

The trip between Gömbe and Kaş is among the first trips where I survived a fatal accident. There is no word to describe

It was an ancient taxi and since there were no constructed roads but only open fields, when we arrived in Gömbe, I got out a man of white hair and eyebrows.

Lycia

Xanthos, engraving of the Prismatic Tomb in Roman Acropolis

the way to fill a jeep with thirteen people, all their belongings and their chickens. One can only live to see it. There I was - sitting on the left of the driver, half of my body inside and the other half hanging outside the jeep. And three more people sitting on the right of the driver. The rest of the company shared the back seats together with their belongings and poultry.

The road between Gömbe and Kaş was not much different from the one between Elmalı and Gömbe: Only more bumpy. The jeep ran on fields and dry river beds. As we arrived at Sinekçi Pass, the jeep stopped at the peak. Since I was young and the other passengers could not even move from their seats, the driver picked me to get out and push the vehicle. And so I did. Of course, the jeep starting running downhill and I started running down with it but one of my feet was still on the jeep and the other was outside on the ground. I told the driver to stop the jeep but instead he replied: 'Quiet! Shut up! The brakes are loose' My only response could be to release the foot inside the jeep. - A reaction that not only released the foot but also dragged me on to the pebbles on the ground. The jeep came to a halt only 50 metres away after I ran on one foot for another 50 metres. I survived this accident with slight bruises.

But as for me, I was invited to the police headquarters as they regarded me a stranger as well as a smuggler - A problem I would resolve thanks to Mr. Lami.

It was around nine pm that I shouted 'There's Kaş!' at the sight of a brightly illuminated city. But the reaction inside the jeep showed the contrary: That was the island of Meis and Kaş would have to be the faintly illuminated city down the hill. The police stopped the jeep as we entered Kaş. Mr. Lami was a well-known figure in the area so he had no problems. But as for me, I was invited to the police headquarters as they regarded me a stranger as well as a smuggler - A problem I would resolve thanks to Mr. Lami.

Though it would be at a very late hour, we had planned to dine at the Kaş City Club located today between the Statue of Atatürk and the Port. But it was not long before we found out that we wouldn't even find a piece of bread to eat, let alone dinner in the Club. Therefore, for dinner, accompanied by a host of gnats, we gobbled up the pastry, which my friends had handed to me back in İzmir.

The next day promised some pleasant and not-so-pleasant surprises for me. Despite all my weariness, I could not skip Mr. Lami's invitation to meet in front of the City Club at eight o'clock next morning. So, I arrived at the place in time. He told me that he had managed to find a motor boat to Kalkan and that we could set out right after breakfast. The not-so-pleasant moment of this day came when we enjoyed our breakfast with a cup of tea and some savory rolls covered with sesame seeds: I read an announcement on a black billboard positioned at the heart of the city. The sign read: "Typhoid epidemic breaks out in the neighbouring town of Elmalı. All inhabitants should be vaccinated…" The idea of the meat-balls and piyaz that I had eaten with such pleasure, under the barbecue smoke in Elmalı only a couple of days ago started inundating my mind as a most dreadful reality. I quickly correlated the intestinal activity that I had been feeling for some time with the notice that I had just read. This was when I concluded, "It must be my mortal fate that dragged me here." My curiosity and passion to look around during the 4-hour motorboat trip between Kaş and Kalkan created nausea as I inhaled a considerable share of the smoke from the exhaust pipe - a fact that I only realized much later. The nausea added to my worries that I was a victim of the epidemic.

*After half an hour of walking, we arrived and
the peasant that had helped me with the
luggage warned me that people were sleeping
on the balconies so I should be careful where
I stepped while going to my room.*

At the peak of the day and the heat, we landed at Kasaba
Port where you couldn't find a single soul and the motorboat
set out on its way back to Kaş. Mr. Lami was heat-struck and
decided to visit his relatives in the town. So, there I was standing
alone on this very remote port. I had the hardest time dragging
my luggage and the saddlebag to a coffeehouse close to the
road between Fethiye and Finike. The coffeehouse was open of
course but without any clients or even the caretaker himself. It
was after six o'clock in the evening when I noticed a peasant
strolling along with his donkey and went up to greet him.

Eventually, I convinced the peasant to use his donkey to
carry my belongings for the price of a car ride - And that
included 3 to 4 hours of walking along with it. When we arrived
in Xanthos, it was around eleven o'clock. I found in the
coffeehouse my colleague, the late Mr. Ismet Ebcioğlu, who was
the excavation commissar, as we then called his position. My
suggestion to have a shower and head directly to bed met with
the reply: "We rented your room, but it is not ready yet. Tonight,
you'll stay over at the teacher's room." We made our plans for
the morning and set off for our rooms. After half an hour of
walking, we arrived and the peasant that had helped me with
the luggage warned me that people were sleeping on the
balconies so I should be careful where I stepped while going to
my room. Ultimately, I made it to the room, which was lit by a
kerosene lamp. There was a mattress on the floor that was so
worn out it was only as thin as a rug rather than a real mattress.
There was also one pillow that had turned completely brown,
as I would find out later in the daylight. Still dressed, I laid my
handkerchief on the pillow and dropped myself on the mattress
although I was covered in dust and dirt. I do remember remotely
watching the door being opened at one time and a swinger held
the kerosene lamp towards my face. Whoever it was, he laid
himself down immediately and fell asleep. And I must have sunk
into unconsciousness immediately thereafter as when I woke
up the next morning at day break, I was once again alone in
the room: The teacher had come and left again much like a
ghost.

How It All Started: My Lycian Adventure And My Passion For Lycia

PRINCIPAL ENTRANCE OF THE HARBOUR OF CACAMO.   PRINCIPALE ENTRÉE DU PORT DE CACAMO

Engraving of Simena

In fact, it is the smallest details that make all the difference: Mr. Ebcioğlu and I finally met two hours after the agreed time. We made a tour of Xanthos until the breakfast at ten o'clock and we also visited the excavation center. At this particular point, I'd like to emphasize one detail, which I would later find out to be of crucial importance for myself and the rest of the excavation team: The drinkingwater in the excavation area came from the nearby Eşen Stream. It must be noted that this stream doubled up as an alfresco public convenience on both banks.

Anyway, I was introduced to the excavation team and we exchanged information about the excavations at Phokaia and Xanthos. Soon, I was telling the team about my slight sickness and my knowledge about the typhoid epidemic in Elmalı. I also drew their attention to the fact that their drinking water exposed them to a great health risk and explained that I should see a doctor. Prof. Demargne suggested that I leave for Fethiye at once. My suggestion to return to Ankara to avoid all risks was immediately accepted. Later on, things did not work so smoothly, either, as you would expect, because the only motor vehicle, ie. the tractor, refused to work. One mishap followed another and eventually, we started looking for a horse to ride. At least, this attempt turned fruitful and we arranged for a horse around noon. The owner of the horse had been quite certain when we hired the animal that I could certainly ride on the

Lycia

ILICREAL GROTS AT THE HEAD OF THE HARBOUR OF CACAMO.   GROTTS SEPULCRALE AU HAUT DU PORT DE CACAMO.

Engraving of the Rock Tomb at Theimiussa

horse along with my luggage. Poor thing! A rather scrubby horse loaded with all my belongings, that is the luggage and the saddlebag! The stomach almost touched the ground... For the sake of safety in this trip, I had to walk alongside the horse, which I did until sunset when we reached Kestep, today called Gölbent. The owner of the horse dropped me at an isolated coffeehouse with an open door, just as the one I had seen in Kalkan. As the owner left, he did not forget to remind me that a bus heading for Fethiye would definitely stop by soon after midnight.

Listening to the tunes of crickets and grasshoppers, I took some rest until eight o'clock on my camp bed under the shadow of the oak tree by the coffee house (at the time, the whole area was lush with oak trees which are, today, too few to mention).

I still remember all so well having to tell every single client in the coffeehouse about who I was, what I did for a living and why I was there that night. After midnight, I woke up to the sound, or better the groaning, of the bus. This sound promised health, sanitation and all the means of transportation and communication again. All the passengers got on the bus, the luggage was tied up in its place and the bus set off. During the trip, everything looked fine - that is, my troubles seemed to be over - so I started to make plans to get to Fethiye and from there

> *I still remember all so well having to tell every single client in the coffeehouse about who I was, what I did for a living and why I was there that night.*

to Muğla, eventually arriving in İzmir again. This optimistic air lasted until we arrived on Fethiye plain right after Eşen. I had had the idea that there wouldn't be any more problems but there were no roads and thus, the driver was following the tire tracks that he, himself, had made on the way up. There we were going up one bank of a rather narrow dry riverbed, and the front right tire wobbled away only to fall over at a distance to the right of the bus. Therefore, the front right part of the bus landed on the ground as the bus was climbing the bank of the riverbed. I can tell you that almost all the passengers remained fast asleep. There was only one lady who was awake and I had to calm her down saying, "It's all-right. They only have to change the front tire." She immediately put her head on the shoulder of her friend and fell asleep. I helped the bus driver to fix the tire that simply abandoned us since it was not fixed well in the first place anyway. This cost us a 45-minute delay. Now, time was getting more and more important. I had a bus to catch in Fethiye at 7 a.m. the next morning so I could set out for Muğla.

We arrived at the central bus station in Fethiye just as the bus that I had to catch had left. Now that I had let life take over, I found it needless to push things too much. Arriving at this relaxed way of thinking must have had something to do with the decline in the frequency of my visiting the WC due to my sickness and that the pain in my stomach was much better now.

Apparently, I was destined to spend 24 hours in Fethiye because the next bus for Muğla was not going to leave before 7 a.m. the next morning. So, I made it to the Rize Hotel the ruins of which I would never see again after the big Fethiye earthquake in 1957. I had a shower, took some rest and decided to disinfect my intestines with the help of some banana liqueur. Only two sips and that was enough. More would be too sweet and way too much. Now, all the perils were over and I was safe again. As a matter of fact, my trip after Fethiye was similarly adventurous, as well; however, it was, basically, Lycia that brought me to the end and brought me back to life. It was beyond doubt that I would have similar adventures and the best place to have an adventure would be Lycia again.

THE PROGRESS WE ACHIEVED

Simena

◄ Andriake, Nymphaeum

Lycia

Kekova, sarcophagus

I n my early years as an archaeologist, it had taken me four days marked with all the problems and adventures you can imagine to reach Xanthos (Kınık) from Antalya.

I would have to make the exact same trip again but backwards this time, and not alone: I would be the young research assistant in charge of a whole group of students. Target: Familiarising ourselves with Western and Southwest Anatolia. Incidents or difficulties that make us lose all our patience today while travelling from Ankara to İzmir and to Fethiye were seen as nothing more than the usual and negligible handicaps of travelling at the time. For instance, you would not be surprised to witness the front tire of the bus abandoning the vehicle and continuing in a separate direction all on its own. Such were the expectation and the means that we had when our group started the exploration from Fethiye. We arrived late at night in Kınık after visiting Pınara. We visited Kınık (Xanthos) in the rain and had to sleep over faced with two big problems: Meals and accommodation. We made it to the house of Mr. Lami, with whom I had had a difficult time in my first trip to the area but later became close friends. Mr. Lami, his wife whose name I could never learn and his son Fahri, who is also deceased now, welcomed us, gave food and shelter together with all the other guests they had had received right on the eve of a religious holiday. Apart from the few students that preferred to sleep over on the bus, that night would turn out to be the last that the students participating in this utterly adventurous trip would sleep comfortably for some days to come. On the morning of the holiday, we exchanged greetings and hit the road again around 10 a.m. The trip continued without too many problems until Fırnaz (today, Yeşilköy). But adventure was imminent when we started climbing the mountains after Fırnaz. The rain getting heavier every minute had totally destroyed the road, which was already covered with mud. The rear tires that were all brand new when we set out from Ankara turned bald around midnight despite all the efforts of the students to push the bus and to cover the road with appropriate materials. The students were exhausted and so was the bus, which made me see that it was high time we slept over in a field.

By now, we had exhausted all the provisions we had brought from Kınık where we had had our last meal. I had to find something to eat and take the bus with its bald tires to Elmalı or, in fact, any place we could reach. Each one of us was equally tired but I still vividly remember the panic of hunger and exhaustion in one of the students, who is deceased now: "I am dying. My brain's not getting any blood!"

We were in serious need of food and support to push the bus. Since I had been there before, I tried to get some help with what I could remember of the area. The most difficult part about this midnight walk into the depths of a forest was trying to convince my companion not to be afraid of the barking of the sheepdogs guarding a far away flock or comforting him when he grew uneasy about the night birds flying around.

In the first field that we could find, though it was early hours of the morning by then, we were lucky enough to bump into a peasant with a donkey and to acquire some picks and shovels as well as some bread to eat. I will never forget the way that the students who were so exhausted and starving to death rushed to eat yoghurt and bread. As the saying goes: Hunger is the best sauce.

I do hope that no one will ever experience what I lived through as the leader of that team. Finally we travelled to Kaş through Elmalı over Sinekçi Pass and only there in Kaş could find bedsto sleep in for all those students who had pushed the bus along the road. And this would not have been possible if it were not for those people who left their beds so the students could sleep, in beds that were still warm with the heat of the other person. I am still thankful to the hotelkeeper and all those hotel guests that I have never seen for their great kindness that night.

The road that I have described takes no longer than an hour or an hour and half today. It is covered in asphalt and although there are some complaints about the curves in the road, today, wherever the road may take you, you are sure to find a place to eat and sleep. And this is exactly why we have to make a multi-dimensional analysis of the progress we have achieved over the years in comparison to the old times.

THE GEOGRAPHY OF LYCIA

Avlan Lake

◀ *Kyaenai, rock tomb*

*A*lthough there are a limited number of seaside plains - the products of streams and rivers - which date back only to the years after the birth of Christ, the landscape of Lycia is almost entirely rugged and generally mountainous.

Aykırıçay

I have regarded it a duty in my life to study the physical geography of Lycia (although I have studied geography academically for only a semester) and I have been able to make good use of the findings of this science to solve a great many problems encountered as part of my job.

However I could never elaborate on the formational stages of Anatolia or Lycia. Therefore, regardless of the age or ages in which the area took its current form, I can only describe the conditions that prevail today and that prevailed in ancient times. For Asia and Europe, the Himalayan Mountains, which many authors call the "Roof of the World" are the extensions of a geological formation that grew over hundreds of thousands of years. The height starting in the Himalayas circumscribes Iran to the north and the south and gathers into a knot at the Caucasus Mountains only to loosen again in Anatolia along which it runs in the shape of a pair of pincers and plunges into the either the Aegean or the Mediterranean Sea. At some point, one can see different branches of the same range creating the Alps or the south-Mediterranean Rif Mountains or the Pyrenees that draw a border in the north of the Iberian Peninsula.

I believe that Lycia lies on the fault line that starts at the Red Sea and affects the whole Western Anatolia on a south-to-north direction and therefore, the area is in constant danger. I am not a geologist, a geomorphologist or a seismologist;

> *The height starting in the Himalayas circumscribes Iran to the north and the south and gathers into a knot at the Caucasus Mountains only to loosen again in Anatolia along which it runs in the shape of a pair of pincers and plunges into the sea at either the Aegean or the Mediterranean Sea.*

however, it is my true belief that we can not afford to remain indifferent to natural disasters like the major earthquakes that hit the region almost every century. I know this well, because I was just a child in Erzincan when the earth shook claiming 39,000 lives according to the official records and I was more of an adult in the time of the Fethiye earthquake in 1957. I have to express with great sorrow that tears dry too quickly and measures that should be taken right away melt into indifference in time. I do hope that the 8 to 10-storey buildings constructed, despite the great risk, in the Lycia region today, conform to the earthquake standards. May God never give anyone any earthquakes.

Eastern Anatolia is Turkey's highland with an average altitude of over 1000 meters. However, Lycia stands as a rival to Eastern Anatolia with its sharp mountainous rises and sharp falls. Although there are a almost entirely rather limited number of seaside plains - the products of streams and rivers - which date back only to the years after the birth of Christ, the landscape of Lycia is almost entirely rugged and generally mountainous.

The major mountains in the region are Mount Tahtalı - Mount Musa, which borders the Bay of Antalya in the west, Beydağları Mountain, which runs northeast-to-southwest in Lycia, Akdağ Mountain Range, which is the eastern border of the Eşençay Valley on a north-to-south direction and the Sandal, Avdancık, Erenler Mountains, which were collectively called Massikytes in antiquity, to the west of the same valley.

The coastline was a lot different in antiquity than it is today. If we were to imagine the earlier ages in history, we would have to carry the coastline all the way to the lower slopes of the mountains. Here is an example of the amount of alluvial soil that rivers carry into the sea: The city of Myra used to be a seaport engaged in regular maritime trade with the city of Limyra - before handing the flag to the city of Andriake to be the seaport.

Lycia

Church of St. Nicholas

Consider that the Church of St. Nicholas was filled with over 5 meters of alluvial soil after its restoration in the 4th century AD and I think, you will get an idea of the terrific amount of soil carried into the sea. The same applies partly to the city of Limyra, as well. As a matter of fact, the city of Limyra has the necessary water for potential maritime transportation in the form of the river Saklısu, which springs from the skirts of Toçak Mountain. It is still navigable for a 10-meter boat (or even larger); however, the Saklısu River meanders into the Bay of Finike, difficult to enter with any boat. We believe that the city of Limyra, which organized chartered maritime transportation with the city of Myra, could not have been too far from the sea, even if using the Saklısu River for the vessels. During the Lycian League, Myra used to be known as a port city with no mention whatsoever of the city of Andriake and such was the case of Limyra too at the time: A port city not at all needing the city of Phoinikos for maritime transportation.

I would like to wrap up this topic with an even more striking example: The distance between the highest peaks in the region, namely Kızlarsivrisi (3070 m.) in Eastern Lycia and Akdağ Mountain Summit (3064 m.) in Western Lycia, and the coastline is no more than 30 to 35 kilometers - and that includes the kilometers that the winding of the actual road adds.

> *Consider that the Church of St. Nicholas was filled with over 5 meters of alluvial soil after its restoration in the 4th century AD and I think, you will get an idea of the terrifying amount of soil carried into the sea.*

(Coming down from a height of 3000 meters to level sea) There is a 70 degree slope in the first 10 kilometers and then the slope declines gradually to around 20 - 10 degrees and then to 7 - 1 degree. It rains worse than cats and dogs around the Mediterranean. These eyes of mine have seen at least 15.000 metre cubes of solid rocks and soil being washed away to the sea in a matter of less than an hour by flooding waters from Şahinkaya. We had spent 4 years carrying that soil to fill up a dry riverbed.

I would like to relate one of my memories: I finished my business in a certain public office, as well as my shopping and told the excavation team that I would be back after taking a few photographs of the city of Limyra. I was busy taking the photographs but couldn't help noticing black clouds gathering on top of the Aykırıçay Valley and Alacadağ Mountain. I thought - and hoped - that they would stop work before the rain came on. I was soaked, myself, around the Theater of Limyra. When I finally made it to the Excavation Center, the weather was beautifully sunny again but since the excavation team had no place at all to shelter from the rain on the road between the ruins and the Excavation Center, a matter of 20 to 25 minutes was more than enough to soak the team so seriously that even their wristwatches were full of water. I still regret very much that for whatever reason, I did not take a photo of the wristwatch hanging and drying along with some laundry on the line.

As I have told you before, Lycia has a rich variety of flora and natural landscape -especially, if we include Milyas and Kibyratis in the region. The flora of any area can be expected to generally reflect the wider region, and you won't be surprised to find indications of both the Mediterranean and the continental climates in Lycia. Eastern Lycia has a rather rugged landscape but a Mediterranean climate and typical Mediterranean flora is dense from the shoreline permeating deep inland until Korkuteli, thanks to the shape of the Alakır Valley. The Mediterranean climate could have permeated even

> *The pines start right at the shoreline turning into forests of larch, juniper, Scots pine and eventually, cedar of Lebanon ("Cedrus Libanesis") as the altitude rises.*

further to the north of Korkuteli if only Çürükdağ Mountain, an extension of Beydağları Mountains, did not lie east-to-west as a natural barrier. Eastern Lycia is a region where the geological structure allows the Mediterranean climate to move freely inland, where there is plenty of water - and right at ground level - and where the general landscape is lush with the calabrian pine forests adorned with the bushes typical of the region. The pines start right at the shoreline turning into forests of larch, juniper, Scots pine and eventually, cedar of Lebanon ("Cedrus Libanesis") as the altitude rises. As the valleys of Alakır and Aykırıçay expand and rise north towards the inner parts of the region, they are among the few places on earth where citrus fruits grow naturally at an altitude of 650 meters!

The coastline of Central Lycia from the west of Finike to the Plain of Kınık however is a considerably difficult region with a serious lack of water resources. Amazingly, fresh water springs from the mountains came to the surface at sea level between Myra and Patara in the form of a fount or a spring or they spring from the middle of the sea as if it were a swimming pool. Furthermore, inland Central Lycia sees a real threat not only to human life but also to the flora in the region due to the excessive use of agricultural growth hormones in greenhouses for the last 30 years.

Both the Eastern and Western Lycia regions possess more regular water systems, if nothing else. The Alakır Stream, Saklısu (Limyros), Başgöz or Aykırıçay (Arykandos) are but a few to mention. In the west, Eşençay (Xanthos), Dalaman Stream (Indos) on the border with Karia and a few other rivers running into the Bay of Fethiye meet the agricultural water needs of the region as well as adding to the natural beauty. However, it is almost impossible to find a river or stream in the Central Lycia that won't dry out during the long summer months. The area certainly gets its share of seasonal showers though and is covered with dry riverbeds where, when it rains, the water simply sweeps away the bridges over them. But in general starting at the end of July, you would be lucky to find any water in these riverbeds (such as Demre or Myros Stream).

Finike

The flora in Lycia has gone through a radical change during the last 30 to 40 years. Although some parts of the area are still rich with calabrian pine forests that are typical to the region and that come down to the coast line, this has only been possible thanks to sheer luck in one hand and environmental protection laws on the other. Vegetables such as tomatoes and potatoes may have made their way to the Old World only after the discovery of America by Christopher Columbus; but, I sincerely believe that even if the citrus fruits - the characteristic fruits of the Mediterranean climate - may have originated in America, they could have existed in this region since the beginning of time as these fruits can grow anywhere in the warm "Mediterranean Climate". Birds and insects have always been the voluntary cross-continental carriers of many seeds in their excrement. Now, we couldn't possibly expect them to make a discrimination between species and not swallow the seeds of citrus fruits, in particular, so that Columbus will have that honour, could we? I am far from being a palaeobotanist; however, I defend my ideas until reaching some sort of a sound outcome. Let's go back to Lycia and the citrus fruits: In 1950's, the plains of Fethiye and Finike were studded with lemon and orange trees. In the aftermath of the WW2, the value of the cotton plant - another typical produce of the Mediterranean climate - doubled as its seeds gained importance in addition to its fiber. I had to witness all those gardens lush with lemon and orange trees turn one by one into cotton plantations. Crops

Lycia

Aykırıçay

that are in worldwide demand and, therefore, bring wealth to the producer, are concurrently grown in a variety of countries. Thus, the whole agricultural philosophy is based on fruits and vegetables that promise wealth. Even today, you can see some of the lemon or orange gardens being converted into greenhouses or cotton fields when cultivation of these produces seem lucrative. I do hope that in a few years, not only the landowners but also the government will pay heed to the cries of the mother earth that brings us wealth and returns our expectations with three to four rounds of crops annually. I hope the government will start to come up with a more sound agricultural policy sometime.

Since antiquity, Lycia has placed its bet on forests as the major source of income. Lycia is not only picturesque with its forests that contain all types of pines - Scots pine, spruce, oak, beech and naturally grown Cedars of Lebanon -("Cedrus Libanesis") - but can be really rich with its forestry products, if operated rationally. Only when we cherish the understanding that trees are not merely timber or wood to burn for heat, can we both save our forests from becoming targets of fire to benefit a handful of individuals or families, and make a dreamland of forests where the green never ends and a much larger range of income is acquired - and with less effort. Narrated in a book like the one that you are holding the ideas and aspirations of an archaeologist who lives in forests only during various excavations can best be summed up in this way.

The wildlife of Lycia is a phenomenon that should be thought of as an integral part of the forest, of nature. Wildlife and forest complement each other. The forest fires don't only destroy the forest, but they also destroy the forest wildlife, the animals themselves, and their habitat, along with the trees. As if the fire were not fatal enough, the irrational shooting of the endangered species under protection kills twice: The mothers and their young still needing their mothers' feeding to survive. To give you an idea about the magnitude of this slaughter: In 1971 when I started the excavation of the city of Arykanda, however distant on the slopes of Şahinkaya, we could still spot small herds of wild goat or deer. It was also fascinating to hear and watch couples of falcons on the rugged slopes of Şahinkaya as they made their dive for the prey. And we laughed a lot when one of the workers had a dog that, soon after we started to work, went chasing a rabbit but returned empty "pawed" but with badly wounded feet. Today, you would hardly see anything like that. We cannot even hear anymore the partridges visiting the springs in the ruins for their share of the water. The wildlife in Lycia is almost totally finished apart from the clever foxes, or the wildboars that reproduce frantically. Badgers, otters and porcupines are among those animals that you will find very rarely, if at all, and nearing their end, as they have no more mates. Most of them struggle to survive all alone in life.

Another way that we have turned nature upside down is with hybrid vegetables and fruits. Unless the necessary measures are taken soon, as animals and human-beings consuming crops that have been fed with growth hormones, we will not be able to avoid developing phallic or testicle-like protrusions in our most unexpected places, just like those vegetables and fruits themselves. Another possibility is that we will have a rapid increase in cancer cases. The dangers of this issue are so severe that I have felt the need to cry out for help to the environmentalists as well as the Ministries of Forestry and Agriculture in this book that is intended to be a cultural guide book.

Lycia is not only picturesque with its forests that contain all types of pines - Scots pine, spruce, oak, beech and naturally grown Cedars of Lebanon -("Cedrus Libanesis")- but can be really rich with its forestry products, if operated rationally.

A SHORT HISTORY OF LYCIA

Limyra, sarcophagus of Xntabura

◄ *Myra, theatre*

Xanthos, sarcophagus of
Payava

Although no research has been conducted into the Neolithic or even earlier ages of Lycia to date, the geological structure in the region allows carstic formations, ie. caves. Moreover, the fact that there are innumerable caves makes one further expect to find a semi-settled life style in Lycia as early as the Palaeolithic age.

LYCIA TIMELINE

2000 BC

We can be sure that Lycians were Luwian people and were mentioned in eastern and Egyptian inscriptions as "Luqqu", "Luqqa" or "Rwk" in the Bronze Age, or around the 2nd millenium BC to be precise.

600 BC

Each new excavation and finding adds to our knowledge about Lycia in the early Iron Age until the mid-6th century BC.

This idea is also supported by the many studies and excavations of caves like Karain or Öküzini on the border between Kabalia, Pamphylia and Pisidia.

I have absolutely no doubt that Lycia was inhabited in the Neolithic age and I believe that, after a series of excavations, the Hacımusalar Höyük, the most striking of its ilk in the region, will become the classic example of the Neolithic Age in the area, as happened with the Bademağacı Höyük in the neighbouring region. Currently, the Neolithic Age is represented by some rather weak findings at the Semahöyük in the Elmalı plain but soon, real findings from those days may be unearthed at the west end of the same plain.

It is quite unfortunate that there are so few excavations and studies of

> *I see it as an Anatolian resistance against outsider invaders, when Lycia ran for the help of the Trojans under the heroic command of Sarpedon as Homer narrates.*

the pre and proto-historical ages in the region. Nevertheless, we have concrete proof that the area was inhabited from the very early ages: Artefacts collected during surface studies or as coincidental findings from the Calcolithic and Bronze Ages in major centers like Semahöyük and Hacımusalar Höyük and around the Kasaba Plateau and Fethiye - the Kibyratis region that became a part of Lycia more recently with Tefenni, Acıpayam and Gölhisar.

It is now widely accepted that names of places and, later in time, proper names that end with -anda and- wanda and wich are spelled with double consonants originate from the Luwian people. The Luwian people settled around southwest Anatolia. We can be sure that Lycians were Luwian people and were mentioned in eastern and Egyptian inscriptions as "Luqqu", "Luqqa" or "Rwk" in the Bronze Age, or around the 2nd millenium BC to be precise. If we analyse the definition by Herodotus of Lycians as "people emigrating from Crete to Anatolia, settling in inner parts of the mountainous Lycia region and naming themselves Tremili or Termili", we have a really hard time finding an explanation as to why Lycians, who have been described as a warrior tribe in the Egyptian records and continued to be so even in the later ages, preferred to settle not on the shoreline but in the mountains.

The inscription about the "Luqqu" or "Luqqa" land that we read on a bronze tablet discovered about 15 years ago in Hattusa and the findings in Kyaenai and Patara combine to point to the very same fact: The shipwrecks found at the Cape of Uluburun and Serçe Port provide the proof we need that Lycia was not only a harbour for commercial ships navigating Lycian waters but these ships represented a trade relation with the inhabitants of the area. The golden seal of Nefertiti that you can see in Bodrum Museum today perfectly matches artifacts of Mycenean origin discovered in Lycian cities.

400 BC

The Akhamenids ruled over the entire Anatolian Peninsula, and therefore Lycia too starting from the year 546 BC, or roughly mid-6th century BC.

310 BC

In 310 BC, the area came under the rule of Ptolemaios dynasty who ruled over Egypt and in 301 BC, under the rule of Lysimakhos, the King of Syria (the nation known as Seleucids).

200 BC

The hardships that Lycia suffered under the rule of Rhodes may have contributed to the formation of the Lycian League in early 2nd century BC.

88 BC

Seeking to erase Roman influence in Anatolia, the King of Pontos, Mithridates I, invaded Lycia in 88 BC along with many other regions in Anatolia.

200 AD

The mid-2nd century AD or the year 141 to be precise was a year of disasters for Lycian cities.

New findings reveal that Persian art influenced Lycian art, especially in ancient times.

I see it as an Anatolian resistance against outsider invaders, when Lycia ran for the help of the Trojans under the heroic command of Sarpedon as Homer narrates. Similarly, we can see the same resistance against the Lydians by the Lycians, although the former and the latter were both Anatolian communities. Although on the basis of individual cities, the same idea of resistance is seen in the struggles of the people of Xanthos against Harpagos, the Persian commander, and of the people of Marmara against Alexander, the Great.

Each new excavation and finding adds to our knowledge about Lycia in the early Iron Age until the mid-6th century BC. The King of Lydia, Alyattes, failed to conquer Lycia; however, Lycia borrowed oriental styles in handcrafts (earthenware, in particular) that were more popular in Western Anatolia or manufactured regional copies of such artifacts in addition to importing terracotta pottery and statuettes, both of which were luxurious for the day. Findings from Xanthos, Patara, Antiphellos, Kyaenai, Phaselis and the Hacımusalar Tumulus are all proof of growing trade relations in the area.

The Akhamenids ruled over the entire Anatolian Peninsula, and

ROCK TOMBS, near THE THEATRE at MYRA

Myra

therefore Lycia too starting from the year 546 BC, or roughly mid-6th century BC. The Persian (Akhamenid) Commander, Harpagos, had a hard time conquering Kaunos and Xanthos and the people of Xanthos chose mass suicide rather than submission. Persian rule was fierce and ruthless, but soon, the iron hand would soften as we can conclude from the fact that some Lycian cities went so far as cooperating with the foes of Persia.

New findings reveal that Persian art influenced Lycian art, especially in ancient times. The Harpies Monument in Xanthos bears a striking resemblance to monuments in Persopolis, in Nakshi Rustem, from the thurible in the ceremony scene to the man sitting on the throne under the umbrella. On the other hand, the man that a servant fans as he lies on the divan as depicted on the Karaburun tumulus does not bear any resemblance at all to any Anatolian man with his brown eyes, humpy nose, mullah beard and especially, his clothes and jewellery.

Kimon's success in Eurymedon contributed greatly to the weakening and fall of the Persian rule over the region. The sides made a treaty which forbade the Persian navy from

300 AD

Lycia appears to have continued developing up to the 3rd century AD when on August 5th, 240, it was hit again by a major earthquake. Lycia wouldn't be so lucky this time.

500 AD

We can find some information about the fate of Lycia during the division of the Empire and fall of Western Roman Empire (5th century AD) in ecclesiastical records.

800 AD

However, I cannot help writing here that the Arab Raids towards Istanbul during the 8th century AD considerably affected the cities in the region and it is very possible that nomadic Turkish tribes and Turkish soldiers in the Abbasi army, who were deployed in the region as patrol teams may have arrived in Lycia even before the Malazgirt War that made Anatolia the new land of the Turks.

navigate west of Eurymedon's mouth (today, Köprüçay), ie. the Pamphylian Sea (Bay of Antalya). However, by that time, Persian rule had gone through a slight change and was dominated by the Karian satrap, Mausolos, or, in other words, the Dynasty of Hekatomnos.

Lycia was home to rather extraordinary happenings in the first half of the 4th century BC when the Karia Satrapy dominated Karia and Lycia, though loosely in the latter: Pericles, the master of Zemuri or Limyra, was working with all his might to unite Lycian cities under one roof. Establishing his rule over both eastern and central Lycia, Pericles had a new target - all the area until Telmessos. He even launched an attack on Telmessos, which resulted in failure and did not help uniting Lycia. Instead, Arbinas and Pixodaros became more powerful, especially in western Lycia. A trilingual inscription (in Arami, Lycian and Greek languages) was discovered in Letoon, which proved to be a diplomatic document about these individuals.

Alexander, the Great launched a military expedition in Asia in search of a world Empire and crossed the Dardanelles. He wouldn't meet almost any resistance in Karia and Lycia, quotes Arrianos. Ada, who was compelled by her own brother, Mausolos, and sister, Artemisia, to reside in Alinda although she was a member of the Dynasty of Hekatomnos as well, opened the gates of the city to meet Alexander and remained so loyal as to call him "My Son". One thing is for sure: Alexander was the one who put an end to Persian rule in Anatolia and continued the satrapy regime, which ruled over Lycia, by assigning one of his supporters, namely Nearkhos,

> *Alexander the Great launched a military expedition in Asia in search of a world Empire and crossed the Dardanelles. He wouldn't meet almost any resistance in Karia and Lycia, quotes Arrianos.*

as satrap. The most critical change that Alexander introduced and his commanders would continue to apply was making it compulsory for the local people, whose problems grew endlessly, to stop using their local languages in favor of speaking and writing in Greek.

After spending the winter in Phaselis, Alexander, continued his long expedition towards Baktria and passed away at a rather early age in 323 in Susa on his way back. His death would be followed by an epoch of successors ("Diadokhs"). In the beginning, Lycia was ruled by the Macedonians under the command of Antigonos Monophtalmos. In 310 BC, the area came under the rule of Ptolemaios dynasty who ruled over Egypt and in 301 BC, under the rule of Lysimakhos, the King of Syria (the nation known as Seleucids). The Syrian Kingdom wouldn't last long in Lycia and came to an end in 296 BC with the reign of Ptolemaios, which lasted approximately a full century. In 197-196 BC, the Syrian King, Antiokhos III, fought to conquer Anatolia - an effort finally turning fruitless on the day he lost the battle of Magnesia around 190-189 BC. The post-war Apameia Treaty left Lycia under the control of Rhodes with the influence of Rome, which was beginning to develop an appetite for the east. The strict attitude of Rhodes received such heavy reaction from the Karian cities and Lycia under their control that they flooded the Roman senate with petitions of complaint. The complaints were found legitimate and the Karia and Lycia cities were freed.

The hardships that Lycia suffered under the rule of Rhodes may have contributed to the formation of the Lycian League in early 2nd century BC. Co-lead by Lysanias and Eudomos, an idea became a reality and the Lycian cities united under a federative state.

Here is some information about the "Lycian League" that Pericles tried but failed to establish in the first half of the

NECROPOLIS OR CEMETERY OF CACAMO.   NÉCROPOLE OU CIMETIÈRE DE CACAMO.

Kekova

4th century BC. All Lycian cities and small federal states were allowed to use coins issued by some cities upon the exclusive entitlement thereto, provided they bear the words ΛΥΚΙΩΝ ΚΟΙΝΩΝ. The six cities of Xanthos, Pınara, Tlos, Patara, Myra and Olympos were the administrative, judicial, military, financial and religious centers and they each had 3 votes in the meetings of the League. Most of the other cities had 1 vote each; however, there were cases when 2 or 3 very small cities were combined under 1 vote.

For instance, Akalissos and Idebessos; Apollonia and Isinda and Aperlai were two groups of cities each represented by a single vote in the meetings of the League.

Seeking to erase Roman influence in Anatolia, the King of Pontos, Mithridates I, invaded Lycia in 88 BC along with many other regions in Anatolia. While the long "Mithridatic Wars" etched a name in history, Sulla defeated Mithridates and reinforced Rome's military authority over Anatolia. The new administrative structure added the region of Kibyratis to Lycia, making the latter a major province of Rome. The four prominent towns of Kibyratis, namely Kibyra, Oinoanda,

Seeking to erase Roman influence in Anatolia, the King of Pontos, Mithridates I, invaded Lycia in 88 BC along with many other regions in Anatolia.

Bubon and Balbura, were granted a special status and admitted to the Lycian League with 2 votes each.

The First century BC brought a lot of trouble for Eastern Lycia, predominantly in the form of intruders from the sea. Pirates from Isauria and Pisidia active in the Bay of Antalya - then called the Pamphylian Sea or Mare Pamphylia - plundered the commercial ships and coastal cities of Rome and other states and based themselves in a number of Lycian and Pamphylian port cities. Manlius Vulso set his mind on protecting the Roman commercial fleet jeopardised in Eastern Anatolia and putting an end to the lack of authority created by pirate activity in the region. He pursued the pirates and their chief, Zeniketes, both on land and sea. Achieving an unprecedented success against the pirates, he earned the title of Conqueror of Isauria, thanks to the Roman historians. The cities of Phaselis and Olympos were accused and punished for their alliance with Zeniketes during the operation against the pirates and Olympos, (which was represented by 3 votes) was dismissed from the League.

Following the killing of Julius Caesar, the power struggle in Rome directly affected a number of Lycian cities. Arriving in Lycia to seek support and finding none, Brutus raided Xanthos, brought the whole acropolis to ruins and slaughtered the inhabitants just like the Persian Commander, Harpagos. A year after Brutus, Mark Antony arrived with the exact same expectations. However, he did exactly the opposite of Brutus: He threw himself into reconstruction works, especially in Xanthos.

The reign of Augustus or Octavian, who eliminated his rivals at the Actium and became Emperor, is the beginning of a promising epoch for Lycia. The financial support, private privileges and facilities granted to certain cities during the reign of Agustus, who did not hesitate to seal his military victories with public favors, all helped to bring peace and

> *The mid-2nd century AD or the year 141 to be precise was a year of disasters for Lycian cities. The great earthquake that hit Lycia and environs was a fatal blow not only to all of Lycia, but some of the neighbouring provinces as well.*

tranquillity over all the provinces; therefore, he managed to stimulate intensive development in the region.

During the 1st century AD, the Emperor or his close circle of relatives visited Lycia, occassions which sometimes ended in the curtailing of some of Lycia's most important powers or rights and even almost placed the region under the authority of another province. However, at the end of the day, this was the one time that the area saw development at such a pace. The region reached its peak during the reigns of Trajan and, most importantly, Hadrian.

The mid-2nd century AD or the year 141 to be precise was a time of disasters for Lycian cities. The great earthquake that hit Lycia and environs was a fatal blow not only to all of Lycia, but some of the neighbouring provinces as well. It would not have been possible to bring the cities up and back to life again were it not for the help of Rome and the support of well-known richmen such as Opromoas of Rhodiapolis, Jason of Kyaenea and Licinius Langus of Oinoanda. We should take time here to mention the name of Opramoas of Rhodiapolis since it was he who helped every single city from Phaselis to Telmessos and went so far as to construct new buildings from scratch in some earthquake-struck cities.

Lycia appears to have continued developing up to the 3rd century AD when on August 5th, 240, it was hit again by a major earthquake. Lycia wouldn't be so lucky this time. Though equally destroyed; now, support was not pouring in but maybe dripping. Rome itself was seriously troubled in terms of administration and military security after the reign of the Severus Dynasty. This may have had something to do with clashes between the growing Christian population and the established pagan population in the Empire, which would even lead to struggles between members of the same family.

TOMBS IN THE ROCK OF ACROPOLIS AT TLOS.

Tlos

And the outside influence on the fall of the Roman Empire was the Goth invasion.

We can find some information about the fate of Lycia during the division of the Empire and fall of Western Roman Empire (5th century AD) in ecclesiastical records.

As a classical archaeologist I should put a full stop to my words at the point of history named in books as the Byzantine Empire. However, I cannot help writing here that the Arab Raids towards Istanbul during the 8th century AD considerably affected the cities in the region and it is very possible that nomadic Turkish tribes and Turkish soldiers in the Abbasi army, who were deployed in the region as patrol teams, may have arrived in Lycia even before the Malazgirt War that made Anatolia the new land of the Turks.

ANCIENT SITES

Simena, sarcophagus

◄ *Lydai, detail of a tomb building*

*O*lbia appears as a Lycian city in the writings of Skylax and Strabon, and lies on a rocky land to the south of the campus of the Mediterranean University and north of Konyaaltı Beach.

Ağırtaş, necropolis

OLBIA (KONYAALTI-PETROL OFİSİ)

We do not know much about the history of the city, except that the city was inhabited around the 4th century BC according to the inscriptions on a sarcophagus unearthed to accidentally the north of the new port in Antalya in a construction site near the junction for Gödene (Altınyaka).

Based on a reading of the "Stadiasmus" monument that gives us an idea about the distances between the Lycian cities in units of "stadia", Prof. Dr. Sencer Şahin locates Olbia on the land where the Kemer Holiday village stands today. (The 'Stadiasmus' monument has been recently discovered in Patara).

Whether the ruins that the 19th century travellers found are still preserved remains unknown, as the area is private property. The only visible remains of the city today are the Late Roman mortared walls to the north of the Petrol Ofisi Filling Station.

Although there is mention of Attaleia being one with or united with Olbia during its days of early foundation, there are no findings or remains to prove this.

AĞIRTAŞ

I participated in the "Symposium on Excavation Findings" in Antalya and because not all the topics were related to my

Ağırtaş, husband and wife or lovers

field of activity and the meeting rooms were extremely hot as it was already end of May, I felt somehow compelled to visit many of the ruins in the region, thanks to my student, Ümit Işın who really knew the area and thus came up with the idea. So, we planned an excursion to Ağırtaş. On the road from Antalya to Saklıkent, right before the Bakacak Pass, you will first see some sarcophagi and then, some well-preserved ruins the size of a whole city discreetly concealed in the forest. This settlement controlled the Bay of Antalya from the west, much like the village of Çitdibi.

The ruins of many rectangular buildings are still standing up to the first floor, though completely filled in with earth, on the west-looking northern slope of the area, which we could call the acropolis of the city. This area was protected by the natural rock formations and therefore, needed city walls only in a few places, if any. For the time being, we cannot say whether these buildings were residences or ruins of family graves since the city is not being excavated.

The surface studies that the Mediterranean University has recently started in the area will shed light on this settlement including the true function of all these buildings. The city is most notable for the sarcophagi with reliefs that you can find on the eastern slope of the acropolis. This must be somehow related to the cult of Men that spread out from

Lycia

Ağırtaş, family relief on a sarcophagus

Phrygia, which is very close to this settlement on the border of Pisidia-Kabalia-Lycia.

Currently, we can see about 10 sarcophagi, which were first discovered by the Italian excursion team of Pace, Mauri and Moretti, who worked in the area during the WW1 and published the inscriptions on these sarcophagi. Most probably, these items belonged to soldiers or watchmen and their families deployed at this garrison. Although the hand of time has worked a lot here, the city is still rich in sarcophagi with reliefs. The inscriptions on the tabula ansatas of some sarcophagi read 3rd century AD in letters. However, the typical Hellenistic structure of the buildings, unless an imitation, could earn this settlement distinction as a good, interesting example of Hellenistic architecture and decorative arts, though in a somewhat rural style. But we must note that the above-mentioned sarcophagi bearing inscriptions date to a later age.

Coming from Antalya, you can see some sarcophagus lids and bodies, which reflect a mixture of styles from various regions, on the side of the road. When you walk southwest towards the acropolis, this mixture of cultures becomes all the more remarkable.

Coming from Antalya, you can see some sarcophagus lids and bodies, which reflect a mixture of styles from various regions, on the side of the road.

Çitdibi, sarcophagus decorated with carvings

ÇİTDİBİ

Going in the direction of Yarbaşçandır on the road from Antalya to Söğütcuma you will arrive in the village of Çitdibi. You can follow the path to the north through a recently burnt field and arrive at the Çitdibi ruins. Driving from Antalya will take between 45 minutes to 1 hour and you will also have to walk for another 45 minutes or so to get to the ruins. Since this path runs through a forest and on a relatively higher altitude, temperatures shouldn't be too difficult to tolerate. However, it would be wise to double up the estimated duration of walking with regular breaks when climbing with people aged over 50 or without the proper experience in climbing.

Most probably, Çitdibi was a military garrison because it overlooks the valley heading for the "new port of Antalya" and the whole coastline to the east of Antalya on one side and the other valleys in the direction of Altınyaka (Gödene) - Kumluca and Korkuteli on the other.

The ruins prove the idea of this city being a garrison, as well. There are a few, well-hidden, megaron-like buildings in good shape on the eastern slope overlooking Antalya. The use of the character "C" for the letter "sigma" in the inscriptions reveal that Çitdibi was not abandoned before the late 3rd - early 4th century AD. The findings that you can see on the surface without any excavation and similar ruins in the region also point to this conclusion.

It must be noted that the sarcophagi in Çitdibi prove that this settlement was either on the border or in the vicinity of one since we can find sarcophagi in both Lycian

> *The use of the character "C" for the letter
> "sigma" in the inscriptions reveal that
> Çitdibi was not abandoned before the late
> 3rd - early 4th century AD.*

Çitdibi, relief of a horseman

style and the Pisidian style, which was characterized by shields and spears.

TREBENNA (CLOSE TO GEYİKBAYIRI VILLAGE)

Take the road from Antalya to Çakırlar-Geyikbayırı to reach Trebenna, which situated on the northern foot of Mount Sivri. If the traffic is light, you can drive to the ruins in 20 to 30 minutes.

The city was found and written up to some extent by the Italian excursion team of Mauri, Moretti and Pace during WW1. Another publication about this city is the article of Prof. Dr. Semavi Eyice that appeared in the periodical of the Touring and Automobile Association of Turkey after his visit to the area in the 1970's. Now, a research team led by Prof. Dr. Nevzat Çevik is working at the site for 'Beydağları Surface Exploration'. The results of the studies will be published soon.

It is beyond doubt that Trebenna and Trebendai are in fact one and the same city named in "Geographica" of Ptolemaios (among the ancient authors) as a Lycian city, on the coordinates of "5.3.6 Trebendai". Since there is no other city in Lycia, Milyas or Pisidia with a similar name, Trebenna and Trebendai must refer to the same city. We have to place Trebenna and Trebendai among the cities on

Trebenna, sarcophagus

the border between Pamphylia, Pisidia and Lycia. As Ptolemaios puts it, Trebenna a Luwian word with the suffix "-nd" and naturally, it is an ancient city where we could expect to find inhabitants from as early as 2nd millenium BC or even earlier.

I was too lazy to see the central settlement in Trebenna because it looked rather simple but I visited the necropolis on the northeastern and north feet of Mount Sivri at least ten times. Therefore, I am basing my words about the ruins on the writings of Prof. Dr. Semavi Eyice and on my personal observations in the necropolis.

Trebenna lived to see the Byzantine Period as well. This is evident from the city walls and the well-preserved ruins of a church on a hill - which could be the acropolis of the city.

Trebenna is noted for the coins of the city issued during the Lycian League and its necropolis spreading over a vast land with many sarcophagi, most of them with reliefs. We can assume that the necropolis was used by many families from Trebenna as on many sarcophagi, especially on the southeastern foot of Mount Sivri, we can read the inscription that bears the name of the deceased followed by "… of Trebenna".

There is a sarcophagus at the beginning of the road leading to Çitdibi along the southern foot of Mount Sivri. The long sides display reliefs of many mythological events although the main scene is rather ordinary. But this sarcophagus is remarkable both for the region and for its

Trebenna, sarcophagus

interest in other mythoses. Moreover, we have discovered over 10 sarcophagi and 5 to 6 family graves in the forest near this interesting sarcophagus. On the "tabula ansatas", we can easily read the word " TREBENDAI" in Greek letters. In this way, we have removed all doubts about Trebenna and Trebendai being the same city as well as disproving Bean's comment (Lycian Turkey s.112) "Trebenna", Trebendai, a mere dependency of Myra, can not come in question.

KITANAURA (SARAYCIK)

This is another city on the border of Pisidia, Kabalia and Lycia that many archaeologist and travellers believe to be the city of "Marmara". This city is one of the many settlements that you can reach by the road from Antalya to Gödene where, at the crossroads for Saraycık, you will have to take the dirt road running through the forest.

This settlement has enthralled many with its orthostats over the podium that even today stand up to the level of architrave and its mausoleum that is famous for its reliefs of military costumes on the ante walls. However, the location of the city does not match with the definition of Marmara

However, the location of the city does not match with the definition of Marmara by both Arrianos and Diodoros as "the city that did not even need city walls, thanks to its rugged landscape".

Kitanaura, acropolis

by both Arrianos and Diodoros as "the city that did not even need city walls, thanks to its rugged landscape". Though standing in the middle of a forest today, Saraycık loses altitude as you walk towards the southwest and is like a peninsula in the middle of pure land. Saraycık is a typical Roman city or town with its eastward pointing acropolis surrounded by city walls, the Roman bath to the south-west of the acropolis and the outer city walls that encircle all of the above. We understand that the necropolis lay westward by looking at the well-preserved mausoleum that Saraycık owes its reputation to, along with the city walls and the family graves spreading to the west, north and south.

Although we were a large group of visitors in this short expedition, we weren't able to locate any buildings in the

Kitanaura, bath

Kitanaura, mausoleum

acropolis that could be easily identified. Nevertheless, we suppose the best preserved public building in Saraycık is the Roman bath on the southwest end of the acropolis where it has been perfectly protected in a corner from the wind. The style is Lycian, ie. the caldarium ends in an apsidal form. The 3 sections of the building were preserved in good condition. The best examples of this type of Roman baths can be seen in Tlos, Pınara, Arykanda, Patara and some other Lycian cities.

We have absolutely no doubt that the building - with an entrance still visible - to the south of the Roman bath is the agora because right behind the entrance is an empty field through which you can walk north and west to see the ruins of some shops.

ALTINYAKA (GÖDENE)

Taking a day trip from Antalya to visit Çitdibi and the ruins as Saraycık, which were mistakenly announced to be the city of Marmara by Kiepert and the Italian team of Mauri, Moretti and Pace, you can also see Altınyaka (formerly, Gödene). At the crossroads, you can visit the necropolis with some sarcophagi near the Çukurca neighbourhood or enjoy a late lunch of trout if you set out late.

Take the old road from Antalya to Finike that turns north right before the end of Konyaaltı Beach and continues west and then, immediately, south where you get to see that the effects of the Mediterranean climate can disappear and reappear in very short distances. Unless lined with valleys

Unless lined with valleys created by rivers, the landscape to the west of Mount Tahtalı and Mount Musa, which draw the western border of the Bay of Antalya, would be that of a steppe such as that you would expect to see in Central Anatolia.

> *Without the exact geographical directions, you could end up in the wrong place and have to deal with a lot of confusion since almost anywhere you go to, you would find some ruins.*

created by rivers, the landscape to the west of Mount Tahtalı and Mount Musa, which draw the western border of the Bay of Antalya, would be that of a steppe such as that you would expect to see in Central Anatolia. The Gödene Mountain Range, or Altınyaka as we call it today, is one of the few places where the green forests grow inland, thanks to the Alakır Stream that runs north-to-south and collects the water of many other streams from the west.

Although not in as good shape as the road following the coastline, this road promises an amazing landscape.

You can see some sarcophagi right by the side of the road around the Çukurca neighbourhood on the left if you are coming from Altınyaka to Antalya. The inscriptions in Greek on their "tabula ansatas" point to the Late Hellenistic or Early Roman ages.

KORMOS (KARABÜK)

You would find similar names used in different places all over Lycia, such as Belen, Belenyayla; Asartepe, Asarönü; Karabük, Gökbük, etc. Without the exact geographical locations, you could end up in the wrong place and have to deal with a lot of confusion since almost anywhere you go to, you would find some ruins. This is exactly the case with Kormos: There are two incidentally very close settlements merely separated by a valley; one of them is within the borders of Altınyaka (Gödene), whereas the other is more connected with Kumluca. Therefore, it would be a good idea to label Asarönü - Karabük in Kumluca as ancient Akalissos and the Karabük in Altınyaka as Kormos.

We can find the roots (or the confusion) of the names in antiquity since Akalissos, Idebessos and Kormos were three cities that were collectively represented by 1 vote in the Lycian League. I believe that this confusion is acceptable considering the unity in their political standing and their geographical positioning.

I have to emphasize that, although Kormos is believed to be where Karabük village stands today, I find it rather

> *Although some of these sarcophagi do bear the name of Kormos, we need further epigraphic documentation or excavation findings to make a final definition.*

misleading to locate an ancient settlement according to administrative titles, i.e. village names of today, since I know of at least two more villages in the area with the exact same name: Karabük. And by chance, there are ancient ruins in every one of them. The ruins that we can see today in Karabük near Asar village and in Kormos on the road leading north from Altınyaka (Gödene) are mostly Lycian style Sarcophagi with "tabula ansatas" from the Roman Period. Although some of these sarcophagi do bear the name of Kormos, we need further epigraphic documentation or excavation findings to make a final definition. Because, when somebody was born in Kormos but died in another city, the sarcophagus would naturally show the deceased as someone from Kormos and it doesn't mean that the person was buried in Kormos as well. Identifying the names of ancient settlements should not be based solely on epitaphs, as the case above is a common problem.

ONABARA

Very few travellers, if any, from Antalya to Finike through Kemer, or the other way round, will have noticed the city called Onabara lying to the west of the shallow waters opposite Sıçan Island.

The area between the Sıçan Island and Onabara was the port where the army of Alexander, the Great set out for Pamphylia and Pisidia from Lycia following their local guide, according to Arrianos.

IDYROS (KEMER)

It was the February of 1979 or 1980 that we started from Cilicia on another of our "Olive Tours", as Dr. Peter Neve called them while he worked in Boğazköy. But you ask: 'What is an Olive Tour?' 'And why is it called that way?' We were a team travelling from Ankara to the Cilicia coasts and naturally, we used to eat at certain intervals. But when we started visiting the ruins one by one as we proceeded towards

Pamphylia and thence, to Lycia, I forced the group to give up on the lunch ceremony. So, we lived on a handful of olives eaten as breakfast that was often unfinished by still sleeping eyes. Hence, the name of the tour, as given by Dr. Neve.

Phaselis was our first stop in Lycia. By pure chance, we had arrived on the day-off of the Museum team working on the initial cleaning of the ancient city. The day-off continued over a fish feast with drinks. We didn't want to leave before seeing the acropolis of Idyros - a desire that took us in a couple of vehicles loaded with people to the summit overlooking Kemer where the watchtower for the forest is today. It was not difficult to locate the city walls because I had been there before. You can still see the walls that I would identify as cyclopic, near the watchtower today.

During my later private and official visits to Idyros, I gained the opinion that the city could be situated where the land descended smoothly eastward from the western summit and that we could find some ruins from the late period between Kemer in the north and the luxury hotels in the south. As a matter of fact, along with other experts, I came back to the region as a member of the Supreme Council of Immovable Antiquities and Monuments and an expert quite well informed about the region to see the "French or Italian Holiday village" as it was then called, which became the Club Med later, in 1981. We put it in our report that the area that is today the location of the tennis courts, which I presume must be the scene of extremely pleasurable games, should be secured as an archaeological conservation area as there were ruins of a church still standing at the time. If I am not mistaken, we were informed by the top level management in the Ministry of Culture and Tourism about the "foreign pressure" (the truth of which has not been validated) from the Italian and French Embassies and we were told in a rather high tone to correct our decision in favor of our country's best

It was not difficult to locate the city walls because I had been there before. You can still see the city walls that I would identify as cyclopic, near the watchtower today.

A German colleague of ours has recently finalized his studies on the findings from that land descending smoothly eastward from the observation tower, which will give us a lot of clues about Idyros.

interests. This Supreme Council had lost all its legal ground after the Military Coup in 1980 but was, in fact, equipped by the Republic of Turkey with a law that could be compared to the Constitution in effectiveness. Soon after, a law was passed that granted two years before the Council would read effectively to re-assert the rights of the people suffering from damage to natural and historical conservation areas. This was a decision that investors, who had already developed an appetite for most of the natural, historical and archaeological conservation areas, were craving for. Forests were burned down. Private projects popped up everywhere. And in the end, innumerable ruins in every bay between Idyros and Ağva were destroyed to develop extremely luxurious holiday villages and hotels in Kemer.

A German colleague of ours has recently finalized his studies on the findings from that land descending smoothly eastward from the observation tower, which will give us a lot of clues about Idyros. His book is about to be published now. However, Prof. Dr. Sencer Şahin seems to be locating Idyros elsewhere in one of his latest articles. I am doing my part by suggesting this idea to the readers and promising a discussion on the issue to come in another publication.

Similarly, the excavation in Ağva produced graves from the late 5th - early 4th century BC and some mosaics from the early Byzantine period, under the supervision of Tanju Özoral, then Manager of the Antalya Museum. The findings proved that Idyros was a port city and an important shelter for the vessels of antiquity, although not as secure as Phaselis against multi-directional winds.

Surprisingly enough, Phaselis and Idyros had more in common: Losing their significance after the 13th century AD, both cities would disappear into history.

Kavaklıdağ, theatrical building

MARMARA (KAVAKLIDAĞ)

Ever since the days of antiquity, some cities have come to be known as "good" or "evil", apparently due to the general attitudes of their inhabitants. However, social values are relative and should be evaluated according to their time and place. Keeping this in mind, the city of Marmara can be described in two extreme ways: It can be regarded as an "evil" city full of thieves - since they had no land to irrigate - or, instead, it can be approached with love and tolerance because of their love for their independence and their power to resist invaders backed by their heroic courage to even commit mass suicide rather than live under oppression.

Marmara is just one of the ancient Anatolian cities that exhibit both these good and bad characteristics. I suppose we should lend our ear to the ancient authors and regard the inhabitants of this city as courageous people who chose to hold on to their freedom despite the rather lawless life they lived. They were gallant, rough fellows.

Our knowledge as to the history of Marmara is quite limited. It is mentioned in ancient writings within the context of the winter that Alexander stayed in Phaselis. We can also read from Diodoros and Arrianos that the inhabitants of Marmara used to pillage the crops of Phaselis.

Travellers and geographers have associated Marmara with the Saraycık ruins because they skipped the readings

Kavaklıdağ, the statue
before the temple

from Diodoros and Arrianos and located cities according to what they knew or saw at that time. But that's not all they neglected: For one thing, while Alexander, the Great spent the winter in Phaselis on his military expedition to Asia, he is reported as having captured the city almost overnight.

Even if we consider that he used cavalry, an army moving for battle from Phaselis towards Saraycık would need more than one day to reach the city, let alone fight and seize it, overcoming all those natural obstacles and breaking through the defences of the city. The road is full of difficult mountain paths and ridges.

We should remember also that the ancient authors tell us that the city was on such a steep landscape that city walls were unnecessary for defence. But, Saraycık is surrounded by city walls and even its acropolis is at a situation and altitude that would be easy to climb and seize. For this reason as well as some others, I presume that we can find Marmara lying in ruins on the summit of Mount Kavaklı, where a middle-aged villager has stated that he would walk from Phaselis in a maximum of 2 hours at a normal pace. So, the idea that the Saraycık ruins might be the city of Marmara is totally undermined. In fact, the most recent studies reveal that the ancient city in Saraycık is Kitanaura.

Also in the vicinity of Phaselis are the Gâvurpazarı ruins; however, the ancient city that these ruins belonged to was surrounded by city walls, which again implies that it cannot be the city of Marmara either because, like Saraycık Gâvurpazarı was an easy target for invasion, owing to its natural disposition.

The city, is extremely difficult to reach. When driving with a guide, you should take the road to the village of Kuzdere from the last turn to Kemer on the road from Antalya to Finike.

The story goes on that the city fell to Alexander in an overnight victory; the young were willing to resist and the elderly to surrender. It also appears that the young decided that the women, children and elderly should escape into the woods at the dark of the night, the married men stay one more night with their wives before the women run out of the city and all young men resist until the last drop of their blood only to commit mass suicide if things turned out to be completely desperate.

Alexander's siege must have taken a couple of days. But, all ended as the inhabitants of Phaselis wished for and the people of Marmara were severely punished. This end is the beginning of silence in ancient writings. Our archaeological findings give us a clue as to what happened afterwards. The ruins on the surface of the eastern end of the town where the temple was located indicate that Marmara survived

Kavaklıdağ, heroon

> *The ruins of this city, on the top of the mountain, run east-to-west. The south of the summit doubled as a stone quarry that provided building material as well as a north-facing protective structure that shielded the city from cold northern winds.*

through the Late Hellenistic - Early Roman Period. Both the surface findings and findings around holes excavated by treasure hunters indicate that the city may have existed even as late as the 2nd century AD. We can even speculate there was a small population in Marmara during the early Byzantine period. This settlement was abandoned most probably in the 8th century AD since we haven't been able to locate any ruins or findings dating after this century in all our five expeditions to the city, two of which turned out to be absolutely fruitless.

The city, is extremely difficult to reach. When driving with a guide, you should take the road to the village of Kuzdere from the last turn to Kemer on the road from Antalya to Finike. After this turning, you should pass Kuzdere and drive west as far as Kesme reservoir, the water resource of Kemer. 1.5 to 2 kilometers after the dam, you will see a crossroads. After the bridge over the riverbed, you should follow the road to the north or the right. Stay on this road until Ovacık village where you should continue to Pınarcık village. Do not enter the village and after the house of the villager, locally called "Parmaksız - The One without Fingers", first take the road leading south of the cemetery and then, follow the path that leads, not south, but north. It is a must that at this point you have a guide who is extremely well informed about the area. From here you will have to walk at least one hour before reaching Kavaklıdağ (Marmara). I would like to make it clear to those above the age of 50 or suffering from various health problems that this walk is a difficult one. I suggest that people in this age group should not attempt to take this risk. If you lose the path and find yourself walking through bushes, it is essential that you go back to the last point where you were on the path and find it. If you really want to see the city, you should have Mount Tahtalı on your back and walk to the left (in a north-to-northwest direction).

Kavaklıdağ, stone blocks and column shafts from the temple

Kavaklıdağ is a summit of c.1400 meters above sea level on south-declining land. The city owes its name to the nature around it: "Marble". The area is so steep that the city really did not need any city walls. Moreover, despite the blocking of Mount Tahtalı, it has a full view over much of Eastern Lycia (since it is situated in the mouth of the Alakır Valley) and of Kabalia Region in the direction of Mount Çürük on the Bay of Antalya.

The ruins of this city, on the top of the mountain, run east-to-west. The south of the summit doubled as a stone quarry that provided building material as well as a north-facing protective structure that shielded the city from cold northern winds. The first building on the southeastern edge is the temple which has three steps in its crepidoma and is in Ionic or Corinthian order, considering the groove incised on the shaft of the columns. We can see that the structure was built to face a certain direction and its antefix, as well as other decorative elements, indicate that the temple was in "prostylos tetrastyle", in other words, its façade was decorated with four columns. The orthostats on the first row of the cella walls were adorned with images of shields richly decorated with what only leather or metal shields would display.

The building material - apart from the frieze - was marble including the ridge tiles as we can understand from the

Kavaklıdağ, temple

findings right on the surface. Wondering how they managed to carry blocks of marble to this city where we could hardly climb with no other load than our own bodies, we studied the area to discover stone quarries that do not turn grey when exposed to air and not crystallized (good lime stone or marble) on the north-west edge of the city.

The temenos of the temple was built by carving out the natural rock in the north and west. However, they either did not build anything else in the south and east of the building due to the difficult, steep nature of the land or walls that did originally stand here collapsed during earthquakes. It's more likely that the latter is true, seeing the shafts of columns lying thirty to forty meters down the terrace where the temple stood.

It is certain that the temple received many statues as gifts. Even now, you can see on the surface, a Hellenistic figurine (Pudicitia type) resting flat at the ground, broken at the neck and waist during an earthquake.

Moving west from the temple is a large cistern that was probably used to collect rain and snow. From this point on until the northwest edge of the city, we can see the ruins of many buildings including none other than heroons, mostly facing south, built of embossed blocks of 1x1.5x2.20 meters, with such great diligence that you cannot even run a razor blade through their joints. Most buildings cannot be identified as they are buried or covered by pine trees, cedar trees and bushes.

However, we identify these buildings to be heroons, based on the sarcophagus lids or pieces in the area, the inscriptions of which are illegible. To the northwest edge of the city lies a vast open field as well as the terrace walls.

We can see the ruins of the agora with excedras (outdoor benches) depicting shield images on their back pieces. To the north of and adjacent to the agora are the ruins of another structure that was probably the bouleuterion.

Another item worthy of note in Marmara is the building to the northeast of the temple, standing almost at the summit of the mountain. It appears that this was a theatrical building which was not built in a semi-circular plan like a regular theatre but rather, on a linear plan and had seating organized in a rectangular plan facing the orchestra's stage, which opened to the cliff on two sides.

The best-preserved examples of this type of unroofed buildings are in the city of Adada in Pisidia or Pessinus in Phrygia. It has to be intended for a certain religious ceremony. This sacred piece of land could have been dedicated to the God Men as well as Selene or Helios. Anyway, overlooking the whole Bay of Antalya all the way to Side, this place should be perceived as an alfresco temple that maybe served Selene or Men, because the big full moon rose from the east in the color of oranges, or maybe Helios, because the sun rose similarly at other times.

PHASELIS (NEAR TEKİROVA)

It was late 1980 or early 1981 that I received a phone call from the General Directorate of Ancient Monuments and Museums - as it was then called - to "cancel all lessons and be present at the Headquarters of the General Directorate at two p.m. sharp" and this is exactly how I got embroiled in the excavation of Phaselis. The reason why I came to define the situation as an "embroilment" is that at the time, I was busy enough working on excavations in both Erythrai and Arykanda. When I got there, the General Manager, the late Mr. Cüneyt Ölçer, gave me a rather hard-

Another item worthy of note in Marmara is the building to the northeast of the temple, standing almost at the summit of the mountain.

hitting and decisive speech: He was proposing that I start the excavation in Phaselis and he would give me all the support he could. I tried to explain that I was already carrying the responsibility of the excavation of two other ancient cities and that a third would be over my limits, at least in terms of the hours in a day, if nothing else. His reaction was all the more violent now and he told me, in a somewhat threatening tone, that the stakes were that I could lose the permits for the excavation I was leading in the other two cities; they could arrange with the University to let me go despite the lessons I was supposed to give; this was a vital

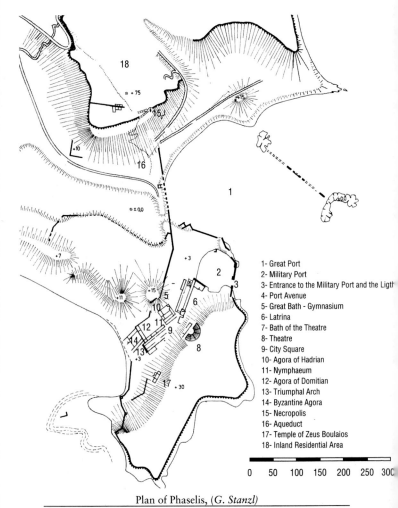

1- Great Port
2- Military Port
3- Entrance to the Military Port and the Ligth
4- Port Avenue
5- Great Bath - Gymnasium
6- Latrina
7- Bath of the Theatre
8- Theatre
9- City Square
10- Agora of Hadrian
11- Nymphaeum
12- Agora of Domitian
13- Triumphal Arch
14- Byzantine Agora
15- Necropolis
16- Aqueduct
17- Temple of Zeus Boulaios
18- Inland Residential Area

0   50   100   150   200   250   300

Plan of Phaselis, (*G. Stanzl*)

> *Remember this was back in 1980, and Phaselis was nothing more than an area of utmost deprivation.*

matter that needed to be resolved with the World Bank and I would be assigned to this duty after consultation with the Prime Minister, Mr. Demirel, who later became President of Turkey. Later, the speech softened and ended with compliments. Soon, he was talking about the resources of the Ministry of Culture and encouraging me about the Phaselis excavation because it could help us obtain all the tools and equipment required not only for this Southern Antalya Project but also for all the "Turkish excavation projects throughout Turkey". After lengthy discussion, I started working in Phaselis under one guarantee: All "bureaucratic barriers" would be raised.

Remember this was back in 1980, and Phaselis was nothing more than an area of utmost deprivation: We had to buy all provisions from Kemer and we did not even have a proper refrigerator. The buildings that are used as service facilities today were under construction. In the semester holiday of 1981, though it was winter, we worked on-site to finish what we had started in summer with the help and support of 2 female and 1 male student and a number of my former students working in the Antalya Museum. We stayed in the unfinished house of our friends in Tekirova - I would like to express my gratitude to dear Tanju and Çetin Anlağan - that we tried so hard to heat with a tiny stove simply called "the duck". My poor female students - they stayed in a metal caravan that we borrowed from the department of roads and they managed to warm themselves not just with blankets or quilts but under 2 or 3 mattresses. These were the conditions we worked under. I owe the girls a thank you: Deniz Kaptan, who became my assistant later, and Ayşegül Arslan.

The excavation ran smoothly between 1981 and 1985, but along with it came many administrative and financial problems, initially not expected. The support that Mr. Ölçer gave for the entire group of Turkish excavation projects basically melted away in the budgets of many Ministries that used it to run their own irrelevant projects. In the beginning, some of our demands such as a crane, some photography tools, a water facility to be connected to Phaselis and fencing around the ruins were declined. Only after lengthy

Lycia

Phaselis, the Peninsula

discussions, could we bring water to the ruins from Yarıkpınar and put up the fence. But the crane needed a bigger effort: I had to talk it over with the General Director of the World Bank.

The crane was mistakenly unloaded in the port of Mersin instead of Antalya and it was locked up in a warehouse in Kemer for over a year. It had the good luck to come into use in Phaselis and Arykanda only when I decided to double up as a crane operator and my son as the guiding car in front of the crane. The same crane was also used in Limyra. I suppose, after these two years of active service, the crane continued to serve in Perge and Side and, at least, paid for itself - although it could have paid for more.

We know that Phaselis was founded in 690 BC by colonists from Rhodes. But, it is certain that there was a settlement in the region before they arrived as confirmed by our knowledge that the locals served smoked fish to the colonists.

Ancient writings sometimes place Phaselis in Lycia (Livius XXXVII-23), and sometimes out of it (Ptolemaios V-3.5). As for Hierokles, he suggests that it was the last city on the border between Lycia and Pamphylia (683.I.). It is surprising to find contradictory information within the writings of Strabon especially about Phaselis (Strabon XIV. 667).

A study of the writings of the ancient authors starting from the earliest would reveal that after the Persian invasion in 546 BC, Phaselis made the surprising move of joining the Attic-Delos Maritime League as a separate entity from Lycia. We understand that Phaselis was on the side of the Greeks against the Persian invasion because, the Persian navy was prohibited by a treaty from entering into the Pamphylian Sea (Mare Pamphylian - Bay of Antalya, today) after Kimon's victory of 446 BC in Eurymedon. Phaselis must have joined the Attic-Delos Maritime League after the Eurymedon War, most probably. Phaselis was a member of the League until 436-435 BC. In his writings about Alexander's Military Expedition to Asia, Arrianos (Anabasis I.24) describes Phaselis as a separate city from Lycia. The same is also true for the writings of Diodoros (XX.27.4). Despite all these writings, Gül and Ümit Işın have recently conducted a study on the "Tomb of the Limping Unbeliever", upon my proposition: They discovered that Phaselis and Lycia had close relations before Alexander's arrival. The rock tomb in Lycian language that was found in the east of Ulupınar appears to be a major challenge to the former opinions. I do not think at all that these ruins that are within the territory of colonial cities such as Phaselis and Olympos serve to demonstrate that Pericles organized an expedition to the east and besieged Phaselis.

This new finding is further supported by the weights that we discovered in Phaselis as we can see the Lycian letter of "I" inscribed on them. But the most outstanding of all evidence is the monument or road sign called "stadios" that was discovered in Patara: The monument tells a lot about many Lycian cities in all directions and their distances to Patara. It even takes account of the border cities of the neighbouring region. Accordingly, Kaunos is the last city in the direction of Karia and Attaleia is the last city in the direction of Pamphylia. Therefore, Phaselis stands as part of Lycia in this monument.

We should pick up the story from the days of Alexander again to be able to make a better assessment of certain facts in the history of Phaselis. Alexander, the Great spent the winter in Phaselis and possibly because the people embraced and served him well, he felt the need to contribute to the city in one way or another. As we learn from the writings of both Arrianos and Diodoros, Phaselis had a serious conflict with the people of Marmara and Alexander organized an expedition to Marmara, which fell to Alexander almost overnight: People of Marmara who would continuously steal

Lycia

Phaselis, entrance to the Military Port; the lighthouses

the crops or damage the fields of Phaselis and even go so far as to kidnapping the women of Phaselis were thus punished for their deeds. We know of the dramatic end of the city where on the night of the battle, the youngmen sent away the women, children and elderly in the darkness of the night to the protecting arms of the forest, defended their city to the last drop of their blood and, when the end drew near, set fire to the whole city with their own hands and committed suicide.

Following the demise of Alexander, his commanders started to fight for power and authority, particularly over Anatolia. The reason was that Anatolia was a land full of potential. The Lycia Region remained for a long time under the rule of the Ptolemaios Dynasty in 309 BC, when Ptolemaios captured Phaselis and the entire region, and the reign of Ptolemaios Epiphanes, V - but with short breaks when the family lost and regained certain cities.

In the Lycian League that Eudemos and Lysanias established around mid-2nd century BC, Phaselis issued coins that, in the beginning, did not bear the inscription of ΛΥΚΙΩΝ - the symbol of the League. Perhaps, in the days of Artemidoros, the city was not a full member of the League. In the early 1st century BC, or around 80 or 79 BC, Phaselis was among the cities conquered by Zeniketes who had a thorough control over all of the eastern Mediterranean and used Olympos or some place close to Olympos as a base for his men. During the reign of Sulla, the Roman navy under the command of Manlius Servilius Isauricus Vulso punished Zeniketes and strove to reinstall peace and tranquillity in Anatolia - a land that Rome inherited from the Pergamon King, Attalos III. Naturally, both Olympos and Phaselis were expelled from the League as punishment for their allegiance with Zeniketes or at least, remaining silent against him. Consequentially, Phaselis and Olympos lost a major entitlement: That of issuing coins, in other words, their autonomy.

I do not wish to go into further details of history. But, I will touch on a few more points of importance. Phaselis was a city of Lycia that was a separate Roman province until the reign of Emperor Vespasian who made an administrative change by uniting Pamphylia and Lycia; thus, the name of the province changed and Phaselis became a city of this new province.

The fact that Emperor Domitian built an agora in Phaselis for some vague reason is a matter that needs thorough reckoning. Soon, he lost his power and his name at the gate of the agora was gone, too: Deleted. I believe it is evident from this incident that internal political matters of Rome changed policy even in the provinces.

Phaselis enjoyed the height of fortune and the most productive period of construction during the reign of Emperor Hadrian. His visit to the city was celebrated with an arch erected in his honor and he must have had some of the best days of his life here before starting the mourning for Antinous.

An earthquake during the reign of Antoninus Pius devastated Phaselis. The fact that we can see the name of Phaselis on the monument of Opramoas is interesting as it is evidence to the feeling of solidarity within Lycia after the earthquake in 141. This monument was erected in honor of Opramoas in gratitude for his contributions to Phaselis, bore an inscription and, perhaps, was decorated with statues, as it stood adjacent to the entrance of the Hadrian agora.

The earthquake of August 5, 240 appears to have hit Phaselis, as well, since Phaselis is among the cities entitled

Following the demise of Alexander, his commanders started to fight for power and authority, particularly over Anatolia.

by Emperor Gordianus, III to issue coins. However, the second half of the 3rd century AD came a great threat to the Bay of Antalya: Pisidians and pirates of Isauria. During the division of the Roman Empire, in addition to the many problems arising due to lack of administrative authority, Phaselis had to fight with the mosquitos reproducing around the former port (near the guard's house and service buildings today) which was turning into a swamp. The silted ports and the fact that all solutions were expected from the authorities must have seriously damaged Phaselis' exports of forestry products. Furthermore, clashes between pagans and Christians and the Arabic expeditions heading for Istanbul obviously made Phaselis a difficult place to live in. We must also keep in mind that Antalya, Side and Alanya - together with their hinterlands - competed with Phaselis, as all were important cities on the same bay.

In 1158 when the region was taken by the Turks, Phaselis was little more than a minor port village or haven for boats despite its three ports perfectly built to protect ships. Sailors and travellers, mostly British, who came to explore the area in the early 18th century should have felt the way Lakios of Kolophon felt when he first visited Phaselis and met Kylabros.

Defined as a completely abandoned area apart from a handful of fishermen's huts since the early 18th century,

The inscription on the gate of the Agora of Domitian

The earthquake of August 5, 240 appears to have hit Phaselis, as well, since Phaselis is among the cities entitled by Emperor Gordianus, III to issue coins.

Phaselis remained out of sight until 1970's, and was difficult to reach by land. Besides, it had a bad name for the many explorers that caught malaria here and passed away. Unfortunately, this evil seems to have struck the Schläger-Schäfer team between 1967 and 1970. The German survey manager, H. Schläger, and Ali Özgür from the same team left this world at a rather early age. I would like to express my heartfelt condolences and wish well-being to the surviving members of this team, which really did a great job in the area. It was their courageous surface survey that encouraged me to agree to do the excavation in 1981. But I, personally, may have gone a little too far - if not insanely too far - with that encouragement and set to work as a crane operator. With what I call today a near-lunatic courage, I lifted from the sea the statue pedestals standing along the sides of the port avenue of Phaselis, and the pieces of stones in the Latrina, bath and the agora. I am still terrified when I think of it today. My son who had only recently qualified for his drivers' license drove as a pioneer in a Volkswagen and we simply placed a signal lamp on top of the car as precaution. Driving the crane this way from Antalya to Finike or Arykanda and back to Antalya, again, sounds like a crazy thing to do today. Although I am already over 60, if I were ever in a position to operate that crane again, I would definitely do it, but maybe with a little more hesitation this time because I've got the virus of archaeology in my blood and it has infected the members of my family, who are mostly archaeologists, as well.

When I first set out to visit Phaselis, I thought I was in a jungle in Africa or South America. Since I was travelling alone, the only tool I had to protect myself was the Swiss knife in my pocket. I struggled to the city on the road connecting the two ports, along which the travellers of our day can easily walk. My only security was the power of my Swiss knife when I noticed the traces of snakes about 20 meters in length. Though scared to death, I looked at the ruins and managed to get a rough idea about the city. The work after 1981 followed this adventure and the ruins you

Phaselis, the ports and the peninsula

can see today in Phaselis are the result of nothing but the devoted efforts of the whole excavation team.

I would like to tell you two stories that, today, make us all laugh but, at the time, they gave me a hard time as the leader of excavation. I suppose, it was the excavation season in 1982. Three large boats from the "Italian or French" holiday village, today, the Club Mediterranée, embarked on the southern port one after another. The first boat carried food and drinks, the barbecue and some kitchenware. Because I did not see the barbecue very well in the beginning, I thought they were big boxes of picnic provisions. The other two boats, however, were full of over 100 men and women. Half the ladies were topless and some were entirely naked. Taking into consideration the general attitude of the time about ladies even in normal bikinis, I told the workers to break off from work and proceed to the military port and I immediately sent out for the tour organizer and forced him to ask the naked ladies to put on their swimming suits in order to avoid any accident or indecent assaults. Naturally, he objected to my words in the beginning. But when asked whether he would like to be responsible for any possible situation when an excavation worker might assault any of the visitors or hit his own brother, kin or fellow peasant with the pickaxe because he was busy staring at the visitors, the organizer was convinced after half an hour of discussion to move the barbecues to a place posing a lesser risk of fire. Apparently, he also considered the fact that although it was only 10 a.m., they had started serving the drinks to the visitors, who were expected to feel the effects of intoxication very soon as the heat of the sun rose. The barbecues were moved to another place where they couldn't start a fire - never to come back again - and the naked ladies and gentlemen started to appear in swimming suits, if nothing else.

And here's the second story: This time it was another foreign tour organizer having his visitors walk on the walls. I warned him that he was risking the lives of his visitors and himself walking on the walls since the walls could collapse or a single stone might break into pieces and they would all end up on the ground. I also explained him that due to the forest fires, the stones weren't as solid as they looked. His reaction was that I was preventing his trip. Just then the stone that he was standing on suddenly broke into pieces and he fell 1 or 1.5 meters. He was lucky to escape with only a few scratches. It happened that I bumped into the tour organizer again after I finished my work in Phaselis. As the old Turkish saying goes, "One misfortune is better than a thousand pieces of advice.": Never again did he forget to warn his visitors not to walk on walls. The excavation of Phaselis generally took place in July and August, apart from one season when we worked in February, as well. To give you a clue about the difficulty of the work we have done there: As a leader of excavation, and a man who loves swimming, I found time to swim no more than a couple of times during the whole campaign.

Although I am already over 60, if I were ever in a position to operate that crane again, I would definitely do it, but maybe with a little more hesitation this time because I've got

Phaselis, theatre

I remember one more incident that is striking as it portrays the conditions in 1980's. I have already told you the story about the crane. So, the crane arrived and stayed locked up for a whole year in Kemer where the treatment plant is today. We tried hard to find a crane operator in Antalya and failed. I notified the Manager of Antalya Museum, Mr. Kayhan Dörtlük, who was a former student of mine, in writing about my willingness to operate the crane in full acceptance of the responsibility arising therefrom. His reply was affirmative. Soon, I was trying to place a block of stone in the southern front of the Hadrian Agora in its original place. The stone was hanging in the air when I was approached by a French lady in horror: "What are you doing?", she asked with astonishment and I told her that we were working on an anastylosis, trying to place a stone back into its original place. Her reaction was violent as well as thought provoking: She said: "We", like a spokesperson for the whole group, "...wish to see it in ruins." This was a reaction worthy of consideration and should be decided on an international platform by "ICOMOS, ICROM or UNESCO". Aren't we allowed anastylosis, anymore? More and more, I am developing the opinion that these international organizations should make a decision, especially as concerns the excavators. Otherwise, each excavation will go on nothing else but its own, self-decided track and this will continue to be the trend so long as there are no other suggestions.

From all the excavated and studied sections of the city at the time-being we do not have findings from before the 6th century BC, which is the rough timing for a Corinthian aryballo that was rescued from a shipwreck by the Schläger and Schäfer team. However, some ceramics pieces have been collected on the surface that can be dated to the mid-6th century BC or the last quarter of the 5th century BC - An indication that the balance of power changed in the city at some point in time: it is a fact that the Persians were more bloodthirsty in some Lycian cities than others, as in the case of Xanthos, and just outside the borders of Lycia, in Kaunos. Still, this is not the case for all of Lycia - or Karia and Pamphylia since the Persians authorized many cities to mint coins despite the fact that they were, in fact, under Persian rule. In the beginning, the Persians were a great enemy of the Lycian people, and in the end, almost a friend, so to

Phaselis, piscina of the Great Bath

Lycia

Phaselis, Necropolis

say. The coins that were issued according to the Persian standards are the best evidence for this thinking.

The intelligent policies of the Persian leaders must be the reason that the Persian invasion was able to last so long in Anatolia, and even in Greece: A strong army devastates an equally powerful kingdom, Lydia, and while doing this, the rulers make sure that the news will spread quickly to all the other strong, revolting cities, reminding them that they, too, may share the same fate. Such a dire threat! The Persians absolutely knew that they could not defend Anatolia and Greece with their army of maximum 500,000 men and more importantly, in a land that is not truly theirs. So, first, they found themselves some supporters and then, went on to develop a safe and sound network of roads. Soon, thanks to their satrapy system, for over three centuries they were the ultimate sovereigns over a vast land where less than 1% of the overall population were of Persian origins. Besides, they would enforce their own standards in issuing coins before anybody knew it, not only in Phaselis but also in many other places.

However, today, if somebody asked me about what is still there in Phaselis to remind us of the more than three centuries of Persian rule, I would have but one answer: Nothing the city's but Persian origins. In our day, Phaselis

Phaselis, as it is today, spreads over a vast area with its necropolis starting at a distance of 3 kilometers before the junction on the motorway from Antalya.

appears more like a prosperous Roman rural city.

Phaselis, as it is today, spreads over a vast area with its necropolis starting at a distance of 3 kilometers before the junction on the motorway from Antalya. I am cognizant that one fourth of the city's necropolis still lies beyond the fences around Phaselis - the fences that I managed to provide for the city. The area that I fenced after overcoming a great many obstacles, at least comprises the city center and much of the necropolis although the fence has been cut in certain places.

You would have to be either illiterate or very absent-minded not to be able to reach Phaselis by land both through Kumluca-Kemer and Antalya. Arriving from sea is equally simple, the ports of Phaselis and especially the southern port, have become a busy haven for yacht tourism agencies and private yachts.

I will introduce the ruins for those arriving by land, ie. the majority of tourists coming here. I would like to start by saying that when you come to Phaselis by land from the junction on the road between Antalya and Kemer or Kumluca, you will be driving through or better on the necropolis since this is where the road runs until you reach the sea. Hitchhikers to Phaselis or slow drivers will notice on both sides of the road innumerable sarcophagus lids or stone tomb covers. This panorama will continue until the visitors get a view of the sea, or the northern port at a distance after the ticket booth.

If you stop at the point where you first see the sea and look north, you will see a terrace and a structure surrounded by column shafts. This structure has been identified as a temple by many explorers; however, I believe it is a large mausoleum constructed by a wealthy family from Phaselis in the form of a temple. Once you get down to the shore, you will see - in the middle of the sea- the ruins of smaller mausoleums and also a number of sarcophagi some of which have lost lids bearing reliefs. On the shore to the west of the northern port, you can see many mausoleums lined up to the north and east around the port. Near these mausoleums, you will find a stairway that leads to the top

Phaselis, Military Port

of the cliff where the civilian residential site was built in Phaselis, to the south of the road today.

I suppose that the first port used to be located on the land on the seaside in the shape of a neck, all the way to the service buildings, land which turns into a swamp to the south. Therefore, if anybody's going to research Phaselis from the Archaic and Classical ages until more recent times, I believe she should start this research not with the peninsula, which was an island until recently, but in this

If you stop at the point where you first see the sea and look north, you will see a terrace and a structure surrounded by column shafts.

Phaselis, city center

direction. I truly believe that an excavation should be started in this area because, recently, circumstances in the city have changed drastically: First, it was an act of nature - wild fire - but the second and third disasters came with a cigarette that was not crushed out properly or a picnic fire. The result is that a lush, green peninsula turned into the rapidly balding head of a man. Therefore, the area is in urgent need of first excavation, second forestation. And the reasoning here is quite simple: No excavator would ever dare again to cut back the green cover that will grow here out of the pine cones or other seeds, incidentally finding a home here. Though a rather unfortunate incident, this is the last chance that we will have for years to get a better idea of the city without cutting down trees and before the rainwater washes the topsoil to the sea.

The peninsula is characterized by early Byzantine buildings, avenues and streets all lying on in a grid plan. We can also see the ruins of churches or chapels covering a larger piece of area and usually in generally perceivable places. However, the early Byzantine city walls following the topography from the military port to the southern port give us the idea that buildings or the remains to the east and west of the city walls were also noteworthy buildings of the city. The first building inside the city walls starting from north is the theatre. The external northern wall of the skene building doubled up as a late period city wall and two gates were constructed at different times on the wall that covered the north of the parados, between the Hellenistic tower and the analemma wall where the northern entrance of the theatron was.

Phaselis, scene building of the theatre

The theater is a typical Roman building in both its plan and appearance. The two-storey skene and the gates survived to our day only to be recently struck by fire which melted the frames and lintels are similar to the Myra Theater. There is a block of stone that bears a single, 0,50 meter tall letter, namely that of "U", on the wall of the stage building - an indication that there used to be an outstanding inscription facing the theatron and the orchestra.

If we were to reach the theater not by the road leading eastward straight from the city square but by the stairway turning in the same direction, we would see, near the late period city walls and the west edge of the stairway, an inscription that can be read only in the afternoon or in the early hours of the day. Some of the words that we can read imply that there used to be the bouleuterion around the ruins with some straight walls that you can find close to the southern parados of the theater. The dimensions of the inscription are approximately 2x1x0.5 meter, and therefore, we cannot imagine that this must have been the original location of the inscription, and it couldn't have somehow been carried here from somewhere far away.

When you walk south following the contour towards the southern port from the level of the southern analemma wall of the theater, you will see an inscription decorated in its upper row of lines with rosettes and bukephalon, which reads DIOS BOULAIOS, and in the east, you will find the temenos of the temple of Zeus with altars and some statue pedestals, bearing inscriptions of Nero and Antoninus Pius. Many column bases and pieces from the upper floors of the temple are scattered intensively in this rather small area. The ruins suggest that it was a small temple for Zeus

Phaselis, the theatre and Mount Tahtalı

Boulaios in the plan of in antis or prostylos because, the total area where the pieces of the building lie is only the size of a small temple.

A short walk from here southeast and then north would take you to an area that has an L-shaped plan full of ungrooved columns lying here and there, surrounded by a stoa. The remains of two temples characterize the area, side by side, with visible crepidomas - unless it is an illusion created by the bushes. The place to see the best-preserved section of the late period city walls, this is where you can walk eastward on the coast of the southern port - you might get a little wet, though - to easily see the city walls built with columns placed horizontally on top of one another. These columns that are preserved to the level of the crepidomas must have belonged to the temples or been part of the stoa. If I am not mistaken, two temples erected side by side were dedicated to the two highly respected local gods in most Lycian cities, ie. the twins, Leto's children, Artemis and Apollon.

I warned you before that people should take extra care when walking in ancient cities and here, on this peninsula, there are many pear-shaped cisterns that are sometimes

> *During Pax Romana I, it was surely solid enough to connect the military port and the southern port.*

covered with bushes or grass. However, there is one special cistern that differs from all others in its structure, diameter and the two 6-meter long massive blocks of stone right at its mouth. It's an interesting cistern and you can find it in the west or northwest foot of the Zeus Boulaius Temple.

We find clues to what happened after the island turned into a peninsula in the many buildings constructed along the avenue that connected the military port with the southern port. It is apparent that the isthmus uniting the island and the mainland had completed most of its formation already in antiquity. During Pax Romana I, it was surely solid enough to connect the military port and the southern port. As a matter of fact, in the second half of the 1st century BC, Emperor Domitian constructed an agora close to the southern port and this is the greatest architectural evidence for our conclusion about the place. But we can still wonder if this was really where the isthmus used to be. Or was it situated more to the north, that is, to the northwest of the three agoras lined up between the southern port and the northern port? We found similar results from our research and observation in two places: The avenue between the military port and the southern port is paved with stone and when we were fixing the blocks of stones broken or misplaced by the raising roots of the trees, we discovered that it was a well-settled and hardened formation of sand dune underneath this avenue.

Back in the 1980's, as long as you took care to find the somewhat harder sand to drive on you could drive on the road, now asphalt, that led to the southern port from the point where the aqueduct enters the ruins of Phaselis. However, driving the crane on that road, I got stuck in soft sand anyway, since the vehicle was far too heavy for this road surface. I mean, the ground was still not well settled at the time. But, of course, it had a lot to do with me being absolutely inexperienced in crane-driving. But, there I was now, stuck in sand. Using all four wheels separately on this special crane, it took me 15 to 20 minutes of tactful driving to get the crane out of this difficult situation. But, then again, you can ask me: "Why were you the crane operator?"

Phaselis, Military Port

The answer is amazingly simple: At the time, there were a maximum of 10 crane operators around Antalya and each one of them was employed at the State's Roads Department or the Water Works Department. The excavation season was also the time that all their work was underway and the men were all very busy; so, naturally, our request for a crane operator had been declined. I thought, now that we had a crane in our hand, we could at least manage some maintenance to the level of anastylosis. This is how we were able to clean and bring back into day light the Triumphal Arch of Hadrian, put some of the pieces of the agoras of Domitian and Hadrian back where they belonged, recreate the latrina to a height of 3 meters on its northern edge and replace 15 to 20 blocks of stone in the bath of the theater as well as some other minor works. Now, this wasn't too bad, was it? I leave it to you and my colleagues to decide.

In this book, I have focused more on Arykanda and Phaselis as they happen to be the two cities that I have actually worked on in the excavations of in Lycia while, I can only retell the other events in the region. Furthermore I would really like you to consider my opinions, when necessary, as bits of self-criticism, which are not meant to disrespect the rights of any other excavators.

A second curious thing happened to me during the excavation in Phaselis, when we were replacing the upper row of lines of a block of inscription that was somehow related to Opromoas. The piece was in the façade of the Hadrian Agora, next to the gate. The lower lines of the inscription were still lying on the floor. Meanwhile, one of the students came up to me at the crane to tell me that Prof. Karl Dörner wanted to see me. He was wondering if I could

Phaselis, Agora of Hadrian

have a moment to say a few words about Phaselis to the people that came along with him in three buses. Once I had placed the inscription where it should be, I told them about my action plan and ended my speech asking Prof. Dörner (who is fluent in Greek) to please correct me if there were any mistakes in the composition of this inscription or if there were any omissions, which we could rectify together by finding and placing the relevant piece. Prof. Dörner was able to read the inscription even before it was up in the air suspending from the crane, and couldn't help saying: "I have never before seen an excavator operate a crane. You have introduced a new dimension to excavating." And he suggested helping with financing. That, we never got to find, but the round of applause from our (mostly foreign) colleagues was enough to raise our spirits.

Let us return to Phaselis and continue with our trip from the Domitian Agora. Since this structure has not been excavated inside, we do not have any idea about the shapes of the shops and the porticos in front of them. The only thing we know is that the gate of the Agora that opened to the port avenue was a vaulted gateway only large enough for pedestrians to walk through and the name of Domitian was scratched out of the inscription on the lintel after Domitian was disgraced.

Between the Domitian Agora and the Hadrian Agora on the same side of the street to the north, there used to be a street that would meet with the avenue there. At this junction, there stood two monumental nymphaeums: One on the side of the Domitian Agora, and the other on the side of the Hadrian Agora. The first of the two nymphaeums was built in a custom-made recess in the northeastern corner of the Domitian Agora whereas the second appears to have been on the side of the Hadrian Agora, as we understand from both the position of the ruins of its drain tiles on the western wall of the agora and the pipe tracks sloping down to about the center of the nymphaeum from the corner on the wall facing the avenue. The ruins prove that each nymphaeum had a basin, a single floor and a columned façade. The ruins on the surface guarantee that the nymphaeum on the side of the Domitian Agora cannot be dated earlier than mid-3rd century AD while the other, the one next to the Hadrian Agora, can be dated to the late 3rd century or early 4th century AD, as we understand from the font of the inscriptions, the architectural decorations and other elements of architecture. However, we would be merely prophesizing if we were to conclude that these two nymphaeums may be dated back to any earlier times, since they haven't been excavated as yet. The traces of drain tiles on the wall of the Hadrian Agora suggest that the nymphaeum next to the Hadrian Agora had drains that were apparently built after the nymphaeum had been constructed. The earliest that we could date this structure would have to be after the second half of the 2nd century AD.

There is no uncertainty about the Hadrian Agora, thanks to the statues above the postaments or the inscriptions stating Opromoas' contributions to Phaselis after the earthquake in 141, on two sides of the gate facing the street. However, the threshold is far too high in comparison to the level of the avenue. The doorstone, which even a young man would have to jump to step on, must have been supported by a wooden staircase since the avenue was prohibited to vehicles on both sides. The goods coming into the Hadrian Agora would be brought in not directly from the avenue in front but from the exact opposite direction,

One on the side of the Domitian Agora, and the other on the side of the Hadrian Agora.

Phaselis, entrance to the Agora of Hadrian

as in the case of the Domitian Agora.

The excavations inside the agora, excepting the basilica, show us that the agora was surrounded by shops on at least 3 of its sides and in front of these shops was a portico, mostly in situ even today. The northern wall of the Hadrian Agora was bordered with a street parallel to the southern wall. The land starting from this street and reaching close to the military port is marked with a building that used to be called the "Bishop's Palace" and which I prefer to call the "Great Baths - Gymnasium". Its praefurnios being in the direction of the southern port, this building has the plan of a bath with two sections similar to the baths in Perge. However, additions and repairs in later ages have transformed the original plan of the structure beyond recognition.

The bath-gymnasium complex reminds us of other buildings dating from the 3rd century AD with its rather jerry built walls made of rectangular blocks of stone, which they tried to hide behind with a soil mixture. We understand that this complex underwent major maintenance and repair in the 4th century AD, most probably as a direct consequence of such low-quality construction: New walls were built, some entrances were closed and most importantly, the repairers had it in their minds to separate the palaestra from the main building.

The floor of the palaestra is decorated with mosaics from the second half of the 5th century or the 6th century AD and the mosaic inscription is in situ even today on its original floor that has now been covered with soil merely for purposes of protection. After the separation of the palaestra

The frieze below the attica of the arch displayed its famed inscription, the proof of which lies in the ruins today.

and the baths, this section developed the appearance of a peristyle and that is exactly the reason why this piece of land was known as the "Bishop's Palace" - although it was not excavated at all. There is absolutely no evidence that the palaestra was indeed used by a Bishop however; and its appearance today is that of a villa, perhaps owned by a wealthy Byzantine family. I think, we should focus on the general outlook of this avenue before moving on to the ruins situated east of the port avenue. This avenue is completely paved with stone and it must have been like a covered stoa with steps on each side, the third step being built from perhaps, wooden boards. At certain intervals alongside the avenue were statues of prominent citizens, just like in the Kuret's Street in Ephesos, as we discovered from column bases bearing inscriptions that we relocated into the recesses. Many pedestals and inscriptions that had once stood along the road were used in the construction of the Byzantine pier. During our excavations in 1982, these pedestals in the pier were rescued from the sea, and although their exact original locations will never be known, placed along the road where they may have been. I give the visitors this particular information so they won't conclude that the pedestals have always been there. The avenue rises to a platform in front of the Hadrian Agora. There are stairways on both sides of this platform -evidence that the avenue was only open to pedestrians. The infrastructure along the avenue provided gutters that would collect not only the rainwater but also the wastewater from the buildings on both sides of the avenue. The wastewater and litter from the latrina and the theatre bath were carried to the military port through a sewerage, of which we can see sewers on the surface today.

The fact that the City Square was marked with columns on both sides, where the steps end in the north, is a rather curious one. They must have done this in an effort to reflect the Hadrian's Arch at the entrance of the city on the southern port.

This arch or monumental gate that was presumably finished by the time Hadrian visited Phaselis for the second time (131 AD) is a single-vaulted arch rising on two square

Phaselis, an aerial view of the peninsula

pedestals, adorned on all four corners with decorations in the form of lion's claws. You can reach this arch or monumental gate from the southern port along the ramp paved with blocks of stone. The side of the arch that faces the southern port is still standing up to beginning of the vault, ie. the niches where busts of Sabina and Faustina once stood. This side was decorated with spiral branches growing out of a kantharos or skyphos on each foot. The frieze below the attica of the arch displayed its famed inscription, the proof of which lies in the ruins today.

The area east of the port avenue is dotted with buildings that we haven't been able identify precisely, so far. Both the travellers of the 19th century and the explorers of our day have the tendency to describe such buildings as customs buildings. They also have the same opinion about the structures adjacent to the military port at the end of the avenue. I really think that it is a remote possibility that this city had so many customs buildings along the road between the southern port and the City Square and also on the other direction - between the military port and the City Square. And as long as these buildings remain unexcavated, I would rather describe them simply as buildings / ruins the functions of which remain unknown.

To the north of the land behind the Port Avenue that I have also referred to as the City Square, there is a building facing this avenue, called the Theatre Bath. Built on a Lycian bath plan, this building must have been constructed after the earthquake on August 5th, 240 because, there are some construction materials, buried in its walls, which were collected from the rubble of other buildings after the earthquake. The Theatre Bath must have remained functional until the end of the 8th century AD, the days of the Arabian raids, since while cleaning and repairing the bath we discovered a silver cross with cornelians and complete with its chain, which we believe establishes a link with either the Arabic attacks or the crusades. Surprisingly enough, Phaselis was abandoned after the 11th century.

Phaselis, the bath of the Theatre

If you walk north of the Theatre Bath, you will see a building decorated with mosaics on the floor, and surrounded with deep gutters on three sides. This must be the latrine, as it has entrances on two sides and the connection of the gutters to the wastewater channels. Apparently, the drain tiles that started from the southeastern wall of the Hadrian Agora and continued along the eastern wall did not only bring water to the nymphaeums but also to the latrine where the water was required for cleaning.

As I have told you before, the buildings standing on the northern end of the Port Avenue have always been described as customs buildings. Only after proper excavations can we decide for sure whether it was really customs operations that these buildings served.

The northern end of the Port Avenue reaches a pier with its bollards, which has survived to our day. The mouth of the military port stands out with two towers that apparently had lights: The lighthouse.

The jetty that was constructed from the rubble of the ruins in the east helped make the northern port a safe place to moor. The pier that was constructed on the rocky surface between the military port and the northern port served as an all-time favorite for ships seeking shelter in Phaselis against the southwest and northeast winds.

OLYMPOS (YANARTAŞ - ÇIRALI)

Twenty-five years ago, Olympos could not be reached by land, but only by the sea. Today, it is an ancient city and natural conservation area that is extremely easy to reach and frequently visited especially by young people of all countries. It would be useful to describe how to get there, despite its popularity. On the road from Antalya to Kumluca and Finike, a few kilometers past the recreational facilities in Ulupınar, you will see the turn on the left (east) that leads to Çıralı and then, a few kilometers ahead, you will see a second turn - the beginning of the road to Olympos. Visitors from Çıralı can reach Olympos in a matter of 15 minutes by an enjoyable walk on the beach. Boats from Antal-ya and Kemer marinas need to go in the direction of Finike and Kaş and boats from Kaş and Finike marinas need to head in the direction of Antalya, if they are to visit Olympos, anchor at the bay and enjoy the day.

Our findings suggest that Olympos was founded in the Hellenistic age. However, we can not be sure that there may not have been an earlier settlement or at least some sort of a port on the site of Olympos. But it was not until the 2nd century BC that Olympos started issuing coins of the Lycian League. Soon, in 100 BC, Olympos would be a major city and one of the six cities represented by three votes in the League. During the early 1st century BC, the Bay of Antalya was under heavy threat of pirate activity, which posed a risk for the interests of the Roman Empire in the Eastern Mediterranean area and Olympos was home to most of the pirates. After the Roman commander, Servilius Isauricus Vulso, chased and captured the pirate chief, Zeniketes, in 78 BC, the area was free of pirate activity and returned to Roman rule. However, one thing we know for sure is that, as punishment for their alliance with the pirates, Olympos was expelled from the Lycian League.

Once under Roman rule again, it did not take Olympos long to develop rapidly and the city owed a lot of this development to the cult of Hephaistos at nearby Yanartaş or Çıralı. A rich Lycian man, a Lyciarkh, namely Opramoas

---

But it was not until the 2nd century BC that Olympos started issuing coins of the Lycian League.

of Rhodiapolis, donated 12,000 Denarii to Olympos "for the festivities in honor of Hephaistos and the Emperor" in the aftermath of the earthquake in 141. The peak of development and construction of public facilities in the city was during the 2nd century and the first half of the 3rd century AD. The second half of the 3rd century AD once again saw increased pirate activity in the region and the city became the target of pirates: Attacked and looted, soon, Olympos would succumb to poverty and shrink into a village.

During the Medieval Age, the city was revived to a certain extent, thanks to the efforts of the Knights of Venice, Genoa and Rhodes. However, the Ottoman navy had already become the ultimate ruling power in the Mediterranean Sea around the 15th century and the city sank into abandonment and oblivion.

The city of Olympos was founded on the two sides of a valley created by a small stream. This valley is a narrow pass on one end; soon it grows into an open space only to narrow down again where it meets the sea. The cliffs to the north and south of the valley's mouth, opening to the sea and the beautiful beach, are marked with city walls and towers dating from the Medieval Age. One of the most striking ruins in this city is the vaulted family grave to the north of this stream close to the sea that has been excavated and restored by teams from the Antalya Museum. The

Olympos, aerial view

Lycia

Olympos, necropolis

sarcophagus that was found in this grave has the relief of a ship and is a must see.

If we walk west along the northern wall - one of the polygonal walls that have steps at certain intervals to board vessels - we see among the trees on the right the ruins of an ancient channel and the remains of a gate, which until recently we have thought to be a temple. To the right of this unfinished gate, there on the floor lies an inscription and some column capitals scattered around the place. Based on the findings, we understand that this building was built during the reign of Emperor Marcus Aurelius. The lush, green land behind the gate is a swamp, making it impossible to pinpoint any other walls.

The ruins of the bath with its back turned northward and resting on the rocks on the east end of the above-mentioned channel, is another ruin of interest, that is if only you can find a passage to get there among the bay trees, turpentine trees and ivies.

We understand that there used to be a bridge in the middle of the city over the stream that flowed through the city. You can see the bridge pier still showing in the middle of the stream as well as the remains of the bridge on the northern bank.

The ramp created by a polygonal wall west of the theatre seems to separate the necropolis from the residential area.

If we follow the southern bank of the stream inland, ie. in an east-to-west direction, as far as possible through the woods, the first building that will come our way is another bath connected to the sea. To the east of this ruin, there are the remains of a church the walls of which are even today marked with (almost invisible) traces of frescoes. Southwest of the church are the remains of a massive excedra or bouleuterion. The path that winds westward will take you to the theatre with vaulted paradoses. It has a semi-circular orchestra, its cavea has been built into the natural rock and the tiers of seats are still there to see.

Olympos, the gate

The ramp created by a polygonal wall west of the theatre seems to separate the necropolis from the residential area. The graves that are closer to the city are more often in the form of sarcophagi and there is one among them that stands out with its reliefs of Eros and the daphne leaves engraved on its lid. Generally, the other graves to be found in Olympos are vaulted family graves standing in a line and bearing inscriptions about the deceased above the gates on their lintels, often made of marble.

GÂVURPAZARI

Gâvurpazarı is an ancient settlement that appears to have been a major Lycian city although its precise name in antiquity remains unknown to us.

The road between Antalya and Kumluca is flat through Kemer, Phaselis and Tekirova all the way until Yarıkpınar. However, after Yarıkpınar, there are both flat parts and slight gradients along the road. Before the final steep hill, there is an asphalt road to "Beycik" turning north from the main road. This is the only way to reach Gâvurpazarı easily. A path leading first northeast and then east from "Aşağı Beycik", now full of summerhouses, takes us to Gâvurpazarı after half an hour of walking. The city is approximately 60 kilometers from the outskirts of Antalya and stands on the southern slope and foothills of Mount Tahtalı and can even be seen by a pair of binoculars from the resorts in Ulupınar.

These ruins, which no ancient author mentioned came to my knowledge thanks to one of my workers at the Phaselis excavations, who is a billionaire today, owns a villa in Beycik and a house and a shopping mall in Tekirova and used to be called "Kavlak" in the past. We even drove to the ruins on his tractor: We left the vehicle in "Yukarı Beycik" and walked the rest of the road. We had to return to Tekirova before sunset because we had to resume excavations early in the next morning in Phaselis. We were a team of 10 to 15 people as we came down the steep hill that begins in Yarıkpınar in the trailer of the tractor that did not have any gears and at a speed

Gâvurpazarı, heroon

Gâvurpazarı is an ancient settlement that appears to have been a major Lycian city although its precise name in antiquity remains unknown to us.

that was extremely unacceptable for any tractor. I remember that we could not even see what was ahead of us as the wind filled our eyes with tears as we sped down the hill. You may be sure therefore that "Kavlak" was really told off when we finally arrived in Tekirova in one piece.

The city used to lie on a slightly elevated plain that lies like a neck from west to east on the slopes of Mount Tahtalı. The mountain rises as we go north and the settlement was protected by the natural formations in the east and the south, as well. The buildings and their foundations - the terrace walls - doubled up as city walls. As a matter of fact, even in our day, we can only enter the city through the well-preserved building about which there is uncertainty: It may be a heroon or a propylon. The building had two west facing gates, one of which was smaller and the other was a regular size. The lintel is made of high quality masonry and is as strong as the city walls. There is an engraving of a lion's raised right claw on the lintel between two half-Ionian columns. This gate with reliefs is still standing and when all its pieces are restored, it will look almost as it did originally. However, we may conclude that what lies behind this gate was added later: as we can see from the foundations of the walls. With straight blocks of stones used in the walls and the general appearance of a parapet, the western and especially, the southern walls give us the idea that originally, this building was planned to be a propylon but later, maybe, its function was altered and then, the building was used for an all together different purpose. The facts that there is a small gate on the west-facing wall, that there are no south facing windows although the landscape is worthy of one, and that there are loopholes are all proof of our hypothesis.

It is clear that to the east and north of this gate or whatever it turned out to be later, there was the agora and the shops with still clear connection points to the rock behind. On a slightly higher level than the floor of the agora, there are the ruins of an Ionian or Corinthian temple, the true character of which we cannot tell for sure since we cannot find its pediment to get a precise idea of its age or order of construction.

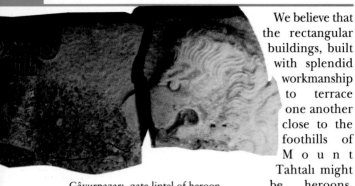

Gâvurpazarı, gate lintel of heroon

We believe that the rectangular buildings, built with splendid workmanship to terrace one another close to the foothills of M o u n t Tahtalı might be heroons. This idea is supported by our experience in other excavated and unexcavated ruins in Lycia and Pisidia.

The reason why the later inhabitants named these ruins "Gâvurpazarı" (The Market of the Unbeliever) still occupies my mind: There are no foreigners (unbelievers in religion or foreign language speakers) in the region and the position of the city is far from being one suitable for a "market" because it lies too far inland to be a marketplace, which are normally found in cities close to the sea. But all of a sudden, it dawned on me that the notorious pirate, Zeniketes, (c. 1st century BC) may have spent some time inland, far from the sea, and if so, he would have chosen a city that both overlooks and controls the sea and promises safety for his men. At this point, I turned for help to photographs and maps of the region. Zeniketes and his predecessors, could they ever have missed the opportunity to find a place to watch over both the Pamphylian Sea and the Bay of Finike? Zeniketes and his men, were they the first gang of bandits? The whole thing may be an indication that, during the epoch of Diadokhs, a number of cities did not remain under the exclusive control of a certain ruler for long periods of time, including some in Lycia. And the safety that a state seemed to offer was easily usurped by gangs of bandits, which is still the case in our times. Each time there was a gap in authority, certain persons or entities were quick to take over the role of the authority, and abuse such power at times. Soon, the market was in the hands of these persons or entities, like it or not.

I can easily imagine such a scenario taking place in ancient Gâvurpazarı and even find an explanation about

Gâvurpazarı, detail from the gate lintel of Heroon

the roots of the name of the area, and perhaps that explanation would be the right one: Pirates did not focus their activities on only bars of gold or accessories of gold, silver and similar precious metals but also, and sometimes mostly, human-beings as commercial goods. Thinking this way, we may wonder whether Gâvurpazarı used to be a place where men and women were traded and whether this commerce continued after the Asian colonization of the Mediterranean in the 8th century AD.

ULUPINAR

5 kilometers after the Ulupınar resort on the road between Antalya, Kumluca and Finike, there is a spring and another resort. Standing in front of this spring and looking northwest, we can see an ancient settlement, probably a small garrison with a part of its defence walls still visible atop steep rocks and its gate still standing.

If you drive slowly from Kumluca to Antalya, on the left hand side or west of the road, you will see the remains of Late Roman or Early Byzantine (mortar) walls, and the body of a sarcophagus on the slope of a small hill close to the spring that I have just mentioned.

You need to look west from the fountain to see the gate of the castle on the crest of the rocks - especially clear in the light of the afternoon hours.

This castle must have been a Late Roman or Early Byzantine garrison. The sarcophagi northwest of the castle give an indication that this garrison was used as an observation and defence post until Early Roman times since the castle, resting on steep rocks to its back and to the west, has a perfect view all the way to Kemer (Idyros) and Olympos (Çıralı) and even to the shores of Adrasan and to some extent, the valley of Alakır in the west.

If you want to see these ruins, look out for the "Potable Water" sign on the road after Ulupınar, park your vehicle near the fountain and climb up to the castle, which could take about half an hour.

It would be enough just to see and photograph from a distance the remains of a sarcophagus and some walls that are about 500 meters or 1 kilometer away from the spring in the direction of Kumluca, unless you are a professional archaeologist or a devotee, of course.

BELEN

When I started excavating Arykanda, Belen village and the hill behind it that lies some 15 kilometers before Kumluca from Antalya occupied my mind as I had a hunch that there could have been a Lycian settlement at the site. And this idea was not all together groundless: There was the lid of a sarcophagus with a relief of Eros on the side of the road until 3 or 4 years ago, and then there were some blocks of stones cut in straight lines, that we discovered in the woods to the south of the road leading to Belen village. These stones were remains of a major monumental grave and my experience of 42 years in the business was telling me that there had to be a settlement around here. We organized an excursion with our excavation team to Belen in 1991 to find out if my experience and observations would prove to be right. Indeed, what we found in Belen village showed that I was right: Walking south (half an hour at normal pace) from Belen village, we found the remains of a settlement over a small hill overlooking the Bay of Antalya all the way to the Finike plain and the vicinity of Adrasan. A small village or a field as it was, the settlement was home to a number of megaron-like structures and we were able to collect right from the surface, pieces of pottery dating back to the Early Hellenistic age - a discovery that made Belen a more important settlement straight away. Apart from a few

> *The position of Belen must have been unique for overseeing both land and sea traffic in antiquity.*

megarons built into the natural rock, two of my students later visited the area only to discover - in line with our expectations - Lycian rock graves in Belen, which we had not discovered in our earlier excursion.

The position of Belen must have been unique for overseeing both land and sea traffic in antiquity. The above-mentioned Hellenistic pottery findings reinforce the idea that the area was a patrol point together with its settlements, controlling the Limyra plain and Adrasan during the rule of Ptolemaios.

GAGAI

The legend goes that a group of people from Rhodes set out in search of a new homeland only to meet the worst of thunderstorms in the waters of Cape Gelidonia. Carried by the wind and waves, they end up on the shores of Yeniceköy. According to the myth, the immigrants shouted out "Ga! Ga!" in Greek ("Land! Land!") when they first saw the land ahead, hence the name of this place: "Gagai". History has seen the awkward currents and waves of "Hiera Akra" or the Sacred Hill or Nose, in other words Cape Gelidonia, swallow many ships into the depths. The oldest shipwreck discovered to date was discovered right here deep in the waters of Gelidonia.

I visited Gagai, which rests on the north and northeast slopes of Yeniceköy many times in the past. However, it's surprising to think that despite all my efforts, I haven't been able to find the ruins of any theater as G. Bean, who visited the area previously, claims to have seen.

Nevertheless, I would like to share with Turkish and international readers another curious thing that happened to me here: It was around 1970's that I had worked through another excavation season in Arykanda and was on my way to Antalya Museum to hand-deliver the findings from the site. I was driving a Volkswagen Beetle, which was not a very common car in the region. Thus, wherever I went, I was quickly recognized. I was stopped by the police in Kumluca and taken to see the Public Prosecutor. As an expert and interpreter I found myself quickly filling in a report about

> *Yeniceköy today is a 20-minute drive from Kumluca or Finike. However, without a guide, finding the ruins could take up to half a day.*

three foreign burglars who were apprehended in Yeniceköy. I have no idea about the further adventures of these three foreigners who were apprehended together with 3 or 4 more people in Yeniceköy; however, I am absolutely positive that Gagai is under continuous threat of treasure hunters. Unless the state and our caring people act now against the new class of quick money-makers that emerged in the last 10 to 15 years, Turkey will be a forgotten country looted and deprived of all of its cultural heritage, before we even realise what is going on.

Yeniceköy today is a 20-minute drive from Kumluca or Finike. However, without a guide, finding the ruins could take up to half a day.

MELAINIPPE

On the road between Finike and Kumluca, there is a road heading east from the point where the highway ends and the road becomes a regular single track road. This road will take you to Mavi Kent after 15 kilometers. Continuing east towards the Bay of Antalya from here, you will reach the Pirate's Bay or Melainippe after about 3 kilometers.

Founded on the side of Cape Gelidonia which faces the Bay of Finike, Melainippe must have been colonised during the first quarter of the 7th century BC, when cities like Gagai, Rhodiapolis and Phaselis were founded. While excavating in Arykanda, a large number of us visited this city no less than five or six times over the years but have been unable to collect any surface findings dating earlier than the Early Roman period, despite all the meticulous efforts of this large team of archaeologists. Our findings were only some pieces of ceramics.

The city walls surround the peninsula and the bay in a bow shape north-to-south and have survived with only negligible damage. Built as the connection point of the city to other settlements, the walls have a west-facing gate around the mid-point of the structure that is, more or less, the shape of a crescent moon.

Although we can see the ruins of a few buildings inside the city walls facing the bay, without proper excavations, it would be impossible to identify these buildings as they are heavily overgrown with trees and other plants.

No wonder the region was called the "Pirate's Bay". Only until 25 to 30 years ago, the bay was a haven for burglars - their base. The easy access to the open sea and the fact that the city was concealed discreetly under the lush, green, overgrown forests must have earned the place its name.

The Byzantine shipwreck that rests on shallow waters in this bay is a sign that Melainippe continued to be a shelter for ships that survived the perils of Cape Gelidonia in late antiquity.

The ceramics kilns that Ms. Ayşe Dinçer photographed on the road connecting the ruins to Mavi Kent can be regarded as a proof that Melainippe was not only a good port but it also had a central role in storing and forwarding certain products - especially fluid ones.

RHODIAPOLIS (HACIALİLER-HACİVELİLER-ŞEYHKÖY)

Follow the road from Kumluca to Turunçova and try not to miss the yellow sign for Rhodiapolis at Hacıaliler or Haciveliler, two villages founded by two bellicose brothers. The road running through the village along the gorge will take you northwest of Kumluca and close to Rhodiapolis, thanks to the citrus fruit garden in the middle of the forest.

If you are driving from Antalya to Kumluca, Finike and Kaş, you would be best advised to take a break at the

Rhodiapolis, the inscriptions of Opramoas

Rhodiapolis, a tomb

roadside cafes - some have names like "manzara kahvesi" ("belvedere café") or "şahin tepesi" ("the hill of the hawk") - in the forest called "Horoz ötmez" ("Where the rooster never crows").

This place has a marvellous view over the Kumluca and Finike plains. From this point, you can easily locate Rhodiapolis. Looking west, you will see the smooth slopes of a small hill northwest of Kumluca, where there are channels or tracks looking like roads and where the forest starts.

This is exactly where you will find Rhodiapolis. When you're looking in the right direction from the belvedere cafés, you will notice that in the center of this hill, there is a valley studded with trees. Once you locate this valley and reach Hacıaliler or Hacıveliler village, to find Rhodiapolis without a guide you must find and reach this valley. The path will turn west and then, north after the citrus fruits garden and will eventually lead you to Rhodiapolis.

Given that nearby cities like Gagai, Olympos, Phaselis and Korydalla were all founded by people from Rhodes and given the name of the city itself, we cannot overlook the possibility that Rhodiapolis was a colony of Rhodes. Besides, Hekataios of Miletos mentions Rhodiapolis in his writings, also affirming this hypothesis.

Until 3 to 4 years ago, Rhodiapolis - if indeed a colony of Rhodes - was the easternmost city where the Lycian language could be seen on a rock grave. The rock grave

> *When you're looking in the right direction from the belvedere cafés, you will notice that in the center of this hill, there is a valley studded with trees.*

near Ulupınar that is commonly called "Unbeliever, the Limp" with its inscription in Lycian language, has now deprived Rhodiapolis of this honour. I can say that this was expected since otherwise, we would be forced to exclude from Lycia the city of Phaselis that, like Olympos, had been a part of, expelled from and then re-accepted into the Lycian League. I must express my happiness for Gül and Ümit Işın, two of my students, who discovered and published their findings about these graves, which I had heard of from villagers during the excavations in Phaselis but actually, never got to find.

Apart from this rock grave bearing an inscription in Lycian language, Rhodiapolis is rather poor in ruins dating back to any time earlier than the 4th century BC. The Hellenistic tower or lookout point must have been constructed during the rule of the Ptolemaios dynasty. However, it is also a fact that Rhodiapolis was one of the last milestones for Alexander, the Great and his army before they could reached Phaselis to spend the winter.

Apart from the rock grave and the Hellenistic tower, Rhodiapolis gives us the impression of a traditional Roman city. We believe that the word of wedrêi' in this inscription must be the name of Rhodiapolis in the Lycian language.

The fact that the city was founded in a forest and offered enough protection from enemies gave rise to the construction of many Early Byzantine buildings. Still, we can find the traces of the time of Opramoas of Lycia who supported a great many Lycian cities in the aftermath of the earthquake that hit in 141 AD. Opramoas was a rich man who contributed thousands of denarii to almost each and every Lycian city after the earthquake and repaired - and in some cases built anew - the temples, theatres and other buildings that were devastated by this terrible disaster in many cities.

Along with his correspondence with the Roman Emperors the monument erected in his honor in the southwest of the Rhodiapolis Theater sheds a lot of light on the cities he has helped and his donations as well. In

Rhodiapolis, cisterns and the Byzantine ruins

particular, his correspondence with Antoninus Pius, the fact that he was appointed "Lyciarkh" as someone from the locals, and the inscriptions collected in "TAM", Tituli Asiae Minoris provide us with all the information we need to understand this particular period of time.

Rhodiapolis lies on a smooth plain, almost defenceless. The residential part of Rhodiapolis used to be on the fairly flat land on the crest of the small hill near Hacıaliler-Hacıveliler or Şeyhköy village.

The settlement is naturally centred around structures that were public buildings. The point where the path first arrives at the city is where the city stood until Late Antiquity (or late Byzantine) and Roman times.

To the southeast edge of the land where Rhodiapolis lies, you can see the ruins of a stadium-like building with three steps on one of its sides. This structure, which travellers and contemporary authors, alike, described as a stadium is nothing but an avenue with places to rest on its sides, the likes of which can be seen in Kadyanda and Phaselis: A stadium with a floor of blocks of stone has never been seen in antiquity or in our times!

Towards the northeast end of this avenue, we can clearly see the theater and some other buildings. Walking on, we can see the ruins of an inscription surrounded by many inscribed blocks of stone lying about.

These are all that is left of an outstanding monument that once honored the good deeds of Opramoas who contributed greatly to Lycia at one point in time and his relations with the emperors.

Towards the northeast end of this avenue, we can clearly see the theater and some other buildings.

After a short northward walk from this monument, we come across the theater that lies in a perfect Greek plan. Its skene is falling apart; however, the theater's best preserved section happens to be the theatron.

Built in a similar plan to Kadyanda, Pınara and Arykanda theaters, this building was definitely hit by the earthquake in 141 and it can be dated to the end of 1st century BC or early 1st century AD.

The southwest end of the avenue that used to be known as the stadium is marked by vaulted and tiled sections of the underground floors of many buildings from the Early Byzantine period. To the north of these vaulted buildings, we can find a bath, typical in its plan, and a caldarium ending in an apsidal form - One of the most striking ruins from the Roman days of the city.

It was after Rhodiapolis was victim to a forest fire that I strolled through the city to find by surprise that walking northward from the bath takes you to a tholos near the Byzantine Basilica. A few years later, the flora was so grown that despite numerous attempts, I couldn't locate the same tholos ever again.

Rhodiapolis, theatre

Rhodiapolis, the late building

Apparently that there used to be official or public buildings around the ruins that can be called city walls or terrace walls. However, we need to excavate the area to be able to arrive at a scientific conclusion as to the real functions of such buildings.

Returning to the theater and walking northeast from here, we arrive at a Hellenistic tower that was terribly despoiled by treasure hunters. Since we do not know of its connection with the Hellenistic city walls, if any, this tower could well have been a watch tower.

The necropolis mainly lies east, southeast and north of Rhodiapolis. The most striking ruins in the necropolis, where there are mostly Roman sarcophagi, are those of the rock grave bearing an inscription in the Lycian language. Until recently, this rock grave was known to be the easternmost example of rock graves in Lycia.

A visit to the ruins of Rhodiapolis can be concluded with one final structure: The aqueduct bringing water to the city from Alakır Stream.

Today, the aqueduct still lies northwest of the city and it must have brought Rhodiapolis the water it needed from a far away source.

Since all the ruins and findings in the area date back to before the 7th century AD, we can presume that Rhodiapolis must have been deserted around this time for a reason that remains unknown to us.

Another way to get there is the poor-quality asphalt-covered road branching off from the Finike - Elmalı road at Turunçova.

KORYDALLA (KUMLUCA)

Korydalla once stood on the plain north of Kumluca approximately 90 kilometers from Antalya on the road to Finike, on the hill northwest of Kumluca where you can see a water tank. Some 18 kilometers before Finike, the place is accessible in a matter of 15 minutes by the highway. Another way to get there is the poor-quality but asphalt-covered road branching off from the Finike - Elmalı road at Turunçova.

Travellers in the 19th century saw many ruins in Korydalla and produced engravings of these ruins. However, even the city walls and the aqueduct that I saw with my own eyes about 30 years ago are eithter nowhere to be seen or are beyond recognition today. We cannot even find the bilingual inscription in Lycian language and Greek that G. Bean reportedly discovered in the wall of a new building.

A large village 30 years ago, Kumluca is today rich in greenhouses and citrus fruit gardens and seems to have developed an tendency to invest all its wealth into buildings of reinforced concrete.

PHOINIKOS (FİNİKE)

I do believe that Phoinikos owes its existence as the port city of Limyra to the rivers around it since it was Limyra that held a vast territory as well cultivating the plains of Finike while Phoinikos hardly had any land to cultivate. Therefore, Phoinikos existed almost until today as merely a tiny port.

As a matter of fact, the city was on a crossroads in antiquity as well and at certain times, thanks to agricultural innovations, they had the potential to harvest a few crops annually; however, perhaps owing to the conservatism of the people of our day as well as of antiquity, the city appears both as an ancient city and a modern city that has quickly become the target of unplanned urbanization in the course of the last decade. We know from a an engraving that appeared in a publication dated 1701 that Phoinikos was surrounded by city walls in the Medieval Age. We also know from the articles of Italian explorers who conducted field surveys in the Antalya area back in 1916 that the ruins of the city walls were still standing near the port until the turn of the last century. Most probably, the Medieval city walls were built on the ruins of Hellenistic or Roman city walls and what is left to se of it today is a tower and a few rows of building blocks that survive intact on a heap of rocks inside the city.

LIMYRA

The city of Limyra had its acropolis on the southern foothills of Mount Toçak on a slope of 40-45 degrees. In the acropolis, you can see buildings mostly from the early ages. The city also filled the area inside the Roman and Byzantine city walls that were built on the plain to the south of the acropolis (now, separated from it by the road). The city's formation and borders in the early ages seem to have spread over the foothills of Mount Toçak. However, in later ages, the settlement concentrated on the islands (and thus, was safer) to the south of the road. The islands were natural formations created by the fast-flowing waters of the nearby springs, although the city was built on a plain. The northernmost section of the land that can be roughly described as the combination of two trapezoid shaped areas connected upside down at their points appears to have been what we can call the "inner castle" with its well-preserved walls. At an altitude of 315 meters from the sea level, the area is

Limyra, a fire altar

> *The third terrace wall after the inner castle is bounded in the south by the Hellenistic or earlier city walls.*

only accessible through a gate in the south. The striking remains in the inner castle are the fire altars that prove the Persian influence on Lycia and Limyra, in particular. These altars are similar in shape and they end in a pouch-like hole used as the place to start the fire. You can reach them by a few steps hewn out of the natural rock. The triangular land that spreads southward from the inner castle is marked with a tumulus in Karian style as suggested by its slightly broader south face and its terrace wall. Another find here is a stella depicting a double-ended axe. There is a path ending in a rock-cut stairway on the northeastern edge of the Byzantine church that stands on a terrace near the terrace wall north of Pericles' Heroon monument. This monument lies north of the ruins of the fire altars mentioned above.

The third terrace wall after the inner castle is bounded in the south by the Hellenistic or earlier city walls. Around the center of these city walls or terrace walls, Pericles' heroon rises in the direction of the natural slope. The monument has the plan of an amphiprostylos and caryatids support its architrave. The building stands on a podium that is plain in decoration right behind the crepidoma and reliefs start after this plainly decorated section. The building was burnt and thus, is currently under conservation and restoration in the Antalya Museum. I would like to give you some information about how the heroon was burnt: It was in 1993, when Prof. Dr. J. Borchhardt organized a feast for the excavation teams working in Lycia and the prominent citizens of Finike. More than one hundred guests were entertained in Borchhardt's island. During the feast, the commissar of the Lycia excavations was slightly wounded from a couple of shots that ricocheted from a sporting gun. But we found out a couple of days later that soon after we, the Arykanda excavation team, left around eleven p.m somebody set fire to the heroon, the protective wooden shelter was bunt down and the caryatids suffered some major damages. One year later, the damaged caryatids were transported by the Turkish Airforce down to the excavation area from the acropolis, thanks to the praiseworthy efforts

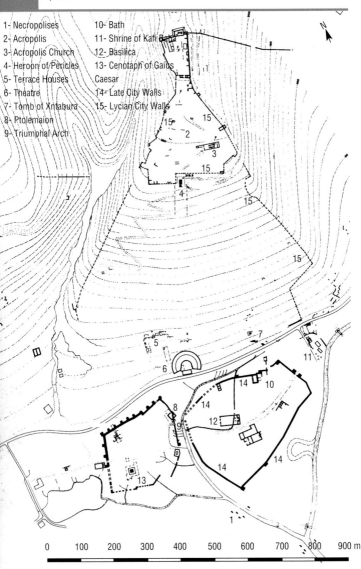

1- Necropolises
2- Acropolis
3- Acropolis Church
4- Heroon of Pericles
5- Terrace Houses
6- Theatre
7- Tomb of Xntabura
8- Ptolemaion
9- Triumphal Arch
10- Bath
11- Shrine of Kafi
12- Basilica
13- Cenotaph of Gaius Caesar
14- Late City Walls
15- Lycian City Walls

Plan of Limyra, (*G. Stanzl*)

of Ms. Emel Örgen, Ministry Representative of Limyra, and Dr. Borchhardt's financial support. The caryatids were carried in helicopters to the excavation center and were later transported to Antalya Museum for conservation and restoration to further great celebration. Today, some parts

> *Of course, the caryatids in the heroon of Limyra are in the shape of Ionian ladies both in their clothes and hairstyles, since they are locals of Anatolia.*

of this monument, which depicts Pericles in its reliefs, can be found in Limyra excavation warehouse and others in the Antalya Museum.

The building, which has the plan of an amphiprostylos, is a mausoleum largely imitating the Nereids Monument in Xanthos, the difference being that the monument in Xanthos is decorated with Nereid statues between the columns whereas the mausoleum in Limyra comes with caryatids in lieu of regular columns. Of course, the caryatids in the heroon of Limyra are in the shape of Ionian ladies both in their clothes and hairstyles, since they are locals of Anatolia. The dominant style is that of Ionic and Aiolic sculpture. Despite the Ionic and Aiolic influence on the caryatids, the friezes show more Phrygian or Persian influence with the Greek-looking persons depicted in the friezes in their clothes and hats. Even the horses stress the existence of various styles in this monument with their different heads and ears: To give you an example, there is a frieze said by its excavators to be part of the eastern face of Pericles' Mausoleum. On this very frieze, the different appearances of horses as well as human beings were intentionally emphasized. The Persians or their supporters were depicted on Persian horses with heads bulging between the nose and the forehead whereas the other characters, probably Greek, are on horses with a furrow above the nose. I strongly believe that this is far from being a coincidence but an intended feature of the frieze. Since we do not have the friezes in their original complete form, we do not have the chance to see the stories in full. The building is now precisely dated to 390 to 370 BC and its pediments are plain, ie. without any

Limyra, a caryatid

Lycia

Limyra, terrace house

reliefs, in contrast to the expectations of many. However, the southern acroterium depicted Bellerophon slaughtering Khimaira while the two acroteriums on the corners depicted the fleeing sisters of the Gorgon. The northern acroterium depicted Perseus beheading the Gorgon and the other figures on both sides showed some other foes of the hero: Khimaira, Amazons or Solyms.

The stairway leading down from Pericles' Monument to the Roman city takes us to the terrace houses near the northern entrance of the theater, which are said to be Lycian houses. One house excavated here is notable for its very special rock-cut niche, which suggests a domestic cult had developed in Lycia.

The most note worthy structure on the foothill or the plain side of the acropolis is the theater that dates back to the Hellenistic age and that was rebuilt after the earthquake in 141 AD with the help of Opramoas. Today, the road between Turunçova and Kumluca runs over the stage of the theater. With its galleries, diazoma and niches on analemma walls, it is clear that the theater - though of a Hellenistic origin - was enlarged and modified during the reign of Augustus and then again, during the Roman Empire. A scaenae frons was appended to the original structure in late 2nd century AD.

The south of the road between Turunçova and Kumluca is in the form of two separate islands divided by the Limyros Stream. Entrance to the island surrounded in the east by

Limyra, theatre

city walls is through the gate controlled by two square-plan towers near the dervish lodge of the Bektashi dervish Kâfi Baba. This gate is connected to the city center in the west via an ancient colonnaded avenue, the west end of which reaches the area used as the excavation center today. North of the avenue, close to the center of the island, are the ruins of what is named by the excavators the "episcopal church" and south of the avenue is the "Bishop's Palace". Both of these buildings are dated to the Early Byzantine Age. The western section of Limyros inside the Early Byzantine city walls is characterized by buildings that are older than those on the eastern section as we can tell from the construction technique and the materials. Inside the southeastern eastern section of the city walls, protected by a circular tower on the side of the road, an excavation has unearthed a large section of the crepidoma and podium of a building named the "Ptolemaion". We suppose that the colonnaded avenue mentioned above continued west to reach this Ptolemaion and was most probably constructed over the ceremonial

The south of the road between Turunçova and Kumluca is in the form of two separate islands divided by the Limyros Stream.

Lycia

Limyra, basilica

road that, in the Hellenistic Age, followed the same path to reach the building of this monarch's cult. This symbolic monument that was dedicated to either Arsinoe or Berenike, has a podium on the ground floor and straight walls rising on the crepidoma, all together ending in what we call a Doric Frieze. The end of the Podium displays lines of triglyphs and metops, which are elements of the Doric order. The metops unearthed during excavations depict scenes from Kentauromakhi, in a more elaborate baroque style than those found on the Altar of Zeus in Pergamon. The second floor appears as a tholos with lion statues on the corners and the tholos is formed by Ionic columns. The roof is thatched with bay leaves. Prof. Dr. Borchhardt concluded that there might well have been statues between the columns of tholos, much like the Nereids Monument in Xanthos, and that a larger-than-normal statue that was discovered in the area could have been that of Arsinoe or Berenike.

During the 2001 campaign, a small church was unearthed in front of the southern corner of the Ptolemaion. South of the church, a colonnaded avenue laid with rectangular blocks of stones begins. This is where the recently discovered ruins of the two preserved pedestals of a monumental arch still stand in-situ.

Excavations at the northwest corner of the island surrounded by Byzantine city walls that we could call the "West City" revealed a Lycian gate with a doorframe in the

> *The excavations further produced quite striking details about the date when Limyra was first inhabited.*

shape of a prism, much like the one in Pınara. The excavations further produced quite striking details about the date when Limyra was first inhabited. A stone axe dating back to the Late Bronze Age and the ceramics to the Late Geometric - Early Orientalist period, all of which were discovered in Patara, Xanthos, Kyaenai, Tlos and Arykanda, were also discovered in Limyra.

Also found in this particular area is an interesting Cenotaph - symbolic monumental grave - erected in memory of Gaius Caesar, the adopted son of Augustus, who passed away in Limyra on the 21st day of February in the year 4 AD on his way back from his excursion to Syria. As a matter of fact, the ashes of Gaius Caesar were shipped to Rome but upon the order of his father, Augustus, the artists of the empire erected this monument in Limyra, the very place where the son passed away. Today, you may imagine the cenotaph as a structure built in the middle of a pool, as the waters have risen since then. However, taking into consideration that Limyra's ground layers during the 4th century AD are below the surface of the sea today, we can see the subsidence in southern Anatolia and the creation of sunk cities as a natural phenomenon. What stands of the original building today is the inner block. The blocks of marble around the building must have been removed during the construction

Limyra, monumental tomb of Xntabura

Limyra, the theatre and the city walls of late period

of the city walls. Despite the truly fastidious work and efforts of Joachim Ganzert, there are still certain issues that are not too clear about the upper structure of Gaius Caesar's Cenotaph. It is generally believed that the building stood on a high, square podium and was covered with a pyramid roof. We are absolutely certain that this building dates back to the reign of Augustus and we believe that the extremely high-quality blocks of friezes belonging to this building surrounded the entrance that stood over the square podium or the building on all four sides. One of the best-preserved sections of these friezes was discovered near the swamp by pure coincidence much later than when Ganzert worked in the area. These findings are currently on display at the Antalya Archaeology Museum.

Limyra is the richest city of Lycia when it comes to rock graves. At first, it may seem that Myra is more important with its outstanding rock graves or Pınara with its pigeon-hole rock graves, however, Limyra is the first of its ilk in Lycia with over 400, mostly real rock graves. And we can name almost each and every rock grave thanks to their inscriptions in the Lycian language (eg. the rock graves of Xntabura, Sidarius, Kuwate, Taburastili, etc.). Some others are famous for their reliefs. Most of them date earlier than mid-4th century BC. If you would like to read more on the subject, please see "Lykische Grabreliefs des 5. und 4.jhds. v. Chr." written by Ms. Dr. Christine Bruns Özgan. The necropolis that truly belongs to Limyra - as opposed to the

I would like to conclude my words about Limyra with its bridges. Apparently, there are a number of bridges over Saklısu in the city.

Limyra, rock tombs

necropolis area of Çavdır and the area called Necropolis No.1 near Limyra - is extremely striking with its beautiful rock graves. The recent excavation in the Necropolis No. IV and No. V. unearthed pieces imported from Attica around the 5th century BC as well as some other graves the precise dating of which is quite possible. The land outside the city walls and the southern plain were also used as a necropolis during the Roman Empire.

I would like to conclude my words about Limyra with its bridges. Apparently, there are a number of bridges over Saklısu in the city. But a rare example is the Roman Bridge spanning 360 meters with its 28 arches that connects Limyra, Korydalla and Rhodiapolis. And it is still in use today! You can reach this bridge over Alakır Stream if you follow the road between Turunçova and Kumluca and turn left - north of the stone quarry. The points where the banisters once stood are clearly visible today on this bridge, which was constructed in a low-arch style with custom-produced bricks.

ÇAVDIR

I would like to start my words by making one thing clear: The excavation team who worked on Limyra have made it a custom to include into their territories two necropolis areas while in fact, these areas have nothing in common with Limyra. My very dear friend the "Master of Zemuri", as he is known among friends, Prof. Dr. J. Borchhardt extended way too far the necropolises of Limyra to the north and west. I suppose he would accept that Limyra's necropolis is bordered by two grave-like monuments. Therefore, the rock graves that the Limyra excavation team named "Necropolis No.1" and the graves in Çavdır are not directly related. Necropolis No.1 is 6 - 7 kilometers from Limyra whereas Çavdır is no less than 10 kilometers away from the city even on the shortest road that we have today. The necropolis of Zemuri or Limyra lies east of Yuvalılar village towards the slopes of Mount Toçak and definitely makes Limyra the richest Lycian city in the number of rock graves.

I am not coming up with this concept to engage in polemics or a professional discussion with a beloved and very successful colleague. Besides, I can defend my ideas in the international forum, if necessary.

I am trying to achieve the setting of the boundaries between the Necropolis No.1 of the Limyra team and the necropolis of Çavdır. Thus, I have discussed it with so many people in Finike, Turunçova and other residential areas in the region. I have studied several times with my small team of explorers Mount Kaklık or Keşlik that had been previously studied by the teams from the Office of National Parks, who went so far as to even register officially that there is a theater in the area. I listened to the shepherds who knew the area by heart as they grazed their livestock here. But, I listened to them having in mind a bad experience with a shepherd. I would like to tell you about it as a proof that in every country and of course, in Turkey, there are people who are half blind or prefer to appear like one: There we were standing in front of the Katabura or Xntabura grave in Limyra. We held a photograph of the grave in our hand

The valley where these graves are found can be reached from the road that leads west near the last mosque (with a minaret) at the end of Turunçova.

and asked the shepherd that walked in our direction if he had ever seen a grave or a structure around here that looked like the one in the photograph. He replied in perfect resolution that he had never seen anything like it, not here and not on the entire Mount Toçak. We simply showed him the grave behind. And now, he gave us the weirdest reply: "Who put it here and when?" This is exactly what we found out after getting to know the region and its people: Those who seem indifferent to their surrounding at first glance may tend to fool you with such naive words.

Let's go back to Mount Kaklık or Keşlik where our team apparently missed the rock graves. These graves must have belonged to the settlement in the area. The valley where these graves are found can be reached from the road that leads west near the last mosque (with a minaret) at the end of Turunçova. Continuing along the foothills of Mount Keşlik or Kaklık and west before strolling too far from the mountain, you will arrive at a few houses, which may be more than few today. This is where you should follow the riverbed northward and reach the necropolis after a 15-to-20 minute walk.

The one and only grave west of the riverbed, which has been partially destroyed by dynamite in the last decade, is the rock grave of a Lycian family and dates back to the 4th century BC. The father, mother, children and servants are all on display here. The excavations of the Limyra team in 1995 and 1996 uncovered the altar in front of the grave as well as the remnants of the channel and the road connecting to the altar.

Right opposite this rock grave and slightly to the north is another group of rock graves that have been seriously impaired by treasure hunters.

ARYKANDA

It was lunch-time in the 2nd Lycian Symposium in

Arykanda, stadium

Lycia

Arykanda, Temple of Helios

Vienna that Prof. Neumann explained - on the back of the bill that the waiter brought to be paid - that the name of the city in the Lycian language was "Ary-ka-wanda", in other words "the place near the high rocks". Later, he would make a publication on the issue and announce it to the rest of the world.

I don't mean to be harsh anymore on Prof. Neumann who, in his article, illustrated that the names of places ending in the suffixes of "-anda" and "-wanda" are of Luwian origins, which is a truth that is now accepted by all philologists and epigraphists. In other words, we can suppose that as early as the beginning of the 2nd millenium BC, there was a new settlement by a group of people on the Teke Peninsula who considered themselves a people that had emigrated from Crete. A bronze tablet that has been recently discovered in Boğazköy (Hattusa) and published by Prof. Dr. H. Otten is especially striking with its content regarding the chronological details of this country. Currently, the most outstanding connection between Arykanda and Lycia is the fact that in the first half of the 2nd millenium BC, there lived a Luggu or Lugga tribe in this region. Since it would be most inappropriate to identify a non-vassal settlement as a place that paid tribute to a vassal state, it is possible to conclude that there was some sort of

Besides, axes dating to the late Calcolithic - early Bronze ages recently discovered in Arykanda, Limyra and Patara are evidencing that the region was intensely populated in earlier ages.

an authority on the Teke Peninsula during and before the reign of Thudaliya IV. Besides, axes dating to the late Calcolithic - early Bronze ages recently discovered in Arykanda, Limyra and Patara are evidencing that the region was intensely populated in earlier ages. The Hacımusalar Höyük that lies no more than 15 kilometers and the Semahöyük that lies 30 kilometers from Arykanda were already suggesting the idea together with other findings in other places.

A stone axe from bronze age

In the beginning the excavation, which I have partly discussed under different headings above, was intended to assemble one complete building in each excavation season. At that point in time, I had no time to consider Sozon or Helios or any other cults or even the ruins and history of Arykanda. The stadium that we restored in a matter of only one season inspired a great acceleration of other excavations that were taking 50 to 75 years to complete, at the time.

I would like to narrate another true story, which I believe has impressed the General Directorate I was working under: I submitted the excavation report to the late Mr. Hikmet Gürçay who was general manager or deputy general manager at the time. I attached "before-and-after" photographs and drawings of the ruins. The allocation for the excavation was 25.000 TL - and it continued to be so until 1976. Out of such allocation, I had spent 10.000 TL to buy equipment, some of which we are still using today, for the camp and I made it clear in the report that it was the balance of the allocation and my own salary that paid for the rest of the excavation. In this stadium, we used sheer man-power to heave fallen blocks of stones that weighed between a couple of tons and 40 tons each, and put them in the hollow on the west of the stadium. Taking into consideration that the stones we built

Naltepesi, the excavation starts

into a wall here roughly measured 13.000 m3 and the fact that all this rubble was used first to fill in a hollow and a dry riverbed, we can easily calculate that in a matter of only 25 days, an approximate of 30 to 40 thousand m^3 of debris was cleared and thus, the hollow on the southeastern wall of the stadium was restored and transformed into a perfect running track for the stadium. As a result, most of the workers employed in this excavation saved enough money to own a car today. What is more, I am currently working with the grandchildren of the same workers today and I can assure you that they are much more hard-working people than to the inhabitants of many other regions.

It was after 1972 that I decided to work on a program to rebuild the whole city. After 27 years of excavating, I can tell you that the Arykanda of our day, with its Agora, temples, 4 baths, Odeon, Bouleuterion, Stadium, Theater and all the other public and private structures that you would expect to find in an excavated city, is a city that can compete with Ephesus or Pergamon where excavations have been going on for 75 or 100 years. Before going on to describe the ruins in the city, it would be most fair to the previous archaeologists to give you some information about how the city was first discovered: Travellers like Leake, Beaufort and Arrundel strolled along the Lycian coast as early as the

> *The honor of really discovering Arykanda, however, would go to Charles Fellows in 1838.*

Reverse of a bronz coin of Emperor Gordianus III, Arykanda

beginning of the 18th century and contributed to the fame of the region with their engravings and travel notes. The honor of really discovering Arykanda, however, would go to Charles Fellows in 1838, who started by noticing that the stream running along the valley happens to be Arykandos. Soon, he would be moving north along that valley from the sea inwards, that is from Finike to Elmalı. This is how he saw the ruins in Arif village. It wasn't until reading the inscriptions on the grave of Themistokles of Arykanda and finding city or league coins with the abbreviation of APY that he finally made his decision: These ruins had to be those of Arykanda! His books titled "Lycia I, II" and "Lycian Travels" would soon make his name all over Europe. His excavations in Xanthos, which he conducted with the ultimate passion of carting off the relics of his choice to the British Museum added to his fame. After him, some travellers came to visit the places described in the books while some others felt just fine for their personal reasons not coming to see the places with their own eyes but simply translating the books about the city and publishing them in their own languages. Among the latter, I suppose, we can mentioned Rott who translated the part about Arykanda in Fellows' book "Kleinasiatische Denkmäler" and published it in his own book, so that anyone fluent in German and English could easily read about Arykanda and notice that not a single sentence is different in the two texts.

An Austrian teacher, Schönborn continued this interest in the region and the relics inside the Trysa Heroon, which he had discovered, were carted off to Vienna by the team of Benndorf-Niemann, who re-discovered the city and wrote a

Glazed vessel decorated with ivies

detailed book about the region titled "Reisen in s ü d w e s t l i c h e n Kleiasien I-II". Later, Kalinka's book, "Tituli Asia Minoris" came as a major hit that focused more on epigraphic findings of his team.

Around the end of 19th and the turn of 20th century, the craze lost velocity. It was the time of the Balkan Wars and the 1st World War. In the aftermath of the WW1, the Lycia and Pamphylia regions were invaded by Italy after which the team of Pace - Mauri - Moretti set out on an excursion from Kuşadası to Antalya, focusing more on the coastline or cities close to the coast. The result of this excursion was their article titled "Da Sklanova a Adalia" that was published by the ASAtene (Athens Italian Archaeology Institute Publications). This was probably the final writing about the region at the time. The region became a military restricted zone after the WW1 and continued to be so during the Turkish Salvation War and until the end of WW2. Therefore, this particular period of time has not been productive as concerns excavations or publications about Lycia.

The excavation that started in 1952 in Xanthos with Prof. Pierre Demargne could be regarded as the beginning of a new era for Lycia studies. In the 1960's, Lycia was again the center of attention: M. J. Mellink excavated Semahöyük and Borchhardt excavated Limyra while Zahle and Kjelsdsen; Wurster, Wörrle; Harrison and Morgenstern's surface surveys and Borchhardt's research in Myra with his crowded team, came one after another as the best examples of the increased attention that Lycia had started receiving.

The 1970's were marked with ongoing excavations in Xanthos and Semahöyük while Limyra was an excavation project on-hold. Surface surveys lost pace and the findings were turning into publications by then. In 1971, I formed the first Turkish team of excavators in the region to start

In 1971, I formed the first Turkish team of excavators in the region to start working on Arykanda. The excavation of Arykanda has continued ever since.

working on Arykanda. The excavation of Arykanda has continued ever since. Between 1981 and 1985, I supervised the excavation in Phaselis and did my part to bring the city's ruins to the way they stand today with the support of the World Bank. But when there was no more support, there was no more excavation.

The team of excavators in Xanthos and Semahöyük are still busy today as new fields of excavation keep coming up. The excavation in the former focuses on Letoon and occasionally on Xanthos while the ongoing excavation in Semahöyük is not simply "excavation" but also restoration and conservation, of the Karaburun and Kızılbel tumuli in particular. The excavation in Limyra is ongoing despite a break until 1973. In the late 1980's, when Prof. Dr. Fahri Işık relocated to Akdeniz University, the excavation in Patara and Tlos or, in more general terms, Lycia studies started off. The Antalya Museum opened the Bayındır tumuli where the findings proved to be plentiful. The Fethiye Museum cleaned the Tlos Theater, unearthed many graves in Pınara where there were some findings and provided a more reliable protection for Kadyanda. Dr. Alan Hall, who left the world at a rather early age, conducted surface surveys in Oinoanda; Prof. Dr. Coulton in Balbura and Prof. G. Frezeuls in Kadyanda. Prof. Dr. J. İnan had to re-excavate Bubon after an illegal excavation and worked devotedly to make an inventory of the relics to publish a list of the ruins that had been smuggled.

Let's go back to Arykanda... It is surprising that there were no findings or ruins other than the stone axe dating from the 2nd millenium BC. We are hoping that cities or tumuli that have not lost their surface soil to rain waters or to erosion, will shed a light on the issue. However, apart from the above mentioned stone axe, Arykanda does not offer any findings or ruins dating earlier than the 5th century BC. To a certain extent, the fire altars might be remnants from the time of the Persian invasion. Besides, we actually hold in our hands some archaeological findings from Arykanda when it

Fragment of a terracotta mould

was under Persian rule: A Late Black and an Early Ceramic Red Figurine both imported from Attica dating back to the 5th century BC which the erosion carried down the slope, (as well as coins of Kuprili and Aquwami, two local magistrates), were coincidentally discovered by villagers. These few findings are followed by the coins of Pericles, the Magistrate of Limyra, (first half of 4th century BC) that are not very promising in terms of stratigraphy.

The writings of Arrianos and the book of Freya Stark titled "Alexandros' Path" give us an idea about the last quarter of the 4th century BC when some of the men of Alexander, the Great passed through Milyas and, then, Arykanda en route to Phaselis. Apparently, the fact that a great many Alexandros coins have been discovered in Arykanda - some of them in good enough shape to be exhibited - cannot simply imply that an emperor or even his entire army has only passed through this city: This fact must be the proof of the influence on the region of the Kingdom of Macedonia, as it was at the time. Perhaps, a certain section of the army of Alexander, the Great, following the coastline to arrive in Phaselis went through Milyas and Arykanda to arrive in Idebessos, while the heavier units stuck to the coastline.

The years after the demise of Alexander, i.e. the epoque of Diadokhs, appear to have been really troublesome times for all cities. Ancient authors relate that the region was soon dominated by the Seleucus dynasty - an idea also supported by both the foundations and the names of the cities. As of the early 3rd century BC, Lycia, and indeed the entire southwest Anatolia, came under the pressure and influence of the Ptolemaios dynasty. This interaction of cultures is more striking in the neighbouring city of Limyra and can be felt, although to a lesser extent, through the cities towards the north. As well as what we call the Ptolemaion ruins in Limyra, we can find traces of that interaction in Arykanda

> *The tension between Limyra and Arykanda, the reasons of which remain unknown to us even today, clearly prevented the influence of Ptolemy spreading inland from the valley of Arykandos.*

in an Egyptian style - Hellenistic statuette that was accidentally discovered by villagers. The tension between Limyra and Arykanda, the reasons of which remain unknown to us even today, clearly prevented the influence of Ptolemy spreading inland from the valley of Arykandos. Moreover, Arykanda signed a defence and cooperation treaty with a city called Trokondos the exact place of which has not been discovered but is known to be somewhere between Myra and Arykanda. I strongly believe that this treaty is also the result of a reaction against Limyra, and therefore the Ptolemaios dynasty.

Arykanda cannot be interpreted according to the remarks of either Lamonier, or Bean. Lamonier describes the building of gymnasium in his book titled "La Gymnase" and he places the reservation that the information included therein is yet "questionable". As for Bean, however, he has made a major mistake when he identified the "Nal Tepesi" to be the acropolis according to the plan he had copied from Lamonier or TAM, despite the fact that this is just a small hill and there are other ruins to the north of it. This is an absolutely false conclusion and nothing but a fantasy.

Let me briefly tell you why: Despite his reservation about the gymnasium, it is quite unexpected for Lamonier to disregard at least the comments made by Vitruvius about some buildings, most importantly, the gymnasium, while he made a thorough study of

Inscription from the Hellenistic period

1- Watchtower
2- Commercial Agora
3- Temple of Helios
4- Bouleuterion
5- Archives
6- Sebasteion / Sacred House
7- Cave Tombs
8- Cistern
9- Stadium
10- Sanctuary
11- Byzantine House
12- Theatre
13- Odeon
14- Civic Agora
15- Prytaneion
16- Nymphaeum
17- Terraca Bath
18- Basilica
19- Sebastaion - Temple of Trajan
20- Roman Villa
21- Western Terrace Houses-Villas
22- Eastern Terrace Houses-Villas
23- Naltepesi, Buildings and Bath
24- Small Bath
25- Great Bath - Gymnasium
26- Eastern Necropolis
27- Winery

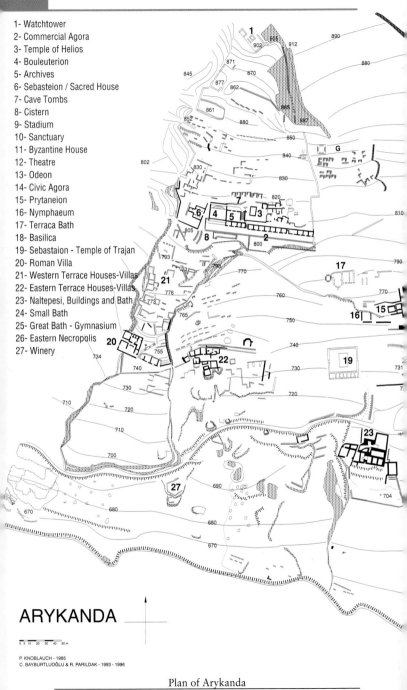

ARYKANDA

0 5 10   20   30   40   50 m

P. KNOBLAUCH - 1985
C. BAYBURTLUOĞLU & R. PARILDAK - 1993 - 1996

Plan of Arykanda

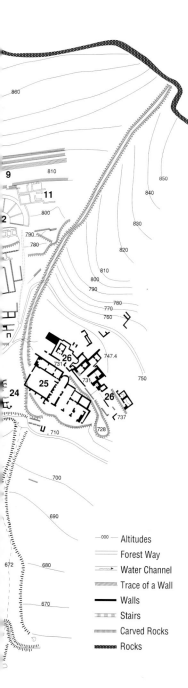

Arykanda. And the only thing we can say about Bean is that his observations are nothing but poor knowledge of archaeology or the desire of an epigraphologist to make speculations when, anyway, there are no experts to prove contrary. Although our faith restricts us from writing ill of the deceased who do not have now or will ever have the chance to defend themselves, I have to make it clear at this point that science and reason are beyond and above logic and the people I have just written about could only arrive at these conclusions given the experience and information they had at the time. Although I am hereby criticising the works of Lamonier and Bean, we have to remember at all times that they were the pioneers in this business.

The city of Arykanda starts on the surface of a very steep rock called Şahinkaya, hence the name of the city. The city stands on a south-incline. The east and west sides of the city are bordered by the cliff while to the north stands the Şahinkaya rock. Therefore, the only weak defence point is the south side, which has been fortified with terrace walls and other structures running north-to-south, built by the people of Arykanda as a solution to the problem of weak defence. Anyway, the city was difficult to locate from a

Watchtower

distance as it was perfectly covered by the forest. It was not necessary to build solid city walls around Arykanda as the main watchtower on the southwest foothill of Şahinkaya had a full view of other watchtowers on the northwest, south and east of the city so they could see danger coming from a distance. The closest structure to a city wall was the wall they made in the crevices or holes on the cliff.

The uppermost structure in Arykanda is the watchtower on the southwest foothill of Şahinkaya. The embossed, rectagonal watchtower was built to a square plan and has terrace walls in front to create a plain area. South of this structure, which stands on the crest of the rock, is an Early Byzantine chapel that probably dates back to the days when Arykanda was recorded in ecclesiastical records as Orykanda or Akalanda. Most of this chapel still stands today.

I believe that the triangular area south of the main watchtower must be the acropolis and most probably, the initial place of settlement. This land was bounded on the south by a high-quality, embossed, rectagonal terrace wall; the cliff in the west; a city wall in the east that resembled the terrace wall in the south in its architecture but served as an aqueduct-city wall that carried brought rain water to the city during the Early Byzantine times. It is here that they created a large space pointing north from the southern wall and this area was connected to a stoa with three steps in the north. The stoa lies east-to-west and was bordered on the north by 12 shops standing in a row that make perfect use of the different elevation. The walls of these shops were hewn out of the natural rock in some places. Right before

It is in this area that they created a large area heading north from the southern wall and this area was connected to a stoa with three steps in the north

the last three shops on the west, you can find a stairway zigzagging up to the propylon of the Temple of Helios as well as houses and graves going north. Under this stairway runs the wastewater channel.

We can see that the stoa continues further west of the last three shops only to end in a rock, the surface of which has been shaped into a wall. At the end of the stoa, we can climb three steps to the north to arrive on a landing. To the east of the landing is a gate made of cedar, its metal pieces remain in-situ even today. This gate opens up to a courtyard with a pebble mosaic paving. There is a hole next to the staircase right opposite the gate. This hole has been quite surprising, the round earthenware relics found in it measure up to 2,5 centimeters in diameter and are slightly puffed in the center. Some of these relics were single printed, some

Stepped street in the west of the Civic Agora

Lycia

Bouleuterion

double printed and some others not printed at all. There are two rock-cut staircases, which provide entrance to the building at, both, east and west ends, adjacent to a south-facing wall with straight rectagonal lines. When we enter the building from these staircases, we can see the semi-circular orchestra with pebble mosaic paving under a pine tree. When we look north from here, we can see the ruins of what looks like a theatron hewn out of the natural rock but lacking a front piece which probably caved in or was shaved off for other reasons. Considering the positioning of the commercial agora and the temple, which I will soon mention, next to this well-preserved structure, we can conclude that these ruins once were the bouleuterion. As for the earthenware relics that came in three different shapes, I think that they should be the ballots standing for "yes", "no" and "abstention" as discovered in other similar cities. The bouleuterion must have fallen into disuse probably due to the destruction of earthquakes. The rock

The findings in the foundations of the temple assure us that the building was constructed after the 4th century BC.

Temple of Helios

to the north at the level of the orchestra has been shaved off so the area could double up as a saloon and capitals and pedestals of some columns or rectangular blocks of stones carried in from other places must have been used to support the wooden vertical members. After the three shops east of the Bouleuterion, you can reach the propylon of the Temple of Helios via a north-climbing stairway under which runs the wastewater channels. The propylon appears to be a simple gate with a single threshold and stone paving. Surely, there used to be a similar gate facing east, as well. The three steps of the temple's crepidoma are complete on the west but missing one row on the east between these gates and the land with stone paving. Unfortunately, we have absolutely no idea about how the temple once looked because some of the blocks of stone in the temple's ante wall, have been used in the construction of a Roman grave in the east, within the temple's temenos. Later, this grave itself was used as a metal melting or a lime mixing spot. Pieces from the upper structure of the temple and many other bronze pieces around the temple were melted here.

Although the design of the temple fits into the normal scheme of Greek temples, the the plan of the Temple of Helios is somewhat out-of-the-ordinary: The shorter sides of the temple are equal; however, the longer sides face east and west, unlike the typical plan of Greek temples.

The findings in the foundations of the temple assure us that the building was constructed after the 4th century BC.

Sebasteion, room with an altar

Another thing that we are sure of is that this temple was devoted to Helios. There were two bomoses (altars) unearthed in the cella of the temple: One of them bears the Hellenistic inscription of "ΗΛΙΟΥ" while the other is a Late Roman - Early Byzantine piece similar to the first one in size and depicting Helios with a halo. The statues of Aesculapius and his daughter Hygeia in the temenos of the temple tell us that Helios shared the temple with other gods. Because Helios is up in the sky the whole day as the god of sun it would be perfectly natural for him to share his temple with one of the gods located all the times on the earth. Remembering that Helios and Aesculapius were worshipped also in the islands of Rhodes and Kos, this influence came to Rhodes and Kos around the mid-2nd century BC and if God Sozon that was mentioned in ancient writings is an equivalent of Helios, the gods worshipped in Lycia at somewhat earlier ages must have been exported to Rhodes and Kos.

The city's acropolis was notable for the Bouleuterion, the Temple of Helios, and the necropolis and some private houses to the north of the temple. Another building of interest stands west of the bouleuterion: This building was apparently intended to be a Sebasteion in the beginning and was later transformed into a private residence, with additions. It has a gate in the east, an almost-square rectangular plan, a hall in the center and a small, vaulted room connected to the hall in the west. The room has a square plan, an altar in the west, a mosaic-laid floor, and a panel with the head of Medusa in the center. The building was originally planned as described here; however, it was

Excluding the watchtower at the top, the Stadium is the uppermost public building of the city.

The bath of the House of Inscriptions

later converted into a villa with an atrium with additions in the south.

Southeast of the acropolis and outside the city walls or the terrace walls is another typically Lycian structure that we have called "The Terrace Bath". The building must have been constructed around mid-3rd century AD and was soon repaired. The building has survived up to the beginning of its vaults.

We understand that Arykanda expanded eastward in the late Hellenistic and Early Roman ages. As a result of the enrichment of the city, two of the most fascinating structures, the Stadium and the Theater, were constructed during the Pax Romana I or slightly earlier, on the foothills of Şahinkaya perhaps by the very same architect and stone mason.

Apart from the watchtower at the top, the Stadium is the uppermost public building of the city. It has a single-directional tribunalis with three steps and a running track that is half the size of the track that a normal stadium would have. This running track was probably composed of two trapezoid areas connected at their narrow ends, following the natural slope of the land. The fact that the running track is half the size of a normal running track may at first seem the most remarkable characteristic of this structure; however, what's really striking about the stadium and what makes this

The structure with niches on the west side of the Stadium

building very special is the northwestern wall, behind the tribunalis on the west, which has the appearance of a temple with a Doric façade with 8 niches. Recent studies looking at its painted pieces of stuccos and the fact that the tiers of seats of the stadium leaned on this very wall have revealed that the building dates back earlier than that of the stadium. As a matter of fact, the excavations at the western end of the stadium, as well as its ground, show that the natural rock in the western end was formed into an apsidal and that there was a wall running southwards from the eastern end of the façade with 8 niches. In other words, the structure that has 8 niches on its north wall has much of the form of a basilica, only its apsis is on the opposite side.

I don't want this section on Arykanda to turn into an excavation report, so I'd better cut a long story short. Finally, there was a medal discovered in this stadium: On this coin, some gods were represented either in person or with their symbols. This was enough proof to conclude that this part of the stadium used to be a Pantheon for Lycia.

Built in the 1st century BC, the stadium underwent major repair especially on its southern wall after the earthquakes in 141 and 240. The Hellenistic wall was partially preserved on the western end. The pillared wall that is connected to the theater with steps must have been built after the earthquake in 240.

On a lower terrace than the stadium, the theater stands

Built in the 1ˢᵗ century BC, the stadium underwent major repair especially on its southern wall after the earthquakes in 141 and 240.

with its cavea built into the natural rock. The stadium and the theater must have been designed and constructed concurrently. This idea is strongly supported by the matching profile of the seats and the general measurements. Built to a typical Greek plan, the theater must date back to between the 1ˢᵗ century BC and the 1ˢᵗ century AD, like the stadium. The earthquakes appear to have hit hardest on the skene building; therefore, the ruins are full of pieces of inscriptions, reliefs and other decorative elements dating back to the 1ˢᵗ century BC and the 2ⁿᵈ - 3ʳᵈ centuries AD. Moreover, it does not take an archaeologist to notice the unskilled repairs on the theatron, especially on the seats of the northeastern and eastern walls.

On a lower terrace than the theater and on the northwest end of the U-shaped, south-facing portico surrounding the civil Agora, you will find the Odeon of Arykanda - that doubled up as the city's bouleuterion - still standing up to its roof. We understand that the building was constructed around the end of the first quarter of the 2ⁿᵈ century AD or slightly earlier, thanks to the style of the statues on its façade as well as the piece of a bust of Hadrian that probably once crowned the central door in perfect harmony with the Corinthian capitals in the inside. The

Lycia

Civic Agora

Odeon must have been decorated both inside and outside with colored, wall-to-wall marble panels. Even today, we can see on the walls the marks of mortar or the holes where these panels were once fixed.

You may ask why I am focusing so much on Arykanda. And the answer is quite simple: I am comparing the structure of Arykanda - a city that I have excavated - with the cities that I have not excavated, thereby seeking to arrive at a conclusion about their similarities and differences and produce answers to many questions without infringing anybody's copyright.

Let's go back to our journey through Arykanda: On a terrace lower than the odeon, there is an Agora without any shops - that's exactly why we call it the civic Agora. The U-shaped building houses what must certainly be the Tykhe Temple right in its center, although the temple has not been thoroughly unearthed yet. To the west of a stairway climbing north-to-south is a Prytaneion that has a similar plan as the other buildings in other excavated cities but it differs in that it has been later used as a private residence. If we take a moment to consider that the grave inscriptions discovered in Arykanda indicate that once here lived Lyciarkhs, members of Boule or Prytans, and that the building has this particular plan, we should not be surprised to find a prytaneion here almost side by side with the civil agora. Intriguingly, this building was used as a private residence during the Late Roman or Early Byzantine times.

This basilica is dated to the late 5ᵗʰ or early 6ᵗʰ Centuries AD.

A clean water channel resting on the natural rock runs southward from the eastern edge of the building known as the "Terrace Bath" and ends in a small building with niches. This building with water supply has three niches on the eastern and western faces each and must have been none other than a nymphaeum. This identification is based on the water channel.

Basilica, the apsides of the first and second stages

On the slight slope that is almost a plain on the south, and west of the dry riverbed, there stands an Early Byzantine Basilica, the frescoes of which are under protection today. This basilica is dated to the late 5ᵗʰ or early 6ᵗʰ Centuries AD because the floor mosaics of this building with three naves are technically quite similar to the contemporary samples of its kind. Most probably, the basilica was devastated by the earthquake of 560 and a rather small chapel was built into its central nave. A small tesseras depicts the name of the person who had the building constructed. On two sides of this name were two scenes - one of them very well-protected - with wreaths and peacocks. The center of the apsis, however, was decorated with a floor mosaic of plant motifs. Today, this mosaic can be seen under protection at the excavation center and the scene with wreaths and peacocks is somewhere outside. What is striking about this building is that although it was a basilica, it was built out of the walls of an ancient temple. As a matter of fact, we found out during the excavation that many of the pieces and building blocks of the temple that was erected in honor of Emperor Trajan and completed during the reign of Hadrian - quoting ancient authors - were reused in the construction of the

Basilica, floor mosaics of the south nave

walls of both the basilica and the newer chapel. It is clear
that the construction of the temple started during the times
of Trajan; however, it is highly probable that its construction
lasted until the days of Hadrian when depictions of Eros,
birds and some other animals shooting from spiral rosettes
of branches were en vogue, as we can see on the walls here.
It must have been quite a ill-fated building in that it
remained in ruins after the earthquake of 141 even before
it was completed, until the "Basilica" came to replace it.
South of this basilica where the cars are parked, there is a
slight slope.

What Bean called the "Acropolis" is, in fact, the

*What Bean called the "Acropolis" is, in
fact, the mausoleum of Hermaios of
Arykanda who served as a Lyciarkh.*

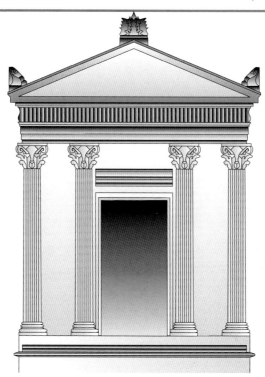

Drawing of the façade of the Grave 5

mausoleum of Hermaios of Arykanda who served as a Lyciarkh. This mausoleum was most probably devastated by the earthquake in 240 and its blocks of stones were later used in the construction of a bath. And an ironsmith apparently used the area as an extension to his premises.

The east bank of the dry riverbed houses the Bath - Gymnasium complex the avenue leading here from the basilica and the graves of rich families that lie along the east of the city. Some of these graves appear in the form of temples and most are vaulted. Approximately 20 different mausoleums have survived, some with restoration.

I am not going into details about these graves; however, I cannot help saying a few words about the Bath-Gymnasium complex so as to be able to make references to other cities.

It is clear that the building was initially planned to be a bath. It is also beyond doubt that it was converted into a Bath-Gymnasium complex probably in the aftermath of the first earthquake (141).

Great Bath-Gymnasium Complex: the pool (piscina) of the frigidarium

The largest building in Arykanda and a typically Lycian bath, the complex was repaired after the earthquake in the 3rd century AD as further indicated by the praefurnios built as an extension to both the caldarium and the tepidarium.

This Great Bath and the connected Gymnasium must have been seriously spectacular buildings for the time. We are certain that the various rooms of the complex were decorated with marble panels imported from different locations and today, you can see the holes were these panels were once fixed.

Clearly, the Great Bath and the connected Gymnasium

> *This Great Bath and the connected Gymnasium must have been seriously spectacular buildings for the time.*

remained functional with ongoing repairs until the 6th century. However, the recession in the city after the 6th century must have had an adverse effect on this complex: It appears that a tiny bath to the southwest of the Great Bath must have taken over the duty of the great complex. This tiny building has many inscriptions on the walls; therefore, in the beginning, we used to simply call it the 'House of Inscriptions'.

The west of the city is dotted with private residences and graves carved into the natural rock. Some of these houses had atriums and others had the plan of a peristyle while some others had a workshop or granary on the first floor and the house on the second floor.

I have discussed Arykanda more than the other cities to be able to make comparisons with and references to other cities and I still have to mention the water and sewerage problem in the city:

Arykanda can be best thought of as an ancient city that not only obtained clean potable water from the two natural springs on its east and west but also cherished the relaxation of spirits from the sound of running water - an idea that mayors of today could quickly pick up! Unlike the common practice today and as a necessity of the technology of the time, the clean water channel would run through the canals or tile drains close to the surface of the avenues and streets

Great Bath-Gymnasium complex: frigidarium and apodyterium

1- Basilica
2- Aqueduct
3- Bath
4- Theatre
5- City Walls
6- Sarcophagi

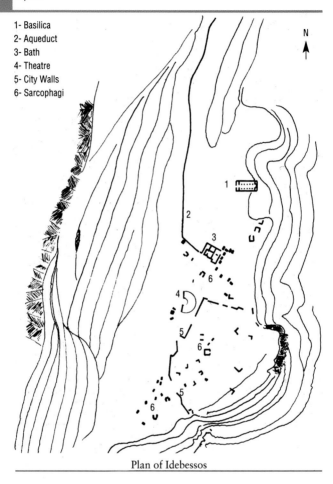

Plan of Idebessos

while the wastewater was transported out of the city through canals or tile drains or other systems running deeper on the other side of the same streets and avenues.

IDEBESSOS (KOZAĞACI OR BADEMAĞACI)

While were excavating Arykanda, we had the opportunity to visit Idebessos every 2 or 3 years with an excavation team comprised of new students and architects. There was even one occasion during the service of my wife as representative of the Ministry in Arykanda when with Dr. Ing. Paul Knoblauch, a few students and the local workers that we hired we were able to clean the theater of Idebessos to the

> *I cannot provide you with any better description due to the existing forestry and new planting.*

level of the orchestra and uncover the true plan of at least the theatron.

Idebessos was visited and written up to some extent by Spratt-Forbes around the mid-19th century and Petersen-Luschan at the turn of the century. Today, you can visit the city by minibus from Finike or Kumluca but if you want to drive there yourself, I suggest you be careful not to damage the car on the road and have to call for a towtruck.

I can tell you the easiest ways to get to Idebessos, by two different routes through which you can visit other ancient cities as well. One route would be this: Set out from Finike, visit Arykanda, stop for a lunch of trout at any of the small restaurants in Arif village and then set out for Idebessos. You will have to turn east after climbing for 2 kilometers if you set out from Çatallar or after declining for 2 kilometers if you set out from Aykırıçay to be able to take the turn for Bağbelen. This road will take you through Bağbelen district and the Belen Plateau en route to Kozağaç-Bademağaç or Payamağaç as the locals call it. If you see a yellowish rocky surface ahead of you in the north, on your left, this means that you are either inside the ancient city or just on the northern outskirts of it. You should be seeing the ruins now. And if you have already seen the sarcophagi and noticed a slight slope to the west, you must be almost in front of the theater. I cannot provide you with any better description due to the existing forestry and new planting. Anyway, the second best thing you can do would be simply asking the first person you see on the road the simple question: "Where is" the ancient city, the ruin or plainly, Idebessos?

The second route to the city would be this: Visit Limyra, and then continue towards Kumluca until the eastern slopes of Mount Toçak where there are stone quarries. At this point, turn north towards Alakır Valley. After only 250 - 300 meters from this junction, stop where the rocks are very close to the road and divide in the shape of the letter "V". This is where you can see probably the longest and the best preserved Roman bridge in all of Anatolia starting right on the point where the rocks meet the road. If you drive slowly

> *We know for sure that Akalissos and Idebessos were represented by a single vote in the "Lycian League".*

and carefully, you will notice to the right of the road this bridge that has 26 well-preserved vaults.

After the Alakır Dam, keep taking the roads leading north west. There is also no harm in going all the way to Karabük or Asarönü since looking east from Asarönü, you will get a chance to see the ruins of Akalissos with its few sarcophagi. Turn back from Karabük or Asarönü and keep driving for approximately 1.5-2 kilometers until you find the road that leads west. This winding road will take you to Idebessos. If you continue on the road leading west from this point, you will again arrive in Arif village and the road between Elmalı and Finike that I have just described. Don't forget to taste the delicious trout dishes here in Çatallar before returning home for the evening.

The ancient writings do not tell us much about Idebessos. The fact that the city's name comes with double "S" indicates that the city is a very ancient settlement.

However, to date, we have not discovered any findings or ruins dating earlier than the "Lycian League". We know for sure that Akalissos and Idebessos were represented by a single vote in the "Lycian League". Freya Stark's observations and comments suggest that a part of the army of Alexander, the Great may have reached Phaselis via Arykanda, Idebessos and Kesmeboğazı.

Mentioned in Byzantine writings as the diocese of Lebissos or Lemissos, the city of Idebessos must have been a settlement that lived under the rule of a minor feudal lord. Its theatre has been dated to the 2nd century BC and the city

Idebessos, family grave

Idebessos, city walls and the theatre

has been mentioned together with Akalissos as part of the Lycian League but we have been unable to discover any findings or ruins from any earlier date.

The city was built partially on a west-facing plain and partially on the two slopes of a hill that declines sharply in the east. The slopes were surrounded by city walls. The theatre lies west of the city walls and it has a theatron of 4 or 5 tiers of seats. The skene building is hard to recognise but its plan reminds us of the Hellenistic age.

To the north of the theater, there is a U-shaped small hill dotted with sarcophagi and klines of a variety of family graves - all from the days of the Roman Empire. Further north, you will find a tiny, typically Lycian bath and next to it, the remains of a church.

Idebessos, family grave

Akalissos

If I tell you that there is a particular section in the city walls where you can see the marks of each and every historical period, I think you will get a rough idea about the history of the city.

AKALISSOS (ASARÖNÜ-KARABÜK)

Probably the most recent victim of grave robbing, Akalissos lies in the direction of Kumluca from Limyra and can be reached after 6-7 kilometers at the northern end of the road that follows the west bank of the Alakır River. You can drive to the city in 1 - 1.5 hours from the Finike-Kumluca plains.

The city was mentioned for the first time, as part of the Lycian League together with Idebessos and Kormos in the writings of Stephanos of Byzantion and Hierokles. Later, this rather small settlement has also been seen in ecclesiastical records.

If you look east from Asarönü village to see the

Akalissos

> *No matter which way you may be coming from, you should pay heed to the road signs indicating these villages.*

ruins today, you will notice at once that the area does not allow much of a settlement, as floodwaters gave the area this rather difficult shape.

Apart from a number of sarcophagi, you will see very roughly carved, simple rock graves in Akalissos, these are as the only major ruins.

ARNEAI (ERNEZ)

Once a very difficult place to reach by the road and considered to be almost detached from the rest of Lycia due to its location, Ernez or Arneai, by its ancient name, can be reached easily today via roads that are probably not the best possible quality but still topped with asphalt to a great extent. You can reach the city from the Elmalı and Kasaba roads or from byroads on the road between Finike and Elmalı. If you are driving yourself, you should turn west to Kasaba from the road sign of Çatallar, at the 30th kilometer on the road between Finike and Elmalı. Approximately 20 kilometers later but before arriving in Kargacık or Küçük Taranır, the road will first turn west and then north and take you to Ernez in 2 kilometers. No matter which way you may be coming from, you should pay heed to the road signs indicating these villages.

Arneai, city walls

Lycia

Arneai, inscription on city walls

For those of you who are staying in or around Kaş, you should first take the road for Kasaba and Elmalı and after Kasaba, you should follow the blue road sign for Çatallar until reaching Karadağ district. Here, you should either ask someone for help or if you have already seen the sign for Ernez, you should continue straight north. In fact, there is a much shorter way to get there: Right after the Avlan Pass towards Finike, there is a road leading west towards the Ördübek plateau. Recently, a number of forest roads have been opened in the area as a precaution against wild fire; however, unless accompanied by a guide, you would be well advised not to take the risk of following this road despite its shortness.

Ancient writings indicate that Arneai used to be a less-than-major city. Arneai was founded on what we can almost call a peninsula on the land, much like Kremna in Pisidia and Kandyba in Lycia. Inside the city is quite a rugged piece of land given its age.

The rocky hill standing south of Mount Eren and the village of Ernez of today, which has pretty much kept its ancient name, made Arneai a naturally well-protected city. On the road between Ernez and the ruins, you will see a few wooden granaries, the kind that you see getting fewer and fewer everyday. On the west face of the south-lying rocks that resemble a peninsula, you will see some house-type rock

> *In the aftermath of the earthquake on August 5th, 240, Arneai would be one of the few cities that Gordianus, III granted the authority to issue coins.*

graves bearing inscriptions in the Lycian language, these are the first ruins in the city.

What we can call the summit of the rocky peninsula is bounded in the south by a terrace wall, where some stones with inscriptions used for building material have been set upside down. Since the slopes of the hill were terraced into agricultural fields and irrigated for so many years, there are no ruins of any major buildings. It is surprising that there are no major public buildings in Arneai although the city received a donation of 30 thousand denarii after the earthquake in 141 from Opramoas and was also later supported by Jason. Moreover, in the aftermath of the earthquake on August 5th, 240, Arneai would be one of the few cities that Gordianus, III granted the authority to issue coins.

An inscription that was published in TAM indicates that Emperor Trajan built a new country house or a guesthouse where the old gymnasium once stood. This must be around the time that the same emperor made donations to Arykanda for the construction of a temple.

Arneai was a well-protected hide-out in late antiquity but

Arneai, rock tomb

Çağman, rock tomb

there is no way we can be sure that the city remained intact from the early Christian movements or buildings in the Kasaba plain. However, we find evidence for this idea in Çağman, which had to be part of the territorium of Arneai, as well as a network of roads that connected these cities to the plain of Demre via Alacadağ, Muskar and Demre or the road between Kasaba and Kaş.

ÇAĞMAN

If you want to see Çağman, you will have to take the turn to Kasaba and Kaş from Çatallar district on the road between Elmalı and Finike. After the Yazır Pass, the asphalt road will take you to Dağbağ village. This is where you should pay utmost attention not to miss the village road to "Çağman". 2 kilometers south of Çağman, you will see a well and a forested hill on your right. You should leave your car here and start climbing the hill slowly. On this very hill that is locally called Bakacak Hill, you will see the ruined walls of the settlement. 500 meters south, you will see the famous grave of Çağman, which was carved into the natural rock. Resembling very much the rock grave in Hayıtlı, this one is notable for its grave chamber housing double graves. Its plan suggests that it must have been built around the 4th century BC for a local rich man.

KANDYBA

If you stop in front of the petrol station at the end of the town of Kasaba on the road from Elmalı to Kaş, you will notice a road climbing the mountain to the west of where

The most striking remains of Kandyba are the acropolis and the rock graves situated east and south of the rocky hill crowned by the city.

you are. This road will take you in 8 kilometers to Gendiye or Kandyba, by its ancient name, or Çataloluk as we call the place today. The name of the city, with its -ND suffix, suggests that this city is among the oldest settlements in the region - a fact further proven by the rock graves bearing Lycian inscriptions and a stone axe that was accidentally discovered on the ground. The city stands on a natural hill resembling an oval table in form that slightly declines from west to east. The city is surrounded by a steep rocky formation to the west, north and east but to the south, where there is more space to move, the city was protected by city walls. To enter the city from the main gate, you will need to take the stairs to the south of the rocks. The main gate is protected by two square-formed towers and stands almost at the center of the hill. As you walk into the city, you reach an area in the west where, most probably, the palace of the magistrate once stood carved into the natural rock. Although the structure is shaded by bushes today, you cannot help noticing the difference of elevation in some sections of the building that followed the natural flow of the rock.

The most striking remains of Kandyba are the acropolis and the rock graves situated east and south of the rocky hill crowned by the city. There is a remarkable rock grave in the east - a must see with its Lycian inscription still carrying its original red color. You will notice right above the main grave chamber a line of frieze similar to that which can be

Kandyba, city walls and city gate

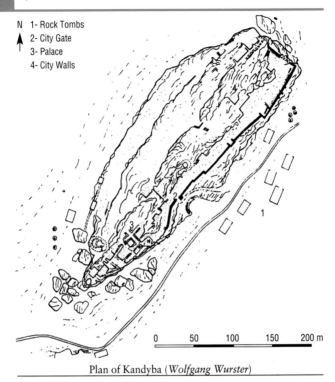

N   1- Rock Tombs
↑   2- City Gate
     3- Palace
     4- City Walls

0   50   100   150   200 m

Plan of Kandyba (*Wolfgang Wurster*)

seen in the Sea Necropolis in the ancient city of Myra. With a little effort, you can even get a glimpse of a seated human figure carved on a piece of rock that has lost much to erosion.

The city is not part of any excavation plan; therefore, we can only guess that the eastern end of the oval-formed rock under the acropolis or the city center was most probably home to the residences of the people of Kandyba.

The city was populated for a short time during the Early Byzantine period. You need proof? Check out the Byzantine walls made of tiles or recycled stones and mortar to the north of the city...

The northwest slope of the hill, or the necropolis of Kandyba, is dotted with rock-cut sarcophagi and other graves. Other points to mention about Kandyba are the granaries dating mostly to the 19th century that would be typical examples to the traditional Lycian residential architecture. You will also notice still-standing old houses with their flat roofs supported by wooden poles - that

> *Approximately 100 tumuli have been discovered near Bayındır.*

decorated gravures of the 19th century travellers more examples of Lycian residential architecture.

BAYINDIR

At the end of the village of Gökpınar on the road between Elmalı and Korkuteli, there is a road leading north from the primary school. It's this road that will take you to the village of Bayındır where the richest tumulus findings have been discovered in recent times. Today, the tumuli in the form of barrows near the village can only be noticed when pointed out by those who have exact knowledge of the area, but the findings discovered in these tumuli are the best quality artifacts that have been unearthed recently. And they sure made a success!

I share the opinions about Uşak and the other findings that Assistant Prof. Dr. İlknur Özgen shared in the book "The Lydian Treasure" that was issued by the Ministry of Culture, which is a first class publication. Although I do not share her views on a number of matters, I would like to take this opportunity to congratulate her on her work. Approximately 100 tumuli have been discovered near Bayındır. The Antalya Museum excavated two of these tumuli, which have been named Tumulus C and D. The findings can be seen today in the Antalya Museum. In general terms, the style of these tumuli is that of Phrygian tumuli and the findings from these two tumuli share characteristics of Lydian and Phrygian art.

It would be a wonderful idea to see these beautiful findings in the Antalya Archaeological Museum even if you do not have the opportunity to visit the tumuli themselves.

PODALIA (AVLAN-GÖLTARLA)

I cannot imagine how Prof. G. Bean could place Podalia at Söyle in his book "Lycian Turkey" on pages 154 and 155. For starters, he is in perfect contradiction with ancient writings. Later, his theory was refuted for good after something special was discovered in Patara following Bean's demise: The "Stadios" or "Milliarium Lyciae" - a running list of Lycian cities with the distances between them

> *The road that turns off towards Ayvasıl*
> *right at the beginning of the road between*
> *Elmalı and Korkuteli will take you to*
> *Geçmen after 3-4 kilometers.*

measured in units of "stadia".

The writings of Pliny (5.28.101) and Ptolemaios (5.3.7), numerous inscriptions about Lycian cities in the Milyas region and finally, the above-mentioned Stadios inscription all help to place Podalia in the vicinity of Avlan, by its ancient name, or Göltarla, today. Transportation inland from the sea or vice versa during antiquity by no means fits in with Bean's suggestions; therefore, his suggestions should be regarded with suspicion. Imagine yourself in ancient times and you want to go to a city which is standing right ahead of you. If there were no obstacles blocking the road, you would just walk straight into the city as the shortest way to get there, wouldn't you? So, I assume that anyone who lived in antiquity would share your reasoning in this matter. Looking at a map of 1/100 thousand scale, you will clearly see the point that I am trying to make here.

It is without question that what appears in old maps as Karamık or Buralye and Bodalye is none other than the city of Podalia. The city walls and graves that Bean identified on the two rocky hills (especially the southern hill) to the west of the Avlan lake - now dried - must have been a part of Podalia as well. This issue has been further proven by our excursion starting from Tekke village and ending in the former Avlan lake during which we discovered some minor ancient graves, but nothing else indicating a major settlement. Therefore, accepting Bean's suggestion about the location of the city would be very much like looking for the ruins of the ancient city of Berolini (or Berlin) in Brandenburg and of Parigi (or Paris) in Lille, regardless of the fact that the real ruins stand right in front of our eyes.

The State's Roads Department once subcontracted the extension and renovation of the road and during road construction, a building with a mosaic floor was discovered around Avlan Pass and the contractor managed to quickly do away with this building as he was very concerned that his construction would be stopped. Anyway, this building does not suggest much on its own.

This structure that was so hurriedly destroyed must have served the same purpose as the caravanserais of the Seljuk or Ottoman ages. The building was probably used as a watchtower as well: from its position, the building must have had a full view of the Avlan Lake in the north and the valley as far as Arykanda in the south.

GEÇMEN

The road that turns off towards Ayvasıl right at the beginning of the road between Elmalı and Korkuteli will take you to Geçmen after 3-4 kilometers. Looking at the Büyük and Küçük Söğle villages that lie only 3-4 kilometers from Geçmen and the building materials on the walls of the country houses dating back to the antiquity and the late antiquity, we can easily conclude that the area has been populated with villages ever since the age of the Roman Empire.

Geçmen must have been a village since antiquity and its location was apparently not the most strategic. That's why the settlement remained trivial. However, Söğle continued to be a village to our day as we understand from the many artifacts shipped to the Antalya Museum from the village as well as many ruins that were melted into lime in later eras. Even today, you can see on some of the walls of the country houses the tombstones or stellae of the many people who once lived here in Geçmen.

SEMAHÖYÜK

On the road between Elmalı, Korkuteli and Antalya, 11 kilometers after Elmalı there is a road that leads southwest towards Gölova. This is the road to Semahöyük. Now an apple garden and agricultural field, the old site has been excavated for a long time by and written up in the books of Prof. Dr. M. J. Mellink.

Today the few ruins in the excavated area that are left are but the wall starting in stones and continuing in mud bricks and a few pieces of pithos graves, if any. Nevertheless, Semahöyük is as important as the Hacımusalar Höyük, thanks to its prehistoric and protohistoric nature. Classical archaeologist that I am, it is extremely difficult for me to

On the road between Elmalı, Korkuteli and Antalya, 11 kilometers after Elmalı there is a road that leads southwest towards Gölova.

elaborate on this mound that is unmistakably marked by the Calcolithic age although beyond recognition. Still, taking into consideration the proximity of the Neolithic settlement in the region and the fact that this mound may have had something to do with these settlements, we can conclude decisively that Lycia, including Kabalia, Milyas and Kibyratis, has been populated ever since prehistoric times.

KARABURUN TUMULUS

Driving from Elmalı towards Antalya or Korkuteli, you can see a road turning off to the north into the fields from the 14th kilometer of the main road. It will lead you up a slight slope which is not always passable. The road turns east to reach the Karaburun Tumulus. If you count the kilometers while driving, on the 14th kilometer of the road, you can catch from a distance the general view of the hill and the tumulus in the north. There are two tumuli in Karaburun.

The first was excavated by late Prof. Dr. Sevim Buluç upon the suggestion of Prof. Dr. Machteld Mellink, soon after the discovery of the second, which is also more spectacular and stands behind the first. The excavation revealed that the first tumulus had already been sacked and destroyed.

The tumulus that wins Karaburun its fame was

Karaburun Tumulus, fresco

Karaburun Tumulus, fresco

accidentally discovered at an illegal excavation by treasure hunters and Prof. Dr. Machteld Mellink was able to publish the findings for the sake of science. It must be noted with gratitude that Prof. Dr. Mellink has taken this tumulus with magnificent frescoes under his protection and assumed all responsibility to solve its problems. The restorator, Ms. Franca Calliori, gave years of unprecedented strength and determination to clean and restore this masterpiece of Anatolian art. Her reproductions of the frescoes in the original size helped bring the paintings to the heart of our time.

I regret to tell you that these frescoes and the tumulus, are not open to the public and even scientists are required to dress in special clothing before they can visit. But the good news is that perhaps in a couple of years, a cultural

> *This exceptional tumulus dates to the late 6th century BC or the early 5th century BC and belonged to a local chief that ruled under Persian influence.*

center will be built in Elmalı and the frescoes will be displayed there. In this way, visitors will be able to see via cameras all the details of not only the frescoes of the Karaburun tumulus but also the Kızılbel Tumulus, without ever really visiting the sites. I believe that this will be possible with the help of Prof. Dr. Mellink and all the other excavators in the region.

A photograph of the Karaburun tumulus that Prof. Dr. Mellink published depicts a fresco that is truly outstanding, a Persian man in his clothes, his tiara, the phial with omphalos that he holds and his men either fanning him or holding the towel for him.

This exceptional tumulus dates to the late 6th century BC or the early 5th century BC and belonged to a local chief that ruled under Persian influence. The front section of the grave chamber is marked with an altar that has plastic decorations on the sides. A rather narrow passage opens into the grave chamber, which has been beautifully adorned with bright and colorful frescoes by a prominent painter of the time. On the wall facing the door across the room, the

Persian ruler is depicted holding a phiale with omphalos in his right hand and lying on the kline. One of the servants holds the towel for him while another fans him. On the sidewalls, there are friezes of war or hunting scenes.

TYMBRIADA (GİLEVGİ CASTLE-ÇOBANİSA)

Approximately 20 kilometres from Elmalı on the road to Antalya, near Çobanisa village the Castle of Gilevgi, by its former

Tymbriada, city walls and the tower

Tymbriada, castle

name, still resists time. Depending on how fast you climb, you will reach the ruins in 45 minutes - 1 hour from Çobanisa or Gilevgi, by its former name. The Hellenistic castle and its walls are still standing, complete with the watchtowers and the parapet.

Behind these very well-preserved walls, lies a settlement that has not been excavated, and thus, there are no identifiable buildings. Despite the good condition of the surrounding walls, the few ruins that we see inside the castle are but a sign that the castle was used solely for military purposes. As a matter of fact, we can read in ancient writings

Tymbriada, city walls

that the settlement or military base on this hill that has been called the Castle of Gilevgi was a perfect natural location to watch and strike, when necessary, the road between Elmalı and Korkuteli.

I still remember Prof. Dr. M. Harrison telling me 5 or 6 years before his demise about a tumulus in the valley southeast of the Castle of Gilevgi, which looked like the Karaburun or Kızılbel Tumuli but he couldn't say anything about the frescoes inside as the structure had already been plundered by treasure hunters. I would like to take this opportunity to remember a dear colleague who passed away at a rather young age and who, for his love for Lycia, broke his leg and had to walk with the help of a cane for quite a long time.

Khoma (Hacimusalar Höyük)

On the road between Elmalı, Akçay and Kaş, 3-4 kilometers after the wooden granaries in Beyler village, look south from the road and you will see an artificial hill 10-15 meters in height. From this road, turn south near the poplar trees, where you can get a good look of the tumulus. In 1 kilometer, you will indeed arrive at the tumulus. Since this is a guide book, I must advise you to take the initiative to stop at the "Beyler" village and visit both the wooden granaries and the old local mansions, which have survived with pretty much their original interior architecture.

The Hacımusalar Höyük is worth mentioning for two reasons: The first is related to its archaeological eminence and the second is that this is the place where intensive smuggling of archaeological artifacts first started. The east

Hacımusalar Höyük, a general view

> *From this road, turn south near the poplar trees, where you can get a good look of the tumulus. In 1 kilometer, you will indeed arrive at the tumulus.*

Beyler Village, a wooden granary

end of Elmalı plain is marked with Calcolithic settlements, as is the Semahöyük. The tumuli around Bayındır in particular have provided a variety of findings dating from between the late 8th and the early 5th centuries BC. The Hacımusalar Höyük, however, differs from the rest in that it has provided findings dating from the Calcolithic age until the Byzantine times. As far as we can understand today, we can almost say that human settlement never ceased in this area.

Antique pieces collected from the surface of the mound date to various points in time between the late 4th or early 3rd millenia BC (ceramics) and the Byzantine times.

Prof. Dr. İlknur Özgen led the excavation, which started with a surface survey exploration. It was also thanks to this excavation that the real dimensions of archaeological smuggling came to the surface: some local people who were accused of smuggling ancient artifacts must have gained their first experience and wealth at this mound.

Prof. Dr. İlknur Özgen stated at the "Symposium on Excavation Results" in Ankara that the mound was

Lycia

İslamlar, heroon

populated until the Early Byzantine period. As far as we can conclude from the ancient writings, the tumulus still houses the ruins of a church or chapel from the Late Byzantine era and a bath the structure of which is now completely beyond recognition - a result of numerous illegal excavations. The excavation of the tumulus has recently commenced and I have no doubt that Prof. Dr. Özgen will find out quite a lot about the early days of Lycia, Kabalia and Kibyratis. The recent excavations on the southeast slope of the tumulus produced ceramics findings from the Orientalisan Age. The quality and variety of the ceramics pieces emphasize the importance of the Hacımusalar tumulus in terms of shedding a light on the relations between Lycia, Milyas and

İslamlar, lid of a sarcophagus

> *You must leave the car at the village and set out on a 15-minute walk to the hill north of the village.*

İslamlar, lid of a sarcophagus

Kibyratis; Lycia, Pisidia and Phrygia; and Lycia and Lydia.

İSLAMLAR

On the road between Elmalı and Kaş and 3 kilometers before Akçay or on the 23rd kilometer of the same road, there is a road that leads north and this is the road that will take you in 4 kilometers to the İslamlar village. You must leave the car at the village and set out on a 15-minute walk to the hill north of the village. As soon as you start climbing out of the village, you will notice a rock grave in the west - the only sample of its kind.

The single major ruin crowning the hill is a rectangular building which still stands up to the level of its stylobate. It must have been a temple or a heroon in Corinthian order and was most probably constructed in the in antis plan. To the north of these ruins and in the field, you can see two pieces with reliefs from the same Roman sarcophagus that probably belonged to a prominent man (other than the one who built the rock grave I have told you before) of the İslamlar village - the ancient name of which remains unknown.

> *Like most Lycian cities, Nisa is secured on three sides by natural formations and the fourth side, the north, is fortified by city walls.*

NISA (SÜTLEĞEN - MERYEMLİK)

When you are driving from Elmalı, Kasaba to Kaş, the road starts climbing after Akçay village. 1-2 kilometers after crossing the Sinekçi pass, to the west of the road where there are coffee houses, you will see another road turning west, that is if the road sign for Sütleğen is still there in its right place. Take this turn and 5 kilometers later, leave the road leading west for Sütleğen and drive south. This is as close to Meryemlik, or Nisa, as you get by car. If you are driving an off-road vehicle, you can drive a little more: First south and, then, east. However, if that's not what you are driving, you would be well advised to leave the car as close to the hill as possible for the good of both the vehicle and the passengers. If you can drive until Sütleğen, you would have a better chance, or should I say mischance, to walk to the ruins because, walking down from the village in 20 to 30 minutes is fine and easy. But when it comes to returning to the car up in the village, you should give yourself double that time.

Like most Lycian cities, Nisa is secured on three sides by natural formations and the fourth side, the north, is fortified by city walls. To the east of the city is the Kıbrıs or Kıbrısçık Stream that runs along what we can call a canyon. To the south, which is the direction of the Beldibi district, is a rather steep slope. It appears that the weakest side of the city in terms of defence was the western slope since the north was properly protected by city walls. The entrance to the city was through the northeastern gate, which implies that the city was fortified in this direction as well.

No matter which road you take to Nisa (the road through Sütleğen or the one above), you are sure to see the necropolis as the first remains of the city. Though an inland Lycian city, Nisa was influenced by Pisidia, especially in sarcophagus reliefs: Shields and spears.

We have almost no precise information about the history of the city. The only evidence that could be traced were the coins they issued during the "Lycian League" and the information that the city received donations from Opramoas during the Roman Ages. The vicinity of the city is rich in

> *There is a block of stone with reliefs next to the rather narrow skene building of the theater, that is if the bushes have not grown to cover it yet.*

Christian hide-outs, monasteries and churches. However, we get the impression that Meryemlik had already been abandoned to a great extent during the Early Byzantine days.

Spreading east, south and, partially, west on quite different positions and planes, the city of Nisa was built on a great piece of land, in fact, greater than its importance in history.

The best-preserved building in Nisa is the theater, which could entertain 500 to 600 people at a time. The structure is in the form of a bow and the uppermost seats have backs. There is a block of stone with reliefs next to the rather narrow skene building of the theater, that is if the bushes have not grown to cover it yet.

Walking east of the theater, you will see the agora laid with nicely shaped blocks of stones on the floor. In the western entrance of the agora, on the side of the path lies an inscription that you can easily read: "Nisa". Another similar sized block of stone bearing an inscription lies in the bushes to the south or southwest of the former. The eastern end of the agora is not clear as it has been heavily

Girdev, sarcophagus

Lycia

Girdev, sarcophagus

overgrown with bushes. However, you can see the ruins of the south-facing bath to the southeast of the agora: The outer walls are still visible.

If you walk towards the rocks protruding eastward and southward, you can see one more ruin: The gate with arches still standing. The rock formation pointing southward is home to many rock graves.

GİRDEV

The road leading to Akatlı from Elmalı and Akçay, climbing north from Gömbe right after the Söğütçük and Belenli neighbourhoods will take you after an hour's drive to Girdev Lake and the ruins.

Driving on a dust-road can be an adventure; therefore, I suggest you do not take this route in the rain or even the possibility of rain because once the vehicle is stuck in mud, you will need a tractor or a towtruck to rescue it. Especially, if you are short of food and lightly dressed, you will be susceptible to bad weather and even, hunger.

A second route would be driving towards Korkuteli from Fethiye and Kemer. 43 kilometers after Kemer, you will see

43 kilometers after Kemer, you will see the road leading east to Seki, which is approximately 10 kilometers away from Girdev.

Girdev, sarcophagi

the road leading east to Seki, which is approximately 10 kilometers away from Girdev. And this is the less risky way to get there! If you are driving from the north or from Kibyra (Gölhisar), you will have to turn west (to the right) at the junction with the road to Fethiye and Korkuteli. Then, you must follow the same road described above after the road sign to Seki.

The Girdev plain is at an altitude of 2000 meters and surrounded on all sides by mountains. As a matter of fact, this plain turns into a lake in both winter and spring, thanks to rainwater, but dries into fertile land for irrigation and grazing in July-September.

There are tumulus remains in the north, northwest and northeast ends of the lake or plain. But in the southwest and west ends, there are ruins of buildings from the Roman ages all the way from the slopes of the hill in the west to the center of the lake or plain. Other ruins of interest in this area are the country style sarcophagi that have reliefs on the lids or sides depicting lions with one front claw in the air or holding an oinokhoe. The tabula ansatas of the sarcophagi depict people of Oinoanda more than anything else - Proof that Girdev was within the territorium of Oinoanda. Besides, Oinoanda is no more than 30 kilometers from here.

1- Theatre
2- City Walls
3- Aqueduct
4- Mausoleum
5- Diogenes Monument
6- Agora
7- Bath
8- City Gates

⊚ Wells
• Trough pipe blocks
▲ Pipe junction blocks
ˣ Other pipe blocks
▨ Bath buildings
⊏⊐ Possible tank locations
--⟨ Possible supply pipe routers

0   100   200 m

Plan of Oinoanda, (*Coulton*)

If you drive out of Girdev from the first route and drive towards Seki, you can see a rock grave at a distance to the north, right outside the village of Değer. Soon, again in the north, you can see another rock-cut grave with the relief of a shield and spear. Of course, if you are not too busy driving. If you look north from this grave, you will see a hill surrounded by city walls. Watching over the Seki plain from the east, this settlement was locally called Asar

> *60 kilometers from Fethiye on the road to Kızılcadağ and Korkuteli, there is a turn for Seki and Elmalı.*

or Ören.

OINOANDA (İNCEALİLER)

60 kilometers from Fethiye on the road to Kızılcadağ and Korkuteli, there is a turn for Seki and Elmalı. A couple of kilometers after this turn, there is another road that is easily accessible for all vehicles, which leads south to the village of İncealiler. If you don't have a guide with you, find the path that climbs south from the village. You would be well advised to either take the watchman of the ruins or almost any villager with you during your visit to the ruins so you will be safe from sheepdogs.

Unless you manage to find someone to accompany you I strongly suggest that you equip yourself with a big stick In the event of an approach by dogs, do not react in any way and calmly stand still with the stick in your hand. The dog will make sure that the flock is not in any kind of danger and this may take a few minutes.

Be patient and of course, careful. Once the dog is

İncealiler Village, viewed from Oinoanda

Lycia

> *Oinoanda makes its first appearance in history as part of a tetrapolis annexed to Lycia.*

convinced that you are not moving and you are harmless, it will return to the sheep to keep guard. But if it does attack you, try to strike the dog in the feet and if you can, move towards it. The only way to survive a dog attack is showing that you are not afraid of the dog.

Give the animal compliments about its effective protection of the flock and try to go on your way without paying too much attention. Such encounters are not uncommon in Lycia and therefore, I think, one should always be prepared.

About an hour of climbing from İncealiler will take you to Oinoanda - a particularly ancient settlement as the name suggests. The suffix "-anda" is a typical local character. However, since the only survey of the area is a surface study conducted by my late friend Alan Hall and his team, there is no archaeological information on hand about the foundation date of the city. Thus, the only idea suggesting the age of the city is the etymology of the city's name, Oinoanda, which gives us the idea that this is a truly ancient settlement.

During our excursions to develop a rough idea about the city, we were able to collect from the surface pieces of

Oinoanda, Diogenes Monument

Oinoanda, the inscription of the Diogenes Monument

Attic ceramics that date to the 5th or 4th centuries BC. More proof that Oinoanda is a very ancient settlement.

The name of the city and the presence of these pieces of ceramics lead me to disagree with Bean's suggestion that Oinoanda was a colony of Termessos Minor. Let's start the discussion with the name of the city: The name with the letters "-nd-" suggests that the city of Oinoanda must have been founded in mid-2nd millenium BC. Termessos Minor, however, did not even exist until the early Hellenistic Age when Termessos Major founded it. Therefore, Termessos Minor could not have founded Oinoanda since there are no buildings in that city dating earlier than the Hellenistic Age.

Appearing in some ancient writings as part of Kobalia (Pliny Hist.Nat. 5.28.101; Ptolemaios 5.3.8) and in some others as part of Kibyratis (Strabon 13.14.17), Oinoanda must have been truly a buffer zone.

Oinoanda makes its first appearance in history as part of a tetrapolis annexed to Lycia. One of four cities led by Kibyratis, Oinoanda was represented along with them by two votes in the Lycian League. The city became an integral part of the Lycian League in the aftermath of Murena's military excursion (81 BC). However, Dr. Alan Hall and Dr. Smiths' surface surveys and the writings of the world famous epicurist - philosopher from Oinoanda, namely, Diogenes, fail to shed light on the pre-Hellenistic Era in the city.

Lycia

Oinoanda, city walls

All the inscriptions and ancient writings clearly point to the early 1st century BC and this is the time of the Mithridates wars that were won by Murena (81 BC). It was only after this war that Kabalia or the Kibyratis Region, to be exact, became a part of the Lycian League beginning with the city of Kibyra and was represented by 2 votes in the League. Soon, the region would accept the sovereignty of Rome (Strabon 631). When Brutus killed Caesar and then started looking for followers to seize power over Rome, Oinoanda had both consenters and dissenters. However, the great majority of the people of Oinoanda had hostile feelings towards Xanthos - A sign that this is where the war had started. The war and the attack of Brutus on Xanthos apparently resulted in the third mass suicide in the region.

We understand from an inscription discovered in Rhodiapolis that, in the aftermath of the earthquake in 141 AD, Oinoanda received donations of 10.000 denarii from a rich man, namely Opramoas, from an Eastern Lycian city, to be used for the construction of a bath. This is how we know for sure that by the 2nd century AD, Oinoanda had become a very important Lycian city. As a matter of fact, slightly before this date, the play of "Isolympia Vespasianeia"

Oinoanda stood on a plain in the crest of a hill west of the village of İncealiler.

Oinoanda, theatre

was staged in honor of the Emperor Vespasian - What could be a better sign that, by the time, Oinoanda was completely Romanized? The festivities celebrating the election of Licinius Langus as Lyciarkh lasted two days. His grandson, Gaius Licinius Langus, would later become military tribune and succeed his grandfather as the Lyciarkh. We understand that relations between the palace of the Roman Empire and the Oinoanda's dignitaries were profound.

Oinoanda stood on a plain on the crest of a hill west of the village of İncealiler. Wider in the north, this plain narrows southward without any serious difference of

Oinoanda, scene building of the theatre

Oinoanda, bath

elevation. The area where the wide land in the north meets with the narrow land in the south is strikingly well-preserved and is rich with ancient buildings.

On the polygonal city walls that are still standing up to the parapet, there is a clearly visible gate to the south and some hidden gates in the middle of the city.

In the northwest of Oinoanda, you can see the theater with a rock-cut cavea. But its plan reminds those of the theaters of Phaselis or Myra. The building must have been repaired during the Roman times.

Walking south from the theater, that is northeast-to-southwest, inside the city walls, you will come to an avenue

Oinoanda, agora and the Diogenes Monument

Oinoanda is surrounded by necropolises in all directions. You can see many rock graves to the east and west of the city center and also, on the rocks west of the theater.

leading to the agora. This avenue closely resembles the avenues of Phaselis with seats on the two sides. I don't think it would be incorrect to name this place the Avenue of Diogenes since there are many inscriptions about the epicurist - philosopher, Diogenes, along the road.

Around the middle of the avenue, which is laid with blocks of stone, you can easily see the bath-gymnasium complex with an apsidal ending that faces west. The style and architectural plan of the building suggests that the complex can be dated to late 2nd century AD.

I would think that the land that lies east of the bath until the city walls of the later ages must have been reserved as the Palaestra. It is impossible to have a precise idea about the function of the building that stood northwest of the bath complex inside the city walls. Still, it could well have been another bath.

The building (30 x 120 m) with a floor laid with blocks of stone that was built in the narrowest land within the city walls of Oinoanda was, without doubt, the agora. This hypothesis is supported by the large avenues leading to this

Oinoanda, theatre

The poor-quality asphalt road from Gölhisar or Altınyayla will take you to Bubon (Ibecik) after half an hour's drive.

structure from both the north and the south.

An aqueduct from the south gave the occupants plenty of water. You can still see the traces of channels and pipes above the still standing walls of this aqueduct, unless, of course, they have somehow been destroyed since my last visit.

Oinoanda is surrounded by necropolises in all directions. You can see many rock graves to the east and west of the city center and also, on the rocks west of the theater. The path leading to the city from İncealiler, the distant lands to the west and east of the theater and, most importantly, the area south of the city are dotted with sarcophagi.

BUBON (İBECİK)

Known for the bronze statues discovered in the 1970's, rather than its ruins, the city of Bubon is among the cities of Kabalia or Kibyratis that were annexed to Lycia by Murena.

We are not well informed about the foundation of the city; however, it definitely shares the same destiny and geography with the city of Kibyra, the capital of Kabalia region. Therefore, like pretty much all of Lycia, the city must have been left under the control of Rhodes after the Apameia Treaty of the Magnesia War (189/188 BC). However I wouldn't expect Rhodes to be as suppressive or influential on Kibyratis as it was in the Southwest and West Lycia. After the Macedonian Wars (168 BC), once again, like pretty much all of Lycia, Kibyratis must have been freed as it was a supporter of Rome. The city remained on the side of Rome during the Mithridates wars during the reign of Sulla (86/85 BC). This is how Bubon and the other cities of the Kibyratis region were gathered by Murena, a commander of Sulla, under one roof, that of the Lycian Province, together with the cities of Lycia. It was Murena who somehow arranged for the cities of Kibyratis to participate and be represented by two votes in the Lycian League. The inscription that gave us all of the above information was discovered in Bubon.

A poor-quality asphalt road from Gölhisar or Altınyayla will take you to Bubon (Ibecik) after half an hour's drive. The ruins of Bubon - if they are still recognisable - are on the Değirmen hill south of the Ibecik village. The city walls, the theater with sandstone seats and the Sebasteion were what remained of the city in the 1960's.

The sebasteion was first excavated by treasure hunters who did not really know what the building really was. The city was not officially excavated until a bronze statue of an emperor - now exhibited in the Burdur Museum - was accidentally found by a treasure hunter. Thanks to this official excavation, we are now sure that the structure was a sebasteion. The pedestals of the statues of emperors and empresses from the Commodus and Severus dynasties were retrieved but the statues, themselves, have been secretly shipped abroad: a head and a statue that you can see today at the Paul Getty Museum were smuggled from Bubon. Unless you are a devotee of archaeology, I would not recommend a visit to Bubon to see the city as it is today: Utterly destroyed...

BALBURA (ÇÖLKAYIĞI)

A foremost city in the Kaballa land or Kibyratis region, Balbura can best be accessed via the road between Fethiye and Korkuteli (350) from which you must take the turn for Altınyayla. 15 kilometers along the road to Altınyayla (the total distance is 20 kilometers), there is a dirt road that turns

Balbura, gate

Balbura, terrace wall of the Scene

left, or southwest. After 2 kilometers, you will arrive at the ruins of Balbura on the plain. I have to warn you about something crucial before going on to describe the ruins: The surrounding of Balbura is susceptible to sudden weather changes. A beautiful blue sky may be covered with clouds before you know and a sudden rain may truly soak you.

The ruins of the city of Balbura can be divided into two: The acropolis and the theater on the southern foot of the acropolis, and the lower city on the plain under the hill.

The acropolis was surrounded by approximately 2 meter high city walls built in a polygonal technique with recycled construction materials in some parts. The city walls date to the later periods of the city. There are no apparent ruins of any monumental building erected with skilled masonry inside the acropolis. Instead, there are remains of houses built in the same poor quality as the city walls. The theater that stands on the southern foot of the acropolis, however, is beautiful, especially the embossed polygonal wall supporting the skene building - A piece that deserves to be in any book on architecture. The orchestra and the seats above the upper 7th or 8th tiers are completely filled with

The city walls date to the later periods of the city.

Balbura, theatre

earth. Another section of interest in this theater is the theatron: Similar to the theater of Milyas in Pisidia, the natural rock across the stage building still stands intact in the middle of the theatron. And this is about all I can tell you about the ruins in the acropolis.

The ruins on the plain can be divided into two as well: On one side, to the south of the stream, you can see a second theater, where blocks of stone from the lower part of the stage building are still preserved, and an Early Byzantine church to the east of the second theater. On the other side of the plain to the north of this stream, you can see the ruins

Balbura, remains of the temples and agora

> *The excedra in the west was built by "Onesimos, the slave of the people" as its inscription reads. Apparently, so was the temple dedicated to Nemesis.*

of a settlement where there are many inscriptions, skilfully carved walls and other ruins of some buildings.

The ruins of the city, unlike the acropolis, are surrounded by city walls built with straight rectagonal blocks of stone and fortified with square watchtowers. You can still see the thickness of the wall and follow the traces of the wall in some parts. If you can get right into the middle of these ruins and locate the intersection of streets, you will get a better grasp of the buildings and ruins. To the northwest of this junction, you can find the bath with three of its sections still visible. The big building north of the bath must have been the gymnasium.

East of the bath and across the street, you can see the agora. The northern entrance to the agora is characterized by two columns. The agora is a rectangular building. On the south end of the agora you can find laid on the floor a Doric frieze and shafts of the columns of a Doric structure in the in antis plan. The function of this building remains unknown. Just south of this group of architectural pieces,

Balbura, mausoleum

you can see a temple dedicated to Nemesis between two excedras. The excedra in the west was built by "Onesimos, the slave of the people" as its inscription reads. Apparently, so was the temple dedicated to Nemesis. East of the temple is another excedra in the in antis plan. This one, however, was dedicated to Meleagros.

There are the ruins of a big church east of the agora, inside the city walls. The apsis of the building is visible. Among the pieces of architecture, you can see many statue pedestals.

There was a mausoleum to the north of the ruins on the plain near the dirt road. Recently, the structure has been seriously damaged, it has been dynamited and its blocks of stones are scattered around. Still, the lid of the sarcophagus in the mausoleum is still there to be seen with the relief of a lion on it.

KIBYRA (GÖLHİSAR)

The greatest and most important city in the Kaballa or Kibyratis region - Kibyra lies some 6 kilometers from the town of Gölhisar. Accessible from Denizli, Aydın, Burdur, Korkuteli, Elmalı and Fethiye by asphalt roads, the town of Gölhisar was connected to Kibyra with a rather poor-quality asphalt road until recently. The road may have been repaired by now due to the increased number of visitors.

Kibyra, the blocks used for the Byzantine restoration

> *With a cavea carved into the natural hill in the west, the theater is one of the biggest in Anatolia.*

Standing atop a hill overlooking the prosperous Gölhisar plain, Kibyra remains unexcavated and what little we know of its history today is limited to the writings of Strabon (Strabon 14,2.1), the brief surface survey report of Prof. Dr. Ümit Serdaroğlu from years ago, and my own observations.

According to Strabon, the city was ruled by a tyrant and despite the immense size of the city, the people of Kibyra did not bother to protect it with city walls, trusting their infantry force of 30,000 and cavalry force of 2,000 men. We also conclude from Strabon's comprehensive writings that these people considered themselves of Lydian origin and spoke the languages of Lydia, Solymos, Pisidia as well as Greek.

Kibyra makes a first appearance in history after the Magnesia war in 189 BC during the military excursion of the Roman Consul, Manlius Vulso, over Galatia. At the time, Kibyra was ruled by the tyrant Moagetes. Vulso only wanted to capture the city without fighting and to make it a tax-payer. Strabon explains that heated negotiations between Moagetes and Vulso took three days and in the end, with the support of his council Moagetes agreed to pay 100 Talents and 10,000 units of corn.

Another point of interest in the writings of Strabon about Kibyra is the annexation of the Kibyratis region to Lycia by Murena during the reign of Sulla. Strabon relates that the cities of Oinoanda, Balbura and Bubon formed a tetrapolis under the command of the city of Kibyra in the Kibyratis region before they were annexed to the Lycian League, while, the city of Kibyra was left under the rule of the Asian province. We understand that Kibyra, in addition to the other cities of the Kibyratis region, was represented by two votes in the Lycian League although this information has not been validated (Strabon 14.3.3).

Another major historical event in Kibyra was an earthquake in 23 AD. Devastated by the disaster, the city was rebuilt by the help of Tiberius and renamed after the

Kibyra, theatre

emperor as a sign of their gratitude: Caesarea Kibyra.

It was during the reign of Hadrian that Kibyra thrived but in the second half of the 3rd century AD came a massive invasion of Goths; an unfortunate end for Kibyra, which soon lost its glamour. The city was largely deserted in the 6th century AD and continued to exist as Horzum or Gölhisar, today, as we can see from the ruins and findings in the area.

If you are driving to Kibyra, follow the main road as far as you can until you see the area intensively covered with graves, and then you can make a U-turn to drive into the

Kibyra, odeon

Lycia

Kibyra, stadium

city where the ruins start appearing. The tire tracks and footsteps of previous visitors will help you with the directions and positions. Proceed until you will have a small hill on the right, park your car opposite the theater and then you can start visiting the ruins.

With a cavea carved into the natural hill in the west, the theater is one of the biggest in Anatolia. The seats have survived in pretty good condition although some are slightly damaged or awry. We can count up to 50 rows after which there is a diazoma of more than two meters in width. There couldn't be any more than ten rows of seats above the diazoma. The stage building is in ruins and covered with earth; however, two of the gates in the exterior part of the skene are still standing in good condition and another is standing in its frame only. The interesting thing about the diazoma is that there are many inscriptions on its walls, just like the theater of Myra.

About a 100 metres south of the theater, you can see the odeon, which is still standing and since the earth inside has been excavated recently, you can also see its marble seats.

The plain east of the theater must have housed some larger buildings. We can easily spot the agora and the stoas leading to it from south and west. The structures that lie on a 250x200 meter field will only be identified after a thorough

> *Strabon writes that Myra was among the 6 largest cities of the Lycian League and the name of the city was spelled 'MYRRH' on the inscriptions in Lycian language.*

excavation of the area.

Now, you can return to the car and take the road to the south that runs west of the hill where the agora stands. On your right, to the south, you will see the largest and best-preserved stadium in the whole region. The U-shaped building has a monumental gate with three arches. The 25 tiers in the west of the stadium, which stand on the natural hill, are particularly well preserved. The eastern side, however, is almost in ruins. Close to the east of the northern entrance of the stadium, you will see the ruins of the gate, up to the beginning of its arch. As you walk east from this gate, you will see a colonnaded street where some of the columns are still standing, though broken.

MYRA (DEMRE - KALE)

The winding picturesque road (D400) between Finike and Kaş will take you in half an hour to Kale, as we call it today. There is another road which is larger but less picturesque, which will take you from Kaş to Kale in 45 minutes. From both these directions, there are scheduled bus or shared taxi trips to the city leaving each half-hour in summer. Sailors will have to moor at Kokar (Andriake) to visit Myra and from Kokar, take a cab or a shared taxi.

Myra appears in ancient writings no earlier than the 1st century BC; however, discovery of inscriptions in Lycian language, coins and

Myra, sea necropolis

Myra, mausoleum

other findings provide evidence that it is a very ancient settlement. The Lycian language was banned after Alexander, the Great, and that the rich necropolises of Myra are full of inscriptions in the Lycian language and reliefs that are dated to very ancient times.

Strabon writes that Myra was among the 6 largest cities of the Lycian League and the name of the city was spelled 'MYRRH' on the inscriptions in Lycian language. Although coins of Myra bearing the abbreviation of "ΛΥΚΙΩΝ MY" have been discovered in many Lycian cities, it is surprising that there is so little information about Myra in ancient writings. The city was mentioned only in connection with certain events: First of all, having conquered Xanthos in 42 BC, Brutus commissioned his commander, Lentulus Spinther, to from Myra return with money and supporters. Spinther broke through the large chain pulled across the port of Andriake and pressed Myra to give money and support and in the end succeeded. The second event is in 18 AD when the adopted son of Emperor Tiberius, Germanicus, and his wife, Agrippina, visited Myra. This visit and the generous donations of Germanicus were commemorated in Myra and its port, Andriake, with a statue raised in the honor of the couple.

Myra was terribly hit by the earthquake in 141 AD and Opramoas of Rhodiapolis helped the city with donations: 56.000 denarii to be spent out of the budget of the League for the construction of the peristyle of the gymnasium and other works; ... denarii (not legible on the inscription) to be spent directly on Myra for the construction of an excedra in the gymnasium and the Temple of Eleuthera after the earthquake; ... denarii (again, not legible on the

In 60 AD, St. Paul stopped in Myra on his way to Rome.

inscription) for the construction of a theater; 12.000 denarii to buy oil; 100.000 denarii for repairs and 10.000 denarii to restore the gold-plated statue of Tykhopolis. The inscription further states that Licinius Langus of Oinoanda and Jason of Kyaenai also contributed to this donation.

Myra had a key role in the spread of Christianity as the city hosted some major personalities: In 60 AD, St. Paul stopped in Myra on his way to Rome.

Myra has a special value in the Orthodox faith, as the home of St. Nicholas (Santa Claus) who was born in Patara and was the bishop of Myra. This must be the reason why Theodosius, II made Myra the capital of Lycia.

An interesting piece of information about a pioneering concept in maritime transportation: The first chartered maritime transport was here between Myra and Limyra during the Roman Empire. Inscriptions indicate that shipping without proper permits was heavily fined.

From late 7th century to mid-9th century, the Arab army landed in Central Lycia en route to Constantinopolis (now, Istanbul). Endless Arab assaults left the inhabitants no other choice than to migrate inland. In 809, one of the

Myra, rock tomb

Lycia

Myra, theatre and sea necropolis

commanders of Harun al-Rashid conquered Myra. Another
Arab attack in 1034 resulted in the destruction of the
church of St. Nicholas, which was later repaired and
fortified by the help of Emperor Constantinos
Monomakhos, IX and Empress Zoe. In 1087, tradesmen
and pirates from Bari destroyed a sarcophagus that they
believed belonged to St. Nicholas and shipped the bones
inside off to Bari.

Myra, theatre

Myra, theatre

The Arab invasions, the unrest that Crusaders brought to the area, the debris that the often-overflowing Myros River (Demre Stream) poured into the region and finally, the earthquakes that hit the city one after another resulted in the city being evacuated: Myra shrunk to a village. Strabon writes that Myra was some 20 stadia inland from the sea. However, today, the city stands at a distance of over 30 stadia from the sea. Similarly, Strabon informs us that the city was founded at the foothills of the acropolis at an altitude close to the level of the sea. However, the mighty power of the Myros River has buried the city under 5 meters of debris.

The ruins of Myra are to be found north of the town of Kale, 6-7 kilometers inland. You can see the necropolis and the acropolis crowning the rocks northeast of the theater. Myra is similar to Simena in that the uppermost section of the city walls were repaired in Ottoman and Byzantine days and use was made of pebbles and mortar. Under this section, you can see the Roman city walls made of larger stones. The bottom of these walls, which can be dated to the pre-Hellenistic or Hellenistic ages have straight blocks

There are 29 rows under and 7 rows above the diazoma.

Relief from river necropolis

of stone.

The theater stands on a plain on the southern slope of the acropolis and its cavea has been partially carved into the natural rock. The lower seats and the upper cavea are supported by a vault in the shape of two large half-circles embracing one another. There are 29 rows under and 7 rows above the diazoma. The walls of the diazoma are full of inscriptions, niches and reliefs.

In the 1960's, the theater was cleaned and both the orchestra and the exterior part of the skene building were unearthed and this is how we know today that the wall of the stage building that faced the theatron was richly decorated. It was not until the orchestra was thoroughly cleaned that we realised that the theater was used as a circus and hosted water sports in the 3rd century AD. Similar to the Perge Theater, the section between the orchestra and the first row of seats was trenched so that the viewers could be safe from a possible attack of wild animals and a special barrier was added.

Travellers in the 19th century wrote that close to the theater of Myra, there used to be the city's agora. But, today, there are no columns or ruins left from the theatre and moreover, there is no clue whatsoever of the direction of the agora from the theater. Near the agora, on the left side

Myra, sea necropolis

> *Myra received its water from the open channel carved into the rocks on the west bank of the Demre Stream.*

of the road to Kale (Demre), you can see the ruins of a bath or a basilica - The only ancient ruins to see in Myra apart from the theater and the church of St. Nicholas.

Myra received its water from the open channel carved into the rocks on the west bank of the Demre Stream. The channel can still be traced above and under some of the rock graves in the river necropolis. The channel is then directed towards the southern slope of the acropolis where it disappears from sight.

Myra's necropolises are important: One of them is the river necropolis on the west bank of the Myros river and the other is the sea necropolis on the southern slope of the acropolis behind the theater. Both are rich in variety of rock graves: Imitating doors and windows, Gothic frontals, triangular frontals, rock graves with reliefs or inscriptions and finally, rock graves in the shape of an entire house - All hewn out of the natural rock. The inscriptions in the Lycian language are still red in color today. The most exciting rock grave with relief in the sea necropolis lies west of the theater: The owner was depicted during a banquet with his family, part of his daily life. A similar theme can be seen on another rock grave that some books refer to as the grave with lions: The owner is depicted on the right-hand side of the grave as he leans on a stick and on the inside as he drinks from a cup. The colors are still visible in this grave. Other reliefs of interest here are the anta capitals in the form of a lion's head and

Myra, Church of St. Nicholas

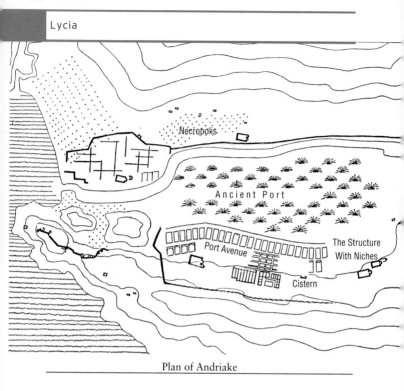

Plan of Andriake

the depiction of a clown next to these anta capitals. The frontal depicts a lion attacking a bull.

Last but not least, among the most notable ruins in Myra is the church of St. Nicholas. Prof. Dr. Yıldız Ötüken excavated the north galleries and discovered a portico in the north end. The frescoes have also been cleaned and restored. Since Prof. Dr. Yıldız Ötüken will soon publish the detailed findings, it would be immoral for me to give you any more information in this book.

ANDRIAKE (KOKAR OR ÇAYAĞZI)

Andriake is among the most easily accessible ancient cities from both land and sea. Blue Voyage boats and daily boat trips to Üçağız and Kekova either make a stop at or begin/end their trips at the dock located in the old mouth of the port at Andriake - called Çayağzı or Kokar today. You can walk to Andriake from the coast in 10-15 minutes but it may take up to half an hour in the heat of summer.

If you are coming by land, take the road between Finike and Kaş (D 400) and just after Kale (Demre), another road will take you to Kokar after 3 kilometers. If you wish to see

> *Andriake is among the most easily accessible ancient cities from both land and sea.*

the view of Andriake from the north, you should follow the new road from Kale (Demre) and drive in the direction of Kaş for 1.2 kilometers after the junction. You will see the view points.

Andriake is known as the port of Myra and a city that existed thanks to Myra. Therefore, it shares a similar history with Myra. However, we know that, around 200 BC, at the mouth of the Andriakos River (Kokar Stream), there was a city called Andriake and in 197 BC, Antiokhos, III arrived in Andriake with his fleet having set out from Antiokheia and conquered the cities under the rule of the Ptolemys. According to Livius (Livius XXXIII 19.9), on the other hand, Andriake was among the cities of southern Lycia. According to the Miliarium Lyciae=Stadios discovered in Patara, Andriake is some stadia away from Patara.

Intending to make war on Parthia and therefore arriving in Asia and Lycia, Trajan made a stop at Myra and noted that a beautiful port should be planned and built to the south of Lycia (Cassius Dio LXUIII 291). However, it turned

An aerial view of Andriake

Similar to the horrea in Patara, this one has 7 chambers and measures 65x32 metres.

Andriake, Nymphaeum

out to be Hadrian who was finally able to plan and build the port.

The city of Andriake was built on the slopes of a hill south of the port, which appears today as sand or marshland. The ruins dating to the later ages and the necropolis are north of the Kokar Stream.

Let's start with the ruins and buildings of the city in the east, ie. from the direction of Kale. The first ruin you will notice will be the aqueduct that watered Andriake. On the face of the rocks that you can find between the new and old roads to Kaş, to the right of the road, you will notice channels carved into the rock and the arches of this aqueduct.

The second well-preserved ruin lies south of the new road and north of the road to Kokar: The nymphaeum, which you will see right after the mud-bath facilities that some clever guy from Kale has built. An arched entrance, inner walls with niches and water springing from the foot of this structure, it's the only drinking water spring in the area.

Another major building to see in Andriake is the agora called Plakoma. Although there are few ruins to see above the ground, you can still follow the walls or column bases and get an idea about the plan of the building. Except on

Andriake, the portraits of Hadrian and Sabina from the Granarium

the south side, the agora is surrounded by shops. You can see the traces of the columns that encircled the area in the center of the agora. And don't miss the columns that were in the corners - They must have been the shape of a heart! Under the center of the agora floor, there was a cistern with a line of columns in the center and two large vaults supported by plaster on the side walls.

To the west of the agora, you will find the Horrea or Granarium that has survived in exactly the same shape that the first travellers into Andriake engraved for their notes. Similar to the horrea in Patara, this one has 7 chambers and measures 65x32 metres. The two corners of its façade are characterized by two square guardhouses and each chamber inside the building is connected and yet, they each have an entrance door on the outside. The walls in the façade were made of perfectly well cut, rectangular blocks of stone whereas the side walls and the back wall are built in the polygonal technique. The archivolt above the gates on the façade displays an inscription that gives us an idea of the time when the granarium was constructed. Moreover, we can see the portraits of Emperor Hadrian and his wife,

Lycia

Andriake, relief on the wall of the Granarium

Sabina, in the center. The writing of "COS III" in the end of the inscription, the fact that Hadrian (119-138) who was elected consul for the third time built this granarium in his second visit to Anatolia (129), and the hair-do of his wife, Sabina, that is similar to the style she used in her portraits dating from the first half of the year 130, all help to prove that the building was constructed in the second half of 129 or the first half of 130. The Granarium bears reliefs of the dreams of an officer or warehouse guard who served in Andriake in the 5th century AD.

The land between the granarium and the port is marked by the Port Avenue and half-open ship shelters and ship building yards. These buildings are notable for the pebble and mortar walls and the straight blocks of stone placed in the corners.

You can see the ruins of the watchtower that you may have seen in the gravures of ancient travellers. The tower stands at the east end of the city walls, on the slope of a hill behind the slope where the other ruins stand. The city walls were built half polygonal and half rectagonal. The base of the watchtower is a square but the main structure has a

You can visit all of Sura in half an hour if you stop close to the graves opposite the acropolis.

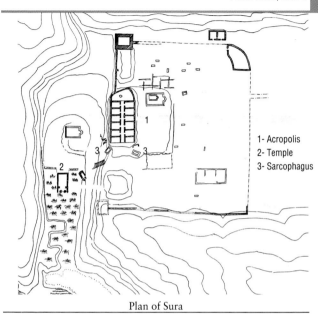

Plan of Sura

circular plan.

The land north of the port is the necropolis characterized by Lycian sarcophagi although there are the ruins of two Byzantine churches.

SURA

When driving between Finike and Kaş, at the end of Kale - formerly Demre - you can take the old road which will take you to a Roman family grave where the road will start climbing. When the road eventually arrives in a plain, you will see a few houses. This is Sura, still called the same name. However, the new road that overlooks Andriake from the north after Demre, runs along the city walls of ancient Sura and finally intersects with the old road destroying a few sarcophagi on its way. From Sura, there is a shortcut to Istlada, Tyberissos and Üçağız along the new asphalt road that meets the other roads at the junction I have mentioned above. This new road is parallel to the main road. If you drive to Sura on the old road, or the road that you see after the mausoleum at the exit of Demre, you will have to take the new road at the junction and proceed in the direction of Kale (Demre) for about 500 meters. You can visit all of Sura in half an hour if you stop close to the graves opposite

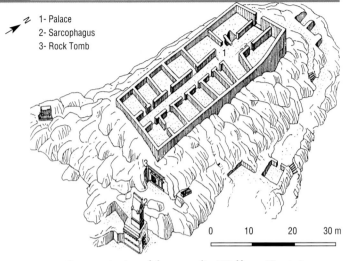

1- Palace
2- Sarcophagus
3- Rock Tomb

Sura, restitution of the acropolis, (*Wolfgang Wurster*)

the acropolis. But if you take the new road to get here, you could park at the parking lot on the left driving towards Kaş. This is where you can see from a distance an oracle of great importance not only for the Lycia region but the entire antiquity: The temple of Apollon Surios. You can also see the water spring where the soothsaying was performed and the nearby Byzantine church. If you are equipped with a pair of binoculars or telescope, you can even see the fallen columns and the row of triglyph-metop of the temple in the prostylos-tetrastyle Doric order. The walls of the temple are still standing up to the level of the architrave. If you are really interested, you will notice that the church next to the temple has three naves. The soothsaying was based on the movements of the fish in this water spring and the Temple of Apollon apparently lasted along time as a place of respect since the Christianized local inhabitants considered the place holy, and built a church here, although it should have been considered a pagan relic.

In a narrow valley stands the Temple of Apollon, the holy spring and the church. Unless you are very interested and want to have a close look at the ruins, you would be well-advised to see the remains from a distance. But if you really want to be close to them, you can follow any of the paths provided to see the ruins atop the hill in the west. You can descend to the temple and the church in a matter of 10-15 minutes but climbing up will take three times more as you will have to make your way through the bushes again.

Sura is a city with an acropolis characterized by a relatively long building with rectagonal walls crowning a small hill in the west, and the main city enclosed in the east and south by city walls standing on the plain east of the acropolis. Similar to other Lycian cities during the feudal Hellenistic Ages, Sura must have been controlled by a minor local chief who ruled over a small piece of land. This ruler and his family lived together with guards in the building standing in a north-to-south in the acropolis.

Sura was always hard to notice unless you knew the area by heart. But now, the new road has destroyed what was left of the city and the only standing building apart from the acropolis is the well-preserved watchtower near the point where the eastern city wall meets with the rocks in the north. Like the city walls around the acropolis, this structure is standing up to the level of its roof or the wooden floor of the second storey. This is all about the buildings to see in Sura. However, Sura is noted for the Lycian style sarcophagus with hyposorion on the southern slope of the acropolis and the nearby rock graves imitating doors and windows bearing inscriptions in the Lycian language. In front of these sarcophagi and graves and on the face of the natural rock, you can see interesting tomb stellae with carved wreathes as the head and a rectangular main body in which there are inscriptions. Among the other ruins in Sura are

Sura, temple of Apollo and the church

the many sarcophagi with tabula ansatas that you can see inside the city and outside the city walls, which the road has destroyed all the way to the flood plain.

There are no ruins or findings in Sura that can be dated to before the 4th century BC, apart from the building in the acropolis, the rock graves south of the acropolis and the sarcophagi. The Temple of Apollon Surios and the Watchtower are remains of the Hellenistic Ages. The sarcophagi inside the city and outside the city walls all date to Roman Times.

TRYSA (GÖLBAŞI)

On the road between Kaş and Antalya, some 30 kilometers from Kaş, you will arrive in Yavı (Kyaenai) 5 kilometers after the road reaches a peak: This is where you

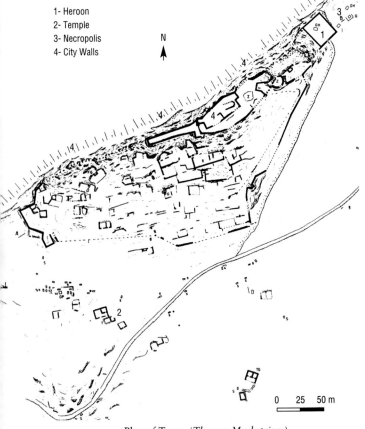

1- Heroon
2- Temple
3- Necropolis
4- City Walls

N

Plan of Trysa, (*Thomas Marksteiner*)

have to park the car if you are driving on your own or get off whatever transport you may have taken here. Once, there used to be rock and a tree as landmarks here and you could drive on the path leading to Gölbaşı from this landmark. However, today, I only recommend you drive an off-road vehicle on this track. If you are coming from the other direction, that is from Antalya or Finike, the ruins lie some 45 kilometers from Finike and you will find the junction for Trysa where the road starts descending after the village of Gürses.

Be prepared for this: The reliefs on the heroon and the sarcophagus of Dereimis and Aiskhylos are items that you cannot see any more in this city where they originally belonged. Discovered in 1841 by Schönborn of Austria and carted off to the coast from an altitude of 866 meters on special wooden sledges by Otto Benndorf in 1882 or 1883, these artifacts are all on display now in Vienna in "Antikensammlung".

Being a very special place for archaeologists with its heroon, the city of Trysa must have existed at the same period as its neighbour, Kyaenai, and given the findings from this neighbouring city, this period of time should be

Trysa, restitution of heroon

> *If you proceed northeast or towards the village of Gölbaşı, you will see Lycian sarcophagi dating from various ages*

before the 8th century BC.

Trysa is a long and narrow acropolis standing east to west on the crest of a rocky hill that is quite steep in the northeast and south slopes. The city is about 30 meters higher in altitude than the village of Gölbaşı. Its current state gives us the idea that the acropolis was just the size to house the estate of a minor local chief and his guards, as was the case in the cities of Phellos, Istlada and Sura.

Although the acropolis hardly has anything more to see than the ruins of some walls, including the city walls, the city must have reached its zenith during the rule of the unknown builder of the heroon.

Trysa is one of those cities that left us few clues as to its history. Most probably, the city was conquered in the first half of the 4th century BC when Pericles, the Magistrate of Limyra, was striving to form the Lycian League. Alternatively the city may have joined the League entirely by their own free-will. The fact that the city was under heavy Greek influence in the second half of the 4th century BC, although it was far from being a sea port or a center of trade, can be explained in one way: The Hellenization movement that Alexander, the Great started with his military expedition over Asia. Soon, you will read more about the heroon but

Trysa, heroon

first, let's imagine why so many scenes of Greek mythology were depicted in the reliefs of the Heroon and why they put an inscription in the Greek alphabet on the sarcophagus of Dereimis and Aiskhylos, which is dated to the same age with the heroon. Although they lived in Lycia, which has always been open to foreign influence in architecture, why did they build during the Roman Ages a theater not to a Roman plan or standards of the time but to a Greek plan of the ancient times? I believe there is only one explanation for this: Lycian conservatism. I would not like to go into such details in a guidebook but I have to because it is an important matter related to the heroon and the sarcophagus of Dereimis-Aiskhylos about which you will read below.

Trysa, heroon

The main road will take you to the fields of Trysa or Gölbaşı on a very flat plain that rises slightly in the north and south. If you proceed northeast or towards the village of Gölbaşı, you will see Lycian sarcophagi dating from various ages. You may notice the depiction of Kybele on the frontal of the lid of a sarcophagus right by the side of the road. You can park your car safely by the side of the road before arriving at this sarcophagus, and you will see a south-facing temple, which loses a block or two every year, to the south of the many sarcophagi on the southwest slope of the acropolis of Trysa - which will be on your left. This temple and the acropolis are the only buildings worthy of note in this city.

There is a path - created over the years by visitors - leading north from the point where you start to see the houses in the village. This path will take you to the famous heroon and the acropolis. A terrace was created at the east end of the acropolis to build the heroon. In an almost rectangular plan, the heroon was accessible through a gate in the middle of the narrow wall in the south. You can see on the outside, above the lintel of this gate, the reliefs of the front part of the bodies of four, winged bulls, rosettes and Gorgoneion. This line of reliefs continues east and west with local engravings and an Ionian kymation that is still in place today. You can see reliefs of the battle between Greeks and Amazons to the west of the upper row at the same height as the lintel. You will notice to the east of the same row reliefs depicting the battle between the 7's and the people of Thebai. The struggle between the Centaurs and Lapithae during the wedding of Peirithos is depicted in reliefs to the west of the lower row whereas the east of the same row depicts a scene that resembles the battle of Troy.

The thickness of the wall is 1 metre and the height is 3 meters and when you enter the building, you will notice on the lintel 8 musicians, dancing demons and funny dwarfs - resembling the Egyptian God of Bes. The frame is carved with dancing figurines the size of normal human-beings.

As for the reliefs inside the building, you will notice that there are two rows on the inside, as well. The upper row west of the gate depicts the suicide of Odysseus, under which you will see the struggle of Meleagros with the wild boar, Kalydon. The east of the gate is decorated with scenes of the cult of the dead, 4-horse chariot races and, in the upper row, Bellerophon's battle with Pegasos. The eastern corners of this dual relief are adorned with the scene of Theseus' arrival at Isthmos in the upper and lower rows.

Almost half of the west wall is decorated with two rows of reliefs depicting battle scenes, the siege of Troy and the battle with the Amazons. The latter is close to the north end of the wall.

The north wall depicts scenes from the battle between the Centaurs and Lapithae (The Abduction of Leukippos) in the upper and lower rows of reliefs running half the length of the wall. The other length of the wall, however, depicts a hunting scene in the upper row and meets the east wall with the reliefs of Centaurs and Lapithae in the lower row.

The lower part of the east wall shows scenes with Perseus on its north end and more scenes of the battle between Centaurs and Lapithae while the upper part depicts scenes of the struggle between Theseus and Perseus.

The grave-chamber of the heroon has the façade of the Lycian rock graves that are hewn out of the natural rock. The chamber is in the northwest corner of the building although slightly tilted today. The piece with the Ionic kymation and the walls are all that are left to see today of the structure - the Heroon of the unknown Magistrate of Trysa. The Benndorf team apparently had in mind to cart off the entire Heroon to Vienna but they changed their minds after they brought the pieces down because the whole thing was too heavy to carry.

I would like to give you some information about the sarcophagus of Dereimis-Aiskhylos that has been shipped off to Vienna. Many archaeologists tend to date this sarcophagus to the same period as the Heroon but I would like to raise a new opinion about this date.

The sarcophagus of Dereimis-Aiskhylos has a typically Gothic frontal and may be in the same category as the similar sarcophagi in Antiphellos, Limyra or Xanthos that are all dated to the years of antiquity. You can also add to this group some of the sarcophagi in Tyberissos, Kyaenai and some other cities as samples with the façade of a rock grave. Now, here is a question for my colleagues who are working on Lycia: Although the people of both Eastern and Western Lycia incised their inscriptions in the Lycian language and decorated their reliefs with figures wearing the local costumes or under the inspiration of the Greek or Persian cultures of the 5th century BC, why, in Trysa, did they decorate the Heroon of Trysa or the sarcophagus of

Trysa, necropolis

Trysa, sarcophagus

The environs of Istlada are rich with high-quality chaste trees and, therefore, called "Hayıtlı".

Dereimis-Aiskhylos with reliefs and inscriptions exclusively influenced by the Greek culture? Trusting my experience of over 40 years about the region and my instinct about the issue, though not recognized scientifically, I can tell you that this is due to one fact: Conservatism over coming the abrupt changes in the area. Therefore, I believe we should date the Heroon of Trysa and the sarcophagus of Dereimis-Aiskhylos to a somewhat later age, such as the last quarter of the 4th century BC, based on an assessment of the style of the heroon - since there are no inscriptions - and of the reliefs on the sarcophagus sharing the same style and masonry with the heroon.

The magistrate of Trysa and owner of the heroon must have heard something that forced him to defend his city or expect some sort of help from somewhere. Or he was a true philhellene.

After this fairly detailed discussion of these artifacts, now we can look into the history of Trysa as a city: It was a member of the Lycian League that was formed in the 2nd century BC. The League coins bearing the first two letters of the city's name, in this case, the abbreviation of "TP", may well be of Trysa, but an alternative is Trebenna, another city far off. Trebenna is a city on the border (Pamphylia-Pisidia-Lycia). We have not found any coins bearing the abbreviation of TP in the site of Trebenna but we have in Central Lycia. Therefore, it is most probable that Trysa issued these coins.

ISTLADA (KAPAKLI - HAYITLI)

Istlada, necropolis

There are two ways to go to Istlada: The first road (400) is the wide but slightly winding road from Kale (Demre) to Kaş where you will have to take a turn to the village of Davazlar from the blue road sign. After the turning, you will be driving on a dirt road ending after 3 or 4 kilometers at Kapaklı. From that point on, you will have to trek to Istlada. The second road is a short-cut, an asphalt road to Uçağız that was constructed only in 1995. If you take this road, you will have to turn left - or west - after Sura. Kapaklı is some 6 kilometers from this turning. Again, from Kapaklı on, you will have to trek to the ruins.

The environs of Istlada are rich with high-quality chaste trees and, therefore, called "Hayıtlı" (a place with chaste trees).

The ancient writings do not tell us anything whatsoever about the city; however, inscriptions in the area point out the name of the city. Istlada has just the right setting and area for a 5th century BC magistrate to settle with his escorts. Off the coast and atop a natural rocky hill, the settlement is surrounded by city walls and stands on a narrow strip of land stretching from east to west. The city walls end in the east with a gate providing access to the castle. The ruin west of this must have been a watchtower overlooking the gate. It is hard to identify any buildings inside the city walls. You can see rock-cut water channels that lead to cisterns and wells. This is how they solved the water problem in Istlada: collecting it. Istlada has been famous since the 18th century

Istlada, necropolis

for the mausoleum, in the village of Kapaklı which has been cited in archaeological literature as the "Hoyran Mausoleum", and the many rock graves, sarcophagi and tomb stellae on the eastern and northern slopes of the acropolis.

When the light is suitable, you can see on the Hoyran Mausoleum an inscription in the Lycian language and the frontal piece depicting the owner of the Mausoleum with his wife and son. The rather low Gothic frontal is bounded by this relief, which shows the owner lying on a sofa with his men at one end of the sofa and his wife, son, daughter and other ladies at the other: The participants of this ceremony. It is highly probable that the man depicted in the reliefs was the Magistrate of Istlada, himself. Moreover, the details of the relief are quite worthy of note: In a good light, you can see the dog of the person lying on the sofa right next to the sofa, a crater on a small stool in front of the soldiers, and an oinokhoe on the floor under the soldiers. There are outward-faced sphinxes on the acroters, one of which is unattached. Looking at other graves, we can assume the top acroter, which was removed long ago, was in the form of a crescent or horn.

From the inscription in the Lycian language and the style of sculptures, the grave is dated to the early 4th century BC. On the northeastern edge of the Istlada acropolis, you can see reliefs on the north side of another rock grave, dating to around the same period of time. These reliefs depict the owner in a feast and the rock grave imitates a

From the inscription in the Lycian language and the style of sculptures, the grave is dated to the early 4ᵗʰ century BC

N   1- Theatre
     2- City Walls
     3- Agora
     4- Churches
     5- Necropolis Areas

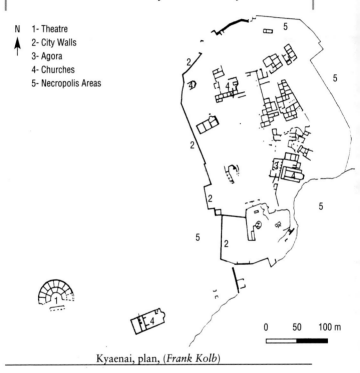

Kyaenai, plan, (*Frank Kolb*)

door or window in its façade. Another relic of attraction in the necropolis is a tomb in the form of a stella on the façade of which the armor of a warrior is depicted.

KYAENAI (YAVU-YAVI)

We do not know the name of the city in the Lycian language and I do not think that we know the true form of the Greek name of this Lycian city, either. If the word derives from "kuaneos" that means "the color dark blue" or "dark rocks", then we should be calling the city "Kyaneri". Anyway, let's leave this problem of whether the name of the city should be Kua-neai or Kua-enai to philologists or epigraphs to solve.

Kyaenai or Kyaneai, the city lies on the crest of a slight

Lycia

Kyaenai, theatre

slope north of the village of Yavu or Yavı about halfway between Kaş and Finike. The new road runs slightly to the south of the old one; therefore, if you are driving from Kaş, you should drive past the roadside stops in Çamlık to take the forest road leading north, 4 or 5 kilometers later. When you begin to see the country houses, you should not proceed towards the village but take the road that will first lead south and then take you to the ruins.

If you are driving from Finike, however, you will follow the road signs to Yavı and Kyaneai. If you decide to climb from Yavı, you would be well advised to procure water and the like before setting out on foot. But if you are to take it the easy way, you can drive past the Yavı village but be careful on the sharp turn to the north that will be approximately three kilometers after. 500 meters after this the forest road that I mentioned above as leading south will take you right in front of the theater of Kyaenai.

Prof. Frank Kolb has been working on surface explorations for almost a decade now. In the last couple of years, he has worked with the Museum of Antalya. It is thanks to his works that, we now know that Kyaneai was inhabited and was a city as early as the 2nd millenium BC. Here, there have been findings from the Late Bronze - Early Iron Ages and furthermore, the excavation of Avşar hill revealed the first evidence of the Lycia region meeting the Hellenistic world. Late Protogeometric and Early Geometric ceramic pieces, shipwrecks carrying goods from Cyprus, Egypt and Phoenicia dating to the 13th and 14th centuries BC, are all signs that Lycia was populated not only on the coastline but also in the cities as early as the 2nd millenium

Kyaneai or Kyaenai was an inland city but still, it had a strategic location, with a fine view over both the coastline and the interior.

BC. Inscriptions on a bronze sheet of Tuthalia, IV, discovered in Hattusa (Boğazkale), the capital city of the Hittite Empire, agree with the findings in the shipwrecks.

Kyaneai or Kyaenai was an inland city but still, it had a strategic location, with a fine view over both the coastline and the interior. Looking south from the theater or the acropolis, the inhabitants could see the entire coastline from Andriake to Isinda; turning 180 degrees, they could see the Lycian heartland all the way to the valleys and Bey Mountains bordering the land in the north. As well as the seaside cities in the south, the city was perfectly situated in a position to overlook Tyrsa in the east, Arneai and Tysse in the north and Phellos in the west. The fact that there are so few ruins apart from the findings in Avşar hill that I have already told you about and the early materials coincidentally discovered in Kyaenai is peculiar to all Lycian cities. This can be explained by one fact: The Lycian cities rich with forestry products used wood as the major construction material. As a matter of fact, the rock graves in this city, though much fewer than you can find in other Lycian cities, provide excellent samples of the use of wood. The Gothic rock graves and their reliefs and inscriptions are still the most ancient

Kyaenai, rock tombs

Kyaenai, view from necropolis

ruins left to see in Kyaenai. Dated to around the 4th century BC, these rock graves with their reliefs and inscriptions are the manifestations of a turning point in history: The Asian expedition of Alexander, the Great. It was after the arrival of Alexander that a severe policy of Hellenization was applied in the area, thereby forbidding the use of Lycian alphabet. After this period, even the reliefs were under the influence of Hellenistic culture. More evidence of this lies with the coins of the "Lycian League": Starting in the 2nd century BC, the coins were no more issued to Persian standards but Attic standards. The inscription of "ΛΥΚΙΩΝ ΚΥ" that we can see on the coins of the League most probably point to Kyaenai. The abbreviation of "ΚΥ" could not refer to Kibyratis or Kibyra as although the Lycian League was formed in the mid-2nd century BC the Kibyratis region did not become a part of it until 80 BC. The coins bearing the inscription of "ΛΥΚΙΩΝ ΚΥ" were clearly minted around the mid-2nd century BC as the official currency of the Lycian League.

Kyaenai is a city that we could simply rename "The City of Sarcophagi". The only identifiable remains are the theater, rock graves and the sarcophagi. The rest of the city is overgrown with bushes and even, an archaeologist or an architect could hardly picture what may be lying underneath.

Kyaenai can best be described as an interesting city, where the acropolis is surrounded by city walls and inside the city walls there is an area with various religious and administrative buildings, family graves and sarcophagi while outside the city walls you can find sarcophagi, rock graves,

> *If you arrive from the west, the first major building that you will notice is the theater.*

tumuli and all kinds of burials encircling the city on all sides. On one side, meanwhile, is the theater. And even the road from the acropolis to the theater is lined by sarcophagi on both sides.

If you arrive from the west, the first major building that you will notice is the theater. The theatron was made in a polygonal technique and stands on a plain land over a wall filled in with stones until the level of the seats. The theater has two diazomas and the uppermost tier of seats behind the first diazoma have backs to rest on. Constructed in a Greek plan, the theater has a stage building, or skene, that was planned to be fairly low, probably to avoid blocking the natural background in the south. As in the case of Antiphellos, a wooden - temporary skene must have been used over some sort of a lower structure because there are no findings that point to the existence of a multi-storey skene. If the skene was indeed a multi-storey structure, the construction material should still be here among the ruins since they could not have been transported elsewhere. All this indicates a single storey skene. The theater is an example of conservatism the like of which you can find in the buildings of some other Lycian cities. Therefore, although the architect adopted the plan of Greek theaters and could well have rested the back (cavea) of the theater on the perfectly suitable natural slope, the theater was constructed as a detached building on the plain land. This is a sign that the theater was constructed around the time of the two famous and contemporary rich men of Lycia - Opramoas of Rhodiapolis and Jason of Kyaenai both of whom served as Lyciarkhs. It is needless to go into more details but, the architectural decoration both inside and

Sarcophagus lid decorated with reliefs

outside the theater can be dated to the times of Antoninus Pius who ruled after the earthquake in 141.

You can reach the acropolis from the theater in two ways: You can take the road lined with sarcophagi on both sides whereby you will reach the south of the acropolis. If you take this road, you will pass by a great many number of Roman sarcophagi as well as the following: Rock-cut niches-aedikulae that you will see as you proceed eastward, a rock grave with a single Ionic column in the middle that you can see down the path as you proceed further east and if you walk still further eastward, house-type rock graves bearing inscriptions in the Lycian alphabet, and some other rock graves with reliefs and Gothic façades. South of this road are lots of mostly Roman sarcophagi all the way to the Yavı or Yavu village.

APOLLONIA (NEAR KILINÇLIKÖY)

Off the road between Kaş and Demre, there is a road turning to Üçağız some 18 kilometers from Kaş. If you are driving, this road will give you the opportunity to visit a number of ancient cities in a daily excursion. Now covered in asphalt, the road to Üçağız will bring you to the village of Kılınçlı. This is where you should leave your vehicle before

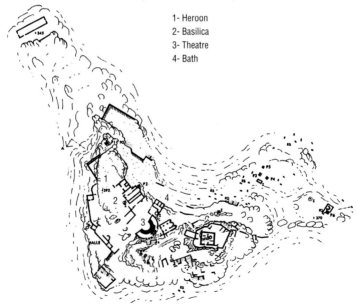

1- Heroon
2- Basilica
3- Theatre
4- Bath

Plan of Apollonia, (*Wolfgang Wurster*)

Kent, doğal oluşumunun verdiği olanaklardan da yararlanarak çok iyi korunma sağlayan bir surla çevrilidir.

Apollonia, city walls

proceeding eastward in the direction of Üçağız. A few hundred meters after Kılınçlı, you should aim for the hill in the west. Half an hour of trekking and you will arrive in Apollonia. Please, bear in mind that the area is short of water, especially if you are visiting in summer, and be prepared with a minimum of 2 litres of water per person. If you are arriving by sea, getting to Apollonia from Aperlai (Sıçak) or Theimiussa (Üçağız) will take no less than two hours on foot.

We do not know much about the history of Apollonia but it may give you the impression of a city more picturesque and rich in terms of its remains than cities like Sura, Isinda and Phellos. Recent surface findings indicate that Apollonia was a fairly ancient Lycian settlement. The city was a city-state represented in the Lycian League by one vote, which it shared with Aperlai and Isinda in the mid-2nd century BC. However, having discovered coins bearing the abbreviation of ΑΠΟ, we have the

Apollonia, prismatic tomb

Apollonia, basilica

perception that Apollonia had a distinct place in the Lycian League.

Findings of ceramic pieces from the late 5th century or early 4th century BC, the polygonal heroon built with very skilled masonry in a prismal body (6 of the walls are still standing) and the fire altars all help to show that Apollonia was a truly ancient city, although we do not know its original Lycian name.

The inhabitants made good use of its natural disposition while building the city walls, which protected the city excellently. The natural slope on which the acropolis stood was enclosed in the form of an inner castle. Sarcophagi and prismal mausoleums can be seen in the necropolis on the north and northeast slopes of the inner castle or the acropolis. A well-preserved late Byzantine Church, built partially in the west of the acropolis, is still standing after years of erosion as probably the only remains of the settlement in the city just before its demise.

West of the church, you can visit the theater where the skene is far from recognition. It is almost the same size as the theater in Idebessos: It has only 5 or 6 tiers of seats. Its plan and the fact that the cavea rests on the natural slope suggests that this theater may date to the Hellenistic ages.

This is where you should be careful not to miss the sign for Hoyran or Kapaklı in this village.

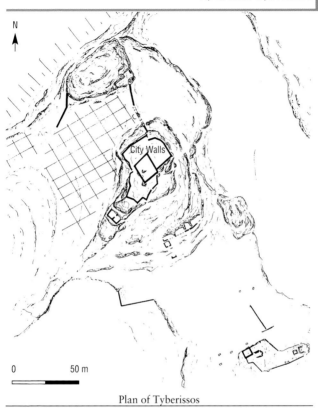

Plan of Tyberissos

The tradition of baths in this region was also carried on in this city as just north of the theater you can see a typically Lycian bath with its apsidal caldarium.

TYBERISSOS (TİRMİSİN-KESMELİ DISTRICT-ÜÇAĞIZ)

18 kilometers from Kaş on the road to Finike, you should take the turn for Üçağız and after the village of Kılınçlı, you should turn east and then south to arrive at the Kesmeli district of Üçağız village. You should be careful not to miss the sign for Hoyran or Kapaklı in this village. Alternatively, you can take the first asphalt road leading east through the houses. After approximately 5 kilometers, you must proceed eastward, you will see to the south both ancient graves and city walls up in the mountain.

As distinct from other Lycian cities, the necropolis of

Tyberissos, detail from the relief of rock tomb

Tyberissos lies on the rocky plain under the city instead of on the rocky slopes of the acropolis.

I was beginning to think that the mausoleum, which I could not see until the early 1980's due to the difficulty of getting to this city was a new finding when my friend, Prof.

Tyberissos, drawing of a rock tomb

Borchhardt informed me that the mausoleum had been a noted remain since the late 19th century. Apparently, I was misled by the drawing errors and typing errors in the publications that I had scrutinised many times. In fact, when I compared the drawings, photos and observation notes of the architects and archaeologists from the Arykanda excavation team with the drawings and photographs that I had made with the same team at different times, I saw differences that were big enough to mislead almost anyone.

I must give you some

This may help us develop an understanding of the basic criteria and variations of a certain type of Lycian rock grave and, even, sarcophagi, to some extent.

information about the rock grave, which, I believe, is the most note worthy and ancient structure in Tyberissos. You may notice that in some regions of the plain where the Kesmeli district of Üçağız stands, there are tiny rocks that appear to be volcanic but are in fact, limestone. Most of these rocks have been used to build late examples of house-type rock graves. However, a giant rock in the direction of Istlada is outstanding with its inscription in Lycian language, its rather pointed Gothic frontal, the space provided in front of it for other graves and the altars on its peak.

This may help us develop an understanding of the basic criteria and variations of a certain type of Lycian rock grave and, even, sarcophagi, to some extent. Of course, this is a generalization based not only on a single element but rather on a combination of elements, some of which may be misleading. According to this general idea, when the façade of a rock grave or the frontal of the lid of a sarcophagus is pointed, this particular item can be deemed among the

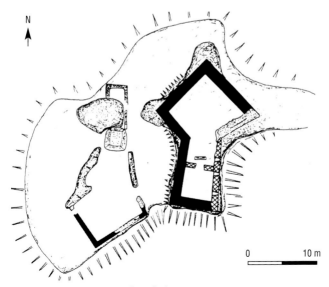

Plan of Theimiussa

Lycia

Theimiussa, necropolis

oldest of its kind.

THEIMIUSSA (ÜÇAĞIZ VILLAGE)

Nearly 20 kilometres from Kaş on the new, large road
to Finike, you will read the road sign to "Üçağız". From this
turning, you have to drive another 20 kilometers on a bumpy
road to the village of Üçağız.

Simena and Theimiussa appear to be two cities that
did not share the same destiny with each other but,
instead, with Tyberissos and Kekova. You can even extend
that destiny all the way to Istlada in the east and Apollonia
and Aperlai in the west. My reasoning behind this idea
is this: Simena, Theimiussa and Kekova were both cities
living on the shores of the very same bay, which was so
small that you could even consider it a lake. In other
words, these cities needed to act in solidarity not only for
transportation but also in matters of defence.
Furthermore, there is a reason why the name of the
region is Üçağız (i.e. Three Openings): The area as it
appears today is the product of a natural formation that
runs from Istlada and Andriake in the east and Aperlai
in the west and that leaves these cities with no other
choice than protecting one another from all evil coming
by sea. Likewise, despite all the new means of
transportation and the increase in tourism revenues, the

population of Üçağız or Kale village does not exceed 500 or 600 throughout the year. And if you consider the recent boom in the population of Turkey, you would have to expect to find an ancient population of no more than one fourth or, even, one eighth of today's population. Take this for instance: when I started primary school back in 1940, the population in Turkey was slightly above 13 million so, the population must have been much less in the first centuries BC or AD. The point I am trying to make here is that the people in the cities that I have mentioned above had to defend themselves with no more than 100 or 150 people of all genders and they were all unskilled warriors. This is why they had to unite their forces in case of danger. Similarly, I do not agree with Bean that Tyberissos was a poorly defended city since the three ruins that you can track in Theimiussa, lying north-to-northeast from the shore, indicate that the people defended their city to the extent they could given that population. And you can also find other ruins of defence structures in the other cities mentioned. The first ruin that you can see of this kind is a rather tiny castle with embossed rectagonal walls on the shore in Theimiussa. This castle served as a focal point when, during the Byzantine era, it was enlarged in diameter to circumscribe the city with walls that may have been begun in an earlier time. On the border of the city with Tybersissos, you can find the acropolis built to an embossed and rectagonal design. Apparently, this building was the last point of defence together with Tybersissos.

The ruins in Theimiussa can be summed up as follows in order of chronology: The city walls, in the bizarre form that I have already described, on the east end of Üçağız Port or the Port district; the relief of a naked young boy on the side of the house-type rock grave to the west of the city wall, a grave that can be dated to mid-4th century BC, bearing an inscription, which reads "Kluwanimi" in the Lycian language, about the young boy.

East of this grave, you will see plenty of Late Hellenistic and Roman sarcophagi around the channel fortified with walls on both sides. These ruins end in the north with what we can call an Early Byzantine building that has not been excavated and, thus, cannot be identified. Based on its direction, we assume that this building cannot be a basilica or a church but still, the exact function of the building

Kekova

remains unknown.

Both in the direction of Simena and on the isles southeast of Theimiussa, you can see that the landscape is marked with many stone quarries that provided the material for these sarcophagi and the buildings in the city.

Anyway, no one can deny that the area was inhabited up

Kekova, Tersane Island

> *You can take any type of vessel from this port, Andriake or Kaş to Kekova Island.*

until the Middle Ages after which it has existed until today as a haven for all kinds of lawless deeds.

KEKOVA (DOLİKHİSTE-TERSANE ISLAND)

18 kms from Kaş on the road to Finike, the large asphalt road that turns south at the road sign for "Üçağız" will bring you to the port of Üçağız. You can take any type of vessel from this port, Andriake or Kaş to Kekova Island.

If you are staying in Üçağız, Kale village, Kokar or Kaş, you could make a tour of the center and north side of Kekova Island both for recreation and as an archaeological visit. You can visit the ruins at Simena, Theimiussa and Kekova, take a walk in the region and enjoy the sea as much as you can.

Kekova Island must have been inhabited at around the same time as the settlements located across the sea in the north. Although we find no word of the island in ancient writings, the east end of the north side of the island was home to many shipyards and careening grounds carved into the natural rock, hence one name of the island:

The church on the Kekova Island

> *Simena fits perfectly with the name it has earned over the years: "Batık kent" or the Sunken City.*

"Tersane" or "shipyard". We do not know precisely until what time these shipyards remained functional. Another ruin of interest is situated near the center of the island on the plain used as a beach today: A church with mosaic decoration in its apses that was made up of millimetric tesseras depicting Jesus Christ, the like of which you can see in the Hagia Sophie Church in Istanbul. Most probably the wall mosaic was also destroyed by treasure hunters. Although we have no documents to prove it, we could imagine that this church was primarily ravaged by the Arabic army under the command of Harun Al-Rashid, who would also conquer Myra. The ruins on the mainland also provide the proof we need to support this idea since, as far as we are concerned, there are almost no ruins on the mainland apart from the Medieval Castle and city walls in the village of Kale.

SIMENA (KALEKÖY)

Simena is a must-see, an ancient settlement that is a long walk by land but it is easily accessible by sea from Andriake (Kokar) or Üçağız (Theimiussa). Simena fits

Simena, Kaleköy

Kaleköy and the Acropolis of Simena

perfectly with the name it has earned over the years: "Batık kent" or the Sunken City. As geomorphologists would agree, southwest Anatolia is slowly sinking into the sea while region of Troy is rising so the coastline is no longer the same as in antiquity.

Here are two extreme examples to help you identify the problem: For starters, if you follow the route from Ayvalık to Edremit and stop for a while near Akçay or slightly south of Akçay to have a close look at the soil of the agricultural fields that lie east of the road, you will find many pieces of sea shells. But, in southwest Anatolia, you will find the exact opposite. Take Limyra, for instance: The ruins dating from the 3rd or 4th Centuries AD are located 3 to 4 meters below the surface today. This means that the ruins are even below the level of the ground water - A clear sign that Anatolia has a tendency to sink from north to south.

There is no way I can tell you why but to the extent I could from the available resources I did feel the need to study the fault lines stretching across Anatolia: The results of the phenomenon are two-fold and extreme: An earthquake may either cause a terrible devastation or nothing at all happens even if the whole world shakes awfully. In either case, you cannot predict which will happen. And this is not only the case for the Lycia region but also many other regions all over Anatolia. You can think of the sunken city as a great warning from the past: Why do you think the ruins dating back to the 4th century AD and later are 4 or 5 meters under the sea today? Yes, the landscape

The Lycia Region has suffered a major earthquake every 25 years and a disastrous and truly devastating one every 100 years

is one of utmost interest for both archaeologists and other visitors and that is for sure. However, nobody can guarantee that the ever changing and uncontrollable geological factors will not emerge in an unusual manner, one day. The point that I am trying to arrive at is this:

The Lycia Region has suffered a major earthquake every 25 years and a disastrous and truly devastating one every 100 years. Nowadays, I am really curious about one thing: In a region that is constantly under this natural threat, how can some people allow the construction of high-rise buildings? Are they trying to challenge the power of nature? I do hope that Mother Nature will not react too strongly.

The village of Kale was home to many civilisations at different ages of history and regardless of which direction you may arrive at the village, you are sure to see walls and sarcophagi raising out of the water.

This is among the few places where you can see traces of the Ottoman, Byzantine, Roman and Lycian periods all in one place and in good, standing condition. The western city wall is the best place to identify the different masonry techniques of each of these civilisations.

Since the only way to reach Kale is by sea, the first

Kaleköy and the Acropolis of Simena

Simena, temple

building you will see is the bath where the coffeehouses and restaurants are today. The bath was constructed during the reign of Titus as a present to all the cities of Aperlai and Sympoliteia.

If you visit the acropolis, inside and east of the city walls, which can be dated to no earlier than the Middle Ages, you can see a rock grave dated to the 4th century BC that has a Gothic façade. The structure was later used as a granary. To the west, you can see another house-type rock grave. On the slope southeast of this rock grave, you will find the ruins of the smallest theater-odeon or bouleuterion hewn out of the natural rock. We are uncertain about the time that this

Kaleköy and the Acropolis of Simena

> *If you wish to visit Aperlai, I still recommend that you take the (slightly more expensive but less risky) journey by sea.*

building was constructed; however, looking at its plan, we may conclude that it was during Roman rule. No matter what its true function was, it can be identified as a theater and apparently, it was connected to the Medieval city walls by a stoa.

Beyond the wall and the olive pressing plant, the plain that lies two terraces below, where there are many country houses, was the temenos of a Domitian or Titus temple, as we understand from an inscription that lies there on the ground. Today, apart from this inscription, the temple is beyond recognition after centuries of being used for other purposes.

Kale village is bounded in the north and west by a necropolis that appears more crowded than that under the sea. I wonder if this necropolis extends northward and westward to blend with the necropolises of Tyberissos and Theimiussa, respectively.

I am certain that the many isles between Kale and Üçağız Port district were used as stone quarries. Therefore, the tiny isles that you may notice during the boat trip from Kale to Üçağız are the places where the material of these graves and buildings came from.

Aperlai, city walls

> *In ecclesiastical records during the Byzantine era, the city appears by the name of "Aprillae".*

Aperlai, city walls

APERLAİ (SIÇAK PORT)

Until only two years ago, Aperlai was not accessible by land. If you wish to visit Aperlai today, I still recommend that you take the (slightly more expensive but less risky) journey by sea. And if you are planning a quick visit to a number of cities, you can rent a boat at Andriake and visit Simena (Kaleköy), Theimiussa (Üçağız) and Aperlai on the northern coast and then sail north of Kekova. Of course, take this suggestion only in the long days and calm weather of summer.

We understand from silver coins minted in the city (bearing the abbreviations of APR, PRL) that Aperlai existed even before the Lycian League. The city is not only cited in the works of ancient authors (Pliny, Stadiasmus, Ptolemaios, Hierokles) but also in the "Book on Navigation" of Piri Reis as an almost-completely deserted shelter for boats where no more than a handful of fishermen's families lived in the 16th century AD. We know that the city was represented in the Lycian League by "one vote" together with three or maybe even four other cities. It is clear that Aperlai signed into a "sympoliteia" with Simena, Apollonia and Isinda. The one vote that they had in the Lycian League was shared by Apollonia, Isinda and Aperlai.

In ecclesiastical records during the Byzantine era, the city appears by the name of "Aprillae".

Today, Aperlai remains as a well-protected castle built close to the shore from straight rectagonal blocks of stone in the lower section and rubble in the upper. The city walls have survived in pretty good shape. Although two of its three gates providing access inside the castle have resisted the centuries fairly well, the ruins inside the castle are beyond recognition. The only building that can be seen and identified on the surface is the Byzantine church.

Ruins of interest outside the city walls are the numerous sarcophagi of polygonal and rectangular design standing between the shoreline and the walls, a sunken dock the like of which you can see in Üçağız and the ruins of which may have been the road connecting the dock to the city. I am sure that many of the buildings inside the city walls would be quickly identified and dated if only the city could be excavated.

PHELLOS (FELEN YAYLA - ÇUKURBAĞ)

You will arrive in Ağullu approximately 2 kilometers after the junction where the road from Finike to Kaş meets the road between Elmalı and Kaş. If you take the asphalt road that leads north of Ağullu, you will see Lycian

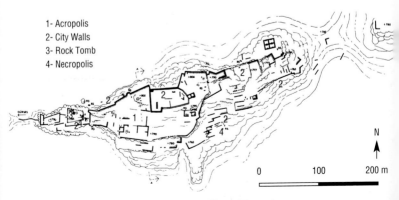

1- Acropolis
2- City Walls
3- Rock Tomb
4- Necropolis

0   100   200 m

Plan of Phellos (*Wolfgang Wurster*)

Aperlai, Phellos

Phellos, necropolis

sarcophagi at a distance crowning the first hill across the road. The road will eventually approach this hill and divide into two, one for the village of Çukurbağ in the west and the other for Pınarbaşı in the north. If you are to visit Phellos, this junction is where you must make a decision. Those of you who would like to climb to the city should go to Çukurbağ and be prepared for a climb (northward) of 45 minutes or an hour. Or else, you can go into Pınarbaşı, find the fountain and then walk (not climb) southwest for 15 to 20 minutes. This is how to get to Phellos - A city that has one thing in common with Kyaneai: Their horizons are vast.

Although we find that the geographer Hekataios (6th or 5th century BC) mentions Phellos in his writings, he made a big mistake when he located the city somewhere in Pamphylia. However, an inscription from the time of Hekataios cites that the name of Phellos was "Vehinda" in the Lycian language. The fact that Skylax (4th century BC) mentions Phellos in his writings provides us with sufficient evidence to conclude that this is a very ancient settlement.

You can even read the Greek inscription on one sarcophagus, if you can catch a good light, of course.

> *But if you want to visit Isinda, you have to slow down and watch out for the road sign for Bayındır and Belenli villages.*

You will not find too many ruins in Phellos apart from the city walls around the acropolis, which stand in a polygonal design in certain parts. The rectagonal structures adjacent to the city walls in the southeast and east of the city were probably watchtowers. North of the acropolis, there are some sarcophagi in the valley and on the slopes of the hill across the valley. These are far fewer than the sarcophagi in other Lycian cities. Some of them have reliefs and are house-type graves. You can even read the Greek inscription on one sarcophagus, if you can catch a good light, of course.

ISINDA (BELENLİ)

Once the road between Finike and Kaş meets the road between Elmalı, Kasaba and Kaş, and after the turn for Ağullu village, you will start descending to Kaş. This part of the road is wide and straight so you may find yourself driving too fast. But if you want to visit Isinda, you have to slow down and watch out for the road sign for Bayındır and Belenli

Isinda, city walls

Isinda, a well

villages. Now, there is a fairly good road, though a dirt road, to the new holiday villages and Bayındır Port. Since the roads keep changing every year with new building in the area, you must be careful not to miss the sign for Belenli or ask for directions from people you meet on the road.

You will drive to the school in Belenli and from that point on, you will have a 5 or 10-minute walk to the hill west of the village, where you will find Isinda.

Isinda was a minor settlement the name of which we do not find in ancient writings and the city was probably ruled by a less-than-powerful family, as was the case in Sura, Apollonia and Trysa. Standing on the crest of a small hill, Isinda was surrounded by jerry built and embossed city walls the ruins of which have survived in good shape in the north and northeast.

The 3 mausoleums bearing inscriptions in Lycian that you can see today in Isinda help us figure out that the city was inhabited earlier than the first half of the 4th century BC.

The city was represented by 1 vote together with Aperlai

Built on steep and rocky land, Isinda could not even last to the Byzantine era owing to the lack of proper land to irrigate as well as shortage of water.

in the 2nd century BC when the Lycian League was established.

On the land between the Balanlı village and the hill that we can assume was the acropolis of Isinda, you can see a number of Roman sarcophagi.

Built on steep and rocky land, Isinda could not even last to the Byzantine era owing to the lack of proper land to irrigate as well as shortage of water. It is a wonder that the city existed for 4 or 5 centuries without interruption on such a piece of land where they had to collect every drop of rainwater knowing that they could never consume it "like water'.

ANTIPHELLOS (KAŞ)

As I explained earlier in the section about my rapport with Lycia, Antiphellos used to be the perfect holiday town with a local population of no more than 2.500 inhabitants who were always ready to help you, the cleanest sea and a location that was very difficult to reach by land. All the hardships of life - except gnats and mosquitoes - were far away behind the mountains. Absolute silence prevailed and beautiful intact nature was everywhere... Even the problems of the real world arrived late into this town as there was no way you could follow the daily press. The people did not disturb one another and neither did the houses that were positioned so cleverly that they were open to the exterior yet, provided all the privacy needed for the inhabitants.

If I am not mistaken, it was in 1958 or 1959 and I was on a stay trip to Lycia that four or five construction workers lost their lives building the road connecting the city to the rest of the world. Kaş would never be the heaven of perfect innocence any more.

These workers were not the ones to blame, of course. They were only poor workers trying to make a living. Their only mistake was probably relying too much on their strength. But today, there is one big mistake that is still being made despite all the warnings: Coastal cities should not be connected via coastal roads but instead, a main road should be constructed inland and parallel to the coastline, thereby preventing all this speculation in land (property), and enhancing growth with cheaper roads connecting the coastal cities to the main road. In contrast to this reasoning, they are still building coastal

Antiphellos, theatre

roads almost the size of highways. Don't forget to add to that the ambition of local mayors who are craving to show off.

The result is roads cutting sharply through the citrus-fruit gardens, if not totally destroying them. The big ambition of making a lot of money out of land, which had its first innocent examples in Erdek, Ayvalık or Edremit would soon destroy Kuşadası, Bodrum and Marmaris. Hardly feeding a population of 2,000 or 2,500 inhabitants, Kaş would soon become the victim of that land speculation, which started in Antalya. From that population, the town would leap to 20,000 to 25,000 or, in summer, 50,000 to 60,000 inhabitants. You would have to be very lucky to bump into someone from the truly local community of Kaş, today, as is the case with Bodrum, Kuşadası, Kemer or Alanya, Antalya, etc. Speculators are everywhere now.

The Lycian name of the town was Habesos and Kaş was a haven for ships between at least the mid-2nd millenium BC and Byzantine times as we can understand from the Serçe and Uluburun shipwrecks.

Although not scientifically excavated, terracotta statuettes of mother goddesses discovered while excavating for the foundations of buildings inside the city, and grave findings imported from Corinthia or Athens are all signs that Antiphellos did exist even before the 4th century BC and was somehow in interaction with other ancient cities.

The Greek name of the city, "Antiphellos" can be translated as "the land opposite the rocks" which fits in perfectly well with both Phellos and Antiphellos.

It is clear that Antiphellos was invaded by Persians around the mid-6th century BC. We figure out from the findings of imported terracotta or ceramic pieces (today, on display in the Antalya Museum) from the same period of time as the Persian invasion that Antiphellos continued to trade with other regions. Despite the invasion, the city prospered through the 5th or early 4th Centuries BC as we can see from the house-type rock graves bearing inscriptions in Lycian and decorated with Gothic frontals.

Unfortunately, the ancient writings fail to provide details of the military excursions of either Pericles or Alexander, the Great. Considering that the rule of Seleucus dynasty did not last long, the Ptolemaic dynasty clearly invested in building up Antiphellos during the era of the Diadokhs.

Antiphellos was represented by 1 vote at the Lycian League but the city remained a center of trade and was known to mint its own coins, as well as coins in the name of the League.

Once under Roman rule, Antiphellos produced coins of Gordianus, III.

As for the ruins of this ancient city, you will notice that the necropolis spread up the mountain bordering Kaş in the east while all other public and private buildings and graves were built around the Bucak (Vathy) port and the center of the city today.

The city walls are still partly visible, with a rectagonal design, in certain sections, starting from the west of the port of Kaş, and ending in front of the theater where the guesthouse of the water authority stands today. On the slope near the actual port of Kaş, you can see a church converted into a mosque and southeast of this mosque are the ruins

A better preserved building than the temple in Antiphellos is the theater.

Antiphellos, theatre

of a temple with its temenos. The temenos was built in an embossed, rectagonal masonry technique, which is a reminder of the Hellenistic age (?) and evidence that the masonry systems in Lycia cannot serve to date buildings. We are uninformed about the god of this temple.

A better preserved building than the temple in Antiphellos is the theater. As a matter of fact, the people of Lycia adopted the Greek norms of architecture; therefore, we just cannot jump to conclusions about the date of structures simply by looking at their architectural plans. However, if we bear in mind that the region underwent intense construction activity during the rule of the Ptolemaios dynasty in the Hellenistic ages, it looks quite likely that the theater was also constructed during this period of time.

The theater does not have a solid skene building of stone, most probably, owing to the fact that they did not want to block the beautiful natural background, the sea, with a solid building. After its construction, the east analemma wall collapsed for some reason, presumably an earthquake. I have reason to believe that this was the earthquake in 141 AD, because Antiphellos was one of the cities that received donations from Opramoas and the purpose of this donation was not set in precise terms and

Antiphellos, theatre

conditions. But, it could well have been the earthquake in the year 27 that hit this wall. If you view the eastern analemma wall of the theater from the south, you will easily notice the repairs. They clearly recycled the original blocks of stone in this repair.

Climb north of the theater and you will see a very interesting grave the like of which is not to be seen in Lycia. Carved into the natural rock in the form of a square prism, this rock grave has an east-facing door in its façade and, on the level of the architrave, a block of triglyphs of limestone next to the grave and another, but in a slightly different decoration, waiting to be fixed into the place that was carved into the rock.

But the most noteworthy aspect of this rock grave is that it bears a relief of girls dancing hand-in-hand on the inside wall across the door. Decorated with rosettes on both sides, this relief can only be seen in the early morning because over the centuries, shepherds used this grave as a shelter and made fires. Therefore, today, the reliefs are covered with a thick layer of greasy smoke. The clothes of the dancing girls are reminders of the female clothing style in Hoyran, Trysa, Pınara and Tyberissos. Accordingly, the rock dates back to the first half of the 4th century BC.

If you trek north of the rock grave towards Vathy, by its ancient name, or the port of Bucak, as we call it today, you will see some other graves that can be dated to the Late Roman - early Byzantine ages. Both on the shore and in the

> *Some bear inscriptions while some others are adorned with reliefs and other architectural decorations but most date to the 4th century BC.*

sea are the ruins of a shipyard similar to that seen in Andriake.

East of this part of the city, which we assume to be the acropolis, the foremost ancient structure of note is the old breakwater that still protects the port, with some recent additions made in the past 20 years. This breakwater (an eastward continuation of the city walls) and the closed port have provided sailors since antiquity with just what they needed, excepting the additions to the east end: An easy access to the port despite the heavy seas from the southwest. The new part of the breakwater and the lighthouse gave in to strong waves soon after construction. Therefore, the port was more unsafe than ever. Later, a better method was used and today, even faster boats can enter the port with confidence although the port never really recovered the status of safety that it once had. The sarcophagi you will see on the docks are not in their original place but roughly in the same area.

When you walk east of the shopping district in the city center, you will see the symbol of Kaş - a rock grave dated to the 4th century BC with its very well preserved hyposorion, inscription in Lycian language and Gothic frontal. Proceed eastward towards the rocks and you will notice, behind the houses now, countless sarcophagi with Gothic frontals or

Patara, sand dune

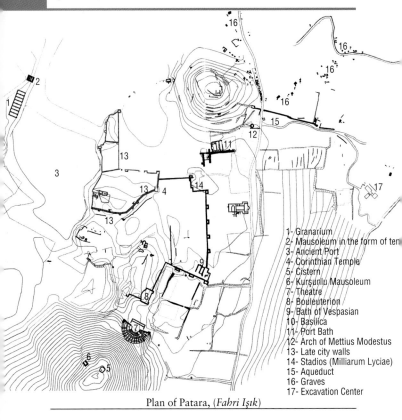

Plan of Patara, (*Fahri Işık*)

1- Granarium
2- Mausoleum in the form of ten
3- Ancient Port
4- Corinthian Temple
5- Cistern
6- Kurşunlu Mausoleum
7- Theatre
8- Bouleuterion
9- Bath of Vespasian
10- Basilica
11- Port Bath
12- Arch of Mettius Modestus
13- Late city walls
14- Stadios (Milliarum Lyciae)
15- Aqueduct
16- Graves
17- Excavation Center

house-type graves. Now, there are even more of them after the arrival of some other sarcophagi discovered during the excavation for new houses on the seaside. Some bear inscriptions while some others are adorned with reliefs and other architectural decorations but most date to the 4th century BC.

PATARA

Like all the other ancient coastal cities, Patara has been continuously and heavily under the threat of speculators as well as the pressure of nature towards its topography. Although the city is still struggling with its initial and most serious problem - urbanization, it seems more or less to have solved its second biggest problem - The giant sand dune.

When I visited Patara for the first time back in 1950's, the city was terribly threatened by erosion and I noticed in my later visits that the sand dune was rapidly expanding while the pine trees that once grew on the edge of the beach were getting scarcer and retreating inland. This serious threat has recently been deterred to a great extent. However, new buildings reproducing like rabbits continue to pose a threat to Patara. In this respect, Patara does not prove to be a city that represents the care we bestow upon our natural and historical heritage. I am sure that the reaction from both local and foreign visitors will help to change many things.

Past Yeşilköy (formerly, Fırnaz) on the road between Kaş and Fethiye, you will drive straight on the plain of Kınık for a while and just before the road makes a 90-degree angle to the north, you will see that there are many water channels and road signs leading south to the sea. This is where you should turn to visit Patara. You just can't miss this turn because of the signs for hotels or motels so numerous that you can hardly see the real road sign.

Patara has been excavated for almost a decade by Prof. Dr. Fahri Işık. I am sure that there are and will be a great deal of new information and ruins unearthed thanks to his work.

The name of the city in the Lycian language was PTTARA and the most recent findings indicate that Patara

Patara, theatre

If you follow the road to the sea, the first major remaining structure you will visit will be the Arch of Mettius Modestus - A triple-arched monument.

could date to as early as the 2nd millenium BC. Stone axes the like of which had been discovered earlier in the other East Lycian cities are quite interesting archaeological findings that shed light on the history of the people of Lycia.

Among the artifacts discovered here, one stone axe earned the honor of being the oldest, followed by some ceramic pieces that date to the end of the 9th century BC. However, we must take into consideration the shipwreck in the port of Serçe from the 14th-13th century BC. So, we cannot be surprised by findings in Patara that date to the same period of time as the Mycenean and, most probably, Minoan cultures or that have been imported from these two places or other inland cities.

The only thing that we are absolutely positive about is that Patara was inhabited as early as the beginning of the 2nd millenium BC. However because the findings do not follow a smooth or uninterrupted chronology, we can conclude that the city was constantly inhabited at least since the 1st millenium BC.

Patara has recently provided brand new information to the world of archaeology with a new relic that was discovered in the city: a monument that Emperor Claudius ordered and which was crowned with his statue - the "Stadios" or "Milliarium Lyciae". This monument documents the

Patara, Arch of Mettius Modestus

Patara, Byzantine city walls

distances between Patara and various cities in all directions. Having collected stones from the monument from all around the Byzantine city walls, we suppose that the monument once stood at the junction of the main avenues in the city center.

Beyond doubt, the best way to learn about Patara, with all its findings and ruins would be the book of Prof. Dr. Fahri Işık who is excavating Patara. However, in case you do not have a copy of his book with you during your visit to the city, I would like to make a brief summary of the ruins starting in the south after the village of Gelemiş. You can reach the village from the road leading to the ruins off the main road. The first ruins coming your way will be vaulted mausoleums with crypts. Next to these structures, you will see rock graves with single or double chambers that were unearthed on both sides of the road.

Before you arrive at the monumental gate of Mettius Modestus, you will notice a slope on your right, to the west. This is the estimated location of the Temple of Apollon since the colossal head of a statue of Apollon had been discovered here. When you look south from here, you can see almost all the major ancient buildings in Patara around the lagoon and on the land north of the hill housing the theater in the south.

If you follow the road to the sea, the first major remaining structure you will visit will be the Arch of Mettius Modestus - A triple-arched monument. Walk eastward from one side of the arch and your eyes can follow all the way to the hills around the city the aqueduct that once watered Patara. You will notice many Lycian sarcophagi around the aqueduct - A sign that the necropolis lies south, southeast and west of the hill where Gelemiş village stands today.

You can follow the asphalt road to reach the theater. Don't forget to have a look at the inscription carved within a very special frame on the east wall of the skene building before you enter the theater through the parados. The builder of the theater, which was constructed with the contributions of the people of Patara has been honored in the center of the text: "Προκλὰ Πάταρέυς ἀνέθεκεν" - "Donated by Procla or Procula of Patara". The theater has 2 diazomas and the theatron, orchestra and the skene building were all until recently filled with sand.

The archaeologist, the late Mr. Ahmet Dönmez, was the first to find traces of the Temple of Athena atop the hill housing the theater and close to the cistern. What some travellers perceived as the ruins of the Temple of Apollon are in fact the ruins of the lighthouse that stood west of the hill.

When you are on the crest of the hill, if you look north and also west of the lagoon, which happens to be the ancient port of the city, you can see the Byzantine city walls that bordered the lagoon in the east start off in front of the theater and head northward. Where the city walls make an angle, you can find ruins of the harbour baths between this angle and the lagoon. Outside the city walls, there is a colonnaded main avenue running north to south at the north end of the city.

The area west of the lagoon is noted for the granarium resembling the one in Andriake both in plan and in time, and north of the granarium lies the ruins of a mausoleum, which was mistakenly taken to be a temple.

You can see on the plain east of the lagoon a temple

Xanthos, Lycian acropolis

What some travellers perceived as the ruins of the Temple of Apollon are in fact the ruins of the lighthouse that stood west of the hill.

with a podium, which has come to be known as the "Temple in the Corinthian Order" and to the east of the avenue and on the same side with the monument of Mettius Modestus, you will notice the ruins of a bath dedicated to Emperor Vespasian and a basilica.

1- Roman Acropolis
2- Agora
3- Lycian Acropolis
4- Nereids Monument
5- Port

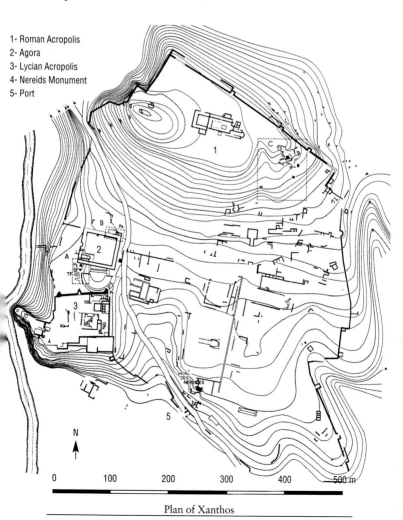

N

0   100   200   300   400   500 m

Plan of Xanthos

> *The last quarter of the 8th century BC saw Lydia striving to expand in Caria and Lycia.*

XANTHOS (KINIK)

Almost halfway between Kaş (Antiphellos) and Fethiye (Telmessos), Xanthos was the religious and administrative center of Lycia and one of the first places to be mentioned in western writings, namely in Homer as part of the account of the Trojan wars. And that's not the only first of this city: Like Kaunos, when they found out that there was no way they could defeat the Persian army commanded by Harpagos, they committed mass suicide, which would occur a second time during the days of Brutus, as well as a third occasion when they did not succeed. Xanthos was also the first city excavated by British teams in Lycia although not with official permission in the true sense of the word. We will find more examples of the city's firsts but I am giving you the last one here: Xanthos was the first Lycian city to be robbed of sarcophagi, reliefs and inscriptions, which had been preserved in more than seventy safe location.In 1838 and 1842 vessels of the British navy anchored near Patara and the findings (Lion Tomb, Harpies Monument, Nereids Monument, Payava Tomb, Merihi Tomb, etc.) from these more than seventy huge collections were carted off to the British Museum as the prize of the excavations. But there is also a positive first about the city: Xanthos was the first city to be scientifically excavated in Lycia, in the beginning of 1950 under the supervision of Prof. Dr. P. Demargne.

We know that the name of the city in Lycian language was ARNNA and since I am not a philologist, I can not tell you whether the name Xanthos had anything in common with "Arinna", a major goddess of the Hittite Pantheon. 'Xanthos' is the Greek word for "yellow" and the city must have earned this name long before the Trojan Wars. However, in the Illiad of Homer, the Lycians of Xanthos under the rule of Sarpedon heroically rushed to help Troy without a second thought, which, in fact, seems rather unlikely considering that the distance between the two cities is approximately 700 kilometers. Given the time that it would take news of Troy's need for their help to reach Xanthos, it seems quite impossible that Sarpedon could arrive in Troy quickly and in time after, first, collecting his men to fight and, then, making his way to Troy through countries that he had never even seen before. Therefore, we can think of two currently debated explanations for the bizarre situation: It is possible that when the works of Homer - a travelling poet - were put into writing, the writers made a big mistake due to their lack of sufficient historical information about the events and their true times. The stories in Illiad and Odyssey were not put on paper until 5 or 6 centuries after the Trojan Wars and until over 1 century after Homer. Consequently, we would not be terribly wrong to suspect that a mistake has been made in the writing. Another possibility, however, is that there used to be another city and river by the name of Xanthos to the east of Troy, around Biga and Karabiga, as we call the area today, and the people of this settlement were also of Lycian origins, according to the writings of some ancient authors (Homer, Illiad 5, 479; 12, 313-314; Illiad 20. 73-74). If we prefer to take the latter seriously, then, Lycians could have really and immediately fought in the Trojan Wars since they always had a leader by the name of "Sarpedon". However, to date, we have been unable to locate a Lycian settlement or a city named Xanthos in the Troas or Mysia regions. Although the city of Zelia may be considered by some authorities as a Lycian colony in the Troas, the idea is difficult to prove for the time being. We may well find the correct answer to this question which seems to have a two-fold explanation by sheer coincidence in a couple of months or just as likely, we might not know the answer for a hundred years to come. I am not trying to confuse anyone here. The only thing I am trying to prove here is that the pieces of the puzzle are too hard to put together as you can understand from the examples I have provided here in relation to a couple of cities.

Although the city existed as early as the second half of the 2nd millenium BC, the findings of the continued excavations by Prof. Dr. Demargne, Prof. Dr. Metzger and Prof. Dr. Le Roy, in chronological order, have only proven that Xanthos was regularly inhabited since late 8th century BC. The time from the 8th, back to the mid-2nd millenium BC still remains a mystery as we have found no artefacts from the period.

The last quarter of the 8th century BC saw Lydia striving to expand in Caria and Lycia. But since they were stopped for good even before arriving in Telmessos, Lycia hardly came under Lydian influence - excepting the Bayındır Tumulus, of course.

The most striking event in the city and the one that you will find in many ancient writings was the Attack of Harpagos, the Persian commander, on Xanthos in 546 - 545 BC. Seeing that they could not fight against Harpagos, the people of Xanthos - women, children, elderly and slaves - gathered in the acropolis with all their precious belongings, set fire on the acropolis and committed mass suicide. When Harpagos finally conquered Xanthos, the city had already burnt to ashes and was without a single soul. Meanwhile, according to Herodotus, 80 families of Xanthos were not present in the city during the battle so they returned to build the city anew.

Another of the firsts of the city, which I have not mentioned above, was the big fire that burnt down the city between 475 - 450 BC. Xanthos clearly remained an ill-fated, unfortunate city in the years before the Birth of Christ as you can well understand from the short list of events cited here. Not too long after this terrible fire, in the year 429 BC to be precise, Melesandros, a commander from Athens, tried to impose new taxes on the region. The Lycians immediately reacted to this attempt and, therefore, waged war against Melesandros who, in the end, would be the one to lose. But as a result ties with Athens were completely cut. Following the destruction of the acropolis in Athens by the Persian army, the hand of Persia was light and smooth on Anatolia despite provocation from Athens. Although invaded, Lycia still continued to develop. To give you some examples from Xanthos, the eastern polygonal wall of the Lycian acropolis, the Nereids Monument and the sarcophagi from early 4th century BC all date to the ages under the rule of Persians.

In the first half of the 4th century BC, Pericles, the magistrate of Limyra, was doing his best to establish a "Lycian League" but the attempt would remain fruitless as he lost a war fought somewhere between Xanthos and Telmessos. But during the whole period, the satrapy of Karia was constantly busy developing, especially in the period after Mausolos and Pixadoras. The activities of Pixadoras spread over Tlos, Pınara, Xanthos and Patara and were even commemorated with inscriptions.

We understand that Alexander, the Great conquered Xanthos with difficulty in 334 BC. According to the writings of Appianos, everybody knew that the people of Xanthos

> *In 42 BC, Brutus' efforts to make Xanthos a supporting city met with determined resistance and once again, the city was on the brink of mass suicide.*

would commit mass suicide again for the sake of their freedom while they resisted Alexander.

Leaving aside some of the legends about the acquisition of the city by Alexander, it is evident that soon after his demise in 323 BC, Xanthos would be one of the cities that of the commanders of Alexander set their eyes on. As a matter of fact, the city fell to Ptolemaios, I in 309 BC. After about a century of living under the rule of Ptolemaios, in 197 BC, the King of Syria, Antiokhos III, conquered Xanthos as we learn from ancient writings. Again, the city would soon change hands, after the Magnesia War in 189 BC, and would be left under the rule of Rhodes. A reaction against foreigners and especially the pressure of Rhodes led many cities, including Xanthos, to petition the Roman Senate. In 167 BC, the Roman Senate made a decision to change some things in the region by first putting an end to the pressure of Rhodes.

Sometime around the mid-2nd century BC, Lysanias and Eudemos were determined to establish a "Lycian League" maybe even in the same year as this change introduced by Rome. Meanwhile, Eudemos found himself in a position to organize an expedition against Tlos to take control of the city. By 167 BC, the "Lycian League" was formally established to a great extent. As Strabon quotes, 23 cities were represented by votes in the "League". As I have told you before under different headings, there were six cities, namely Xanthos, Pınara, Patara, Tlos, Myra and Olympos, that had three votes each in the meetings. However, there were some other cities that were collectively represented by 1 vote in the Lycian League, such as Isinda, Apollonia and Aperlai or Idebessos, Akalissos and Kormos, despite being self-governing cities.

If we are to discuss the issue from the specific point of Xanthos, as opposed to Lycia in general, Xanthos was not only the religious center thanks to the neighbouring Letoon but also the administrative center, the capital city of the Lycian League established by Lysanias and Eudemos. Naturally, being the center allowed certain privileges, beginning in the Hellenistic perod. When, during the reign of Sulla, the cities of Kibyratis were annexed to the League,

Xanthos, Lycian acropolis

Xanthos simply benefited from the situation. This change extended the borders of Lycia to include the 4 major cities of Kibyratis, which were represented by 2 votes. This was the time that the borders of Lycia attained, and preserved, their maximum extent in their history, until the Mithridates, I War or even until the 80's BC when Sulla continued to reign.

The conflicts of interest after the killing of Julius Caesar plunged Lycia into chaos again. First, Cassius arrived in search of support and then, came Brutus. In 42 BC, Brutus' efforts to make Xanthos a supporting city met with determined resistance and once again, the city was on the brink of mass suicide. This time, however, Roman soldiers prevented this suicide. Consequentially, Mark Anthony took control of the area and it was thanks to his work that, in 41 BC, the city went through major repairs and continued to thrive.

Driving his competitors off the field at the Triumph of Actium, Octavianus granted autonomy to Lycia for their support in the battle and their particularly heroic contributions. During the reign of Emperor Claudius, Lycia was united with Pamphylia and reduced to the status of a province again in 43 AD only to regain independence during the days of Nero (54 - 68 AD). But fate had it that Lycia and its annexes would be united with Pamphylia into a province again in the days of Emperor Vespasian (69 - 79 AD). We are still surprised to find a monumental gate erected in honor of Emperor Vespasian in Xanthos despite all these recurrent major changes in the city's administrative status.

The days of Emperor Trajan and Hadrian were active

> *The Lycian acropolis was in fact a Persian acropolis because most of the findings are of Persian origin.*

years in the development of Lycia; however, findings from these days are rare. We understand that in the wake of the earthquake in 141, rich people of various far away cities contributed to the re-building of Xanthos. The fame of rich men of Lycia such as Opramoas of Rhodiapolis and Jason of Kyaenai endured due to their help and support. Inscriptions indicate, for instance, that Licinius Langus made donations for the construction of a bath in Xanthos.

During the Byzantine era, Xanthos was a diocese, as we understand from the ecclesiastical records. Xanthos must have shone for the last time during the early Byzantine period. But, the Arabic raids that started with Harun-al Rashid and the construction of a permanent garrison in Finike were no less than the worst nightmare for most cities in the region. The city would soon lose its glory and be reduced to a village.

Almost until the research and excavation in Xanthos by Fellows in 1838, the village of Kınık continued to live the way they did when I visited the place in early 1950s. I can even tell you that the buildings along the road leading to the site were almost the same as in photographs taken

Xanthos, Lycian acropolis

around 1900.

The city of Xanthos was founded east of the Xanthos or Eşen River on a few hills and on the south and east slopes of these hills. The city was fortified with walls.

The studies of Prof. Dr. Demargne, Prof. Dr. H. Metzger and later Prof. Dr. C. Le Roy inform us that the Lycian acropolis is home to many artifacts from earlier ages.

The first hill near the Eşen River has come to be known as the "Lycian Acropolis" by the excavators and we shall stick to that name without question. This acropolis is bounded in the east by a polygonal terrace wall dated to the early 4th century BC, and the city walls running north to south. When entering the site from the village of Kınık, you can see south of the Nereids Monument, a monumental gate from the Hellenistic period. Spreading away from this gate you will find the rectagonal and slightly embossed city walls that border the Lycian acropolis in the south. The structure continues until the River Eşen. Meanwhile, the city walls that border the Lycian acropolis in the west made good use of the natural slope in certain sections. There are secret passages dated to the Lycian days in the lower parts of these city walls. But the upper parts are exactly in the same style as the Roman or Byzantine city walls that surround the rest of the city. As for the city walls that bound the Lycian acropolis in the north, the structure is inherently Byzantine with three of its triangular counterforts still standing in-situ. The counterfort in the east, in particular, is worthy of note for the Lycian open-air temple or mausoleum that it stands over.

The Lycian acropolis was in fact a Persian acropolis because most of the findings are of Persian origin. The ruins dated to Lycian age and named from A to E by the excavators must be mausoleums or open air temples generally from the first half of the 4th century BC.

North of the Lycian acropolis, you can find a typically Roman theater. With its vaulted entrances and high-rise stage building, the Xanthos theater must have been built in the second half of the 2nd century AD. As the Lycian acropolis remained in use even in later eras it became

The Harpies Monument is memorable for the subjects on its reliefs as well as being the best example of Persian influence in Anatolia.

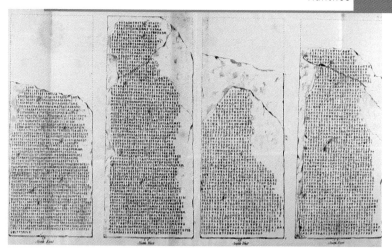

Xanthos, Stela with Inscription

necessary to run a network of water channels through the theatron. The water channels that you can see lead not only to buildings in the Lycian Acropolis but also to other structures to the east.

There are three andesite ruins west of the theater, and one among them is outstanding. The first ruin in the north is the Harpies Monument. The part that surrounded the grave chamber in a decoration of reliefs has been shipped off to the British Museum. Until my French colleagues provided the plaster copies cast from the originals, the Harpies Monument stood in the exact poor state that Fellows and his team had left it.

The Harpies Monument is memorable for the subjects on its reliefs as well as being the best example of Persian influence in Anatolia. The reliefs have found an established place in archaeological literature as the "Throne Scene": A typically Persian leader sits on his throne under an umbrella on the left, in front of him are thuribles in the style that you would see in Urartian and Persian reliefs, and next to these thuribles are various persons blessing the leader and showing their loyalty. The lower part of the grave is a monolith square prism and underneath is what we can call the crypt: The main grave chamber where the deceased lay. Dating to the first quarter of the 5th century BC, this prismal mausoleum was decorated with reliefs of Harpies, which had the bodies of birds and carried off souls of the dead.

> *The sarcophagus of young girls or dancing girls has recently been restored and re-erected.*

South of the Harpies Monument, you will find another sarcophagus with a Gothic frontal and hyposorion from the 4th century BC. The excavators call the structure "sarcophage pilier". During the excavation, some reliefs of wrestlers were found in the hyposorion and dated by the excavators to around 540 - 530 BC. These reliefs must have been brought from somewhere else and left here.

The third monument near the theater is a grave with a raised pedestal dated to the 1st century AD.

Next to the theater and almost adjacent to the skene, you will find the agora with its shops on all three sides. The agora dates to the 2nd century AD. On the southwest corner of the agora, there are the ruins of an Early Byzantine chapel almost adjacent to the Harpies monument and the theater.

On the northeast corner of the agora, however, you will find another mausoleum named the "stela with inscription". The structure is very much like the Harpies Monument and its monolith body is incised with inscriptions in the Greek and Lycian languages. Compared to the Harpies Monument, this one is decorated with reliefs of sportsmen in the grave chamber. Dated to the end of the 5th century BC, this mausoleum is still standing in its original place.

When you reach the Roman acropolis through the east of the Lycian acropolis, you will notice that there are some major ruins. The land is flat to a great extent and here was the location of a great basilica, agora and many other buildings with stoas. No wonder this is where the city stood most of its days under the Roman Empire. However, the details are unknown to us.

The Roman acropolis is in much the appearance of a Byzantine acropolis except for the ruins on its east and southeast corners. The major ruins to be seen here are the very delicately made Early Byzantine mosaics, which have been repaired recently, and a basilica connected to this mosaic floor.

East and southeast of the Roman acropolis the area is marked by many house-type rock graves dated to the 4th century BC. North of these rock graves, you will notice another prismal mausoleum similar to the "Stela with Inscription" or the "Harpies Monument". However, this one does not have reliefs in the grave chamber. Proceeding south of this area, you can see the pedestals of the Lion Tomb, Payava Tomb and the Merihi Tomb on the southern slope of the new Roman Acropolis. The sarcophagus of young girls or dancing girls has recently been restored and re-erected.

Leaving the city in the direction of the village of Kınık, the first of the ruins you will find is the Gate of Vespasian with its arch still partly standing. If you walk south of the gate, you will come to the Nereid Monument behind the building that is used as the excavation warehouse today. The lowest two rows of the blocks of the monument are still there, in-situ, to be seen.

I believe the Nereids Monument was not only the product of a Greek - Persian synthesis but also of western culture. As far as I have noticed both in the British Museum and the photographs of the monument in Prof. E. Akurgal's book, "Griechische und Römische Kunst in der Türkei", I can assure you that, in terms of architecture and sculpture, the monument is a typically eclectic structure. For example: The triangular frontal, tetrastylos and Ionic order, the upper part of the monument and the style of the sculptures are representations of a typically Ionic architecture. In this respect, the influence of Ionia - or even Attica is more dominant on the monument. On the other hand, we can not deny that the raised podium of the monument can be attributed to both the eastern and western styles because monuments of similar structure have been discovered both in Etruria and the Akhamenid lands. Most of the subjects in the reliefs are scenes from the Greek mythology and the local culture is depicted in the scenes from the urban life.

Letoon, temple area

Letoon, gate of the theatre

Therefore, we would not be mistaken to describe the Nereids monument as the work of a rich variety of cultures. Going into more detail would exceed the purpose of a guide book and turn it into a scientific book, so this is where we should put a full stop.

LETOON (BOHSULLU- BOZOLUK- KUMLUOVA, TODAY)

It is a must to visit Letoon, the major religious center of Lycia, if you are visiting Xanthos. The asphalt road leading south 1 kilometer after Kınık takes you in 4 kilometers to the village of Bohsullu by its old name, Bozoluk by its newer name, or Kumluova by its latest name. Near the village, you will find Letoon.

Letoon must be thought of not as a settlement but a religious center, just like Didyma near Miletos, where one should expect to find temples, as theaters or stadiums to hold various games and festivals, public buildings like fountains and baths as well as residences for the priests to live in.

The name of Leto was "Lada" or "Latta" in Lycian language and together with her twins, Apollon and Artemis, they were the national god and goddesses of Lycia. During the Lycian League, Letoon continued to be the religious center of the federation and the Chief Priests of the League served in the sacred places of these god and goddesses.

Excavation in Xanthos and Letoon since 1962 has unearthed the temples of these three national gods and goddesses as well as revealing many trilingual inscriptions

> *Southwest of the temples is an enormous nymphaeum where the holy water used to spring.*

Letoon, theatre

and official documents that have contributed greatly to the decipherment of the Lycian language.

The excavations in Letoon brought to light three temples standing side by side. We understand from the inscription in the middle of the northern face of the temple that it was dedicated to Artemis (Ertemidi in Lycian language). Based on a study of its architectural elements, the building can be dated to the early 4th century BC. Exploration in the foundation of the building produced materials from the 6th and 7th centuries BC. Either side of the Temple of Artemis, there are two more temples, one built in the Doric Order and the other in the Ionic order. Both are built on 6X11 columns. We are not certain which of these two temples was dedicated to Leto and which to Apollon.

Southwest of the temples is an enormous nymphaeum where the holy water used to spring. On both sides of the square nymphaeum stood semi-circular excedras. The visible ruins date to the 3rd century AD: however, they must have been built over earlier and most probably Hellenistic structures. North and west of the temples, you will notice

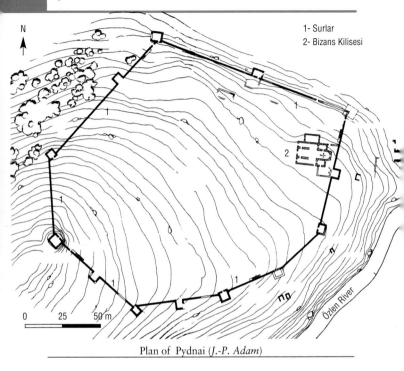

N

1- Surlar
2- Bizans Kilisesi

Özlen River

0   25   50 m

Plan of Pydnai (*J.-P. Adam*)

Hellenistic stoas. To the north - northeast of the sacred land, there is a well-preserved theater, altough the skene building is far from recognisable. The entrance to the theatron differed from the other theaters in that here, there were vaulted passages on the sides, the like of which can be seen in the theater of Alabanda in the Karia region. On the inner faces of these vaults, 16 masks were depicted. The inscriptions discovered in Letoon imply that there used to be a stadium in the city: however, to date, we have been unable to locate its place or any of its ruins.

PYDNAI - KYDNAI

Referred to in the Stadiasmus (248) as Pydnai and in Ptolemaios (5.3.5) as Kydnai, if the latter was indeed

The building that you can see on the seaside south or southwest of Pydnai looks very much like the lighthouse that is west of the acropolis of Patara.

referring to the same place, the city lies some 5 kilometers west of Xanthos, near the village of Özlen in a region that is given the name of Gavurağılı by the locals.

Charles Texier saw the inscription of the city and identified the ruins as the city of Pydnai. The city walls of Pydnai or Kydnai are still standing with parapet, battlements and watchtowers. The walls are embossed, polygonal and works of skilled masonry, similar to the city walls of Oinoanda even with the parapet. The same skill of masonry can be seen in the back wall of the granarium in Andriake. As a matter of fact, setting the date of a building just by looking at its masonry is not a totally unsuccessful method in the Lycian region; however, the granarium in Andriake certainly dated to the days of Hadrian based on the inscription on the structure, and the city walls of Oinoanda were dated to an earlier age: These two facts bring to mind that the castle of Pydnai was constructed in the 1st century AD or around the first half of the 2nd century AD.

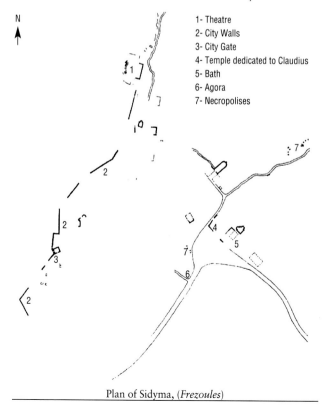

N

1- Theatre
2- City Walls
3- City Gate
4- Temple dedicated to Claudius
5- Bath
6- Agora
7- Necropolises

Plan of Sidyma, (*Frezoules*)

Sidyma, mausoleum

The ruins you can see inside the castle are those of a Byzantine church.

The building on the seaside south or southwest of Pydnai looks very much like the lighthouse west of the acropolis of Patara. The endless pirate activity in the southern coasts of Anatolia during the Late Hellenistic or Early Roman ages must have made it a necessary to protect the port and granarium in Patara despite the implementation of Pax Romana, I and II. The watchtower in Andriake, which the travellers of the 18th and 19th Centuries depicted in their gravures as still standing and in good shape, must have had a similar purpose behind its construction.

SIDYMA (DODURGA ASARI)

According to the "Sign Post Monument" in Patara (Miliarium Lyciae=Stadios) that was erected and dedicated to Emperor Claudius by the governor of Lycia, Q.Veranius, Sidyma was 104 stadia, or approximately 20 kilometers, from Xanthos. Sidyma (Dodurga asarı) is today a similar distance using the road between Kaş and Fethiye that follows pretty much the ancient route.

If you follow directions connecting the new road (400), (which you will not find on the road maps of 2002 and earlier), to the old road at two separate points (one in Eşen and the other in Eskiköy), you will reach Dodurga via an asphalt road. The village is connected to the ruins by a poor-quality asphalt road of approximately 1 kilometer. The ruins are known by the name of "Dodurga asarı".

Sidyma ismi tıpkı İdyma, Didyma gibi Anadolu'nun yerli isimlerindendir.

Sidyma, sarcophagi

The name Sidyma is a local Anatolian name as is the case with Idyma and Didyma and therefore the settlement can be expected to date as early as the 10th century BC or even earlier. Surface collections of ceramic pieces have shed light on the city only until the Classical Ages. The ancient writings mention Sidyma for the first time in the 1st century BC - Maybe, a sign that the city remained insignificant until that time. The truth will only be revealed after a scientific excavation in Sidyma.

Our knowledge of the city's history is quite limited but we know that Sidyma started to grow and develop during the late Hellenistic era. I believe, of all the coins of the Lycian League, those bearing the abbreviation of "ΛΥΚΙΩΝ ΞΙ" should be related with Sidyma because, an alternate city that could use the same abbreviation of "ΞΙ" in Central Lycia would be Simena but that one has always been mentioned in combination with Theimiussa. Besides, considering that cities such as Aperlai, Apollonia and Trysa were represented in the League by a single vote, these coins cannot have been minted by any other city than Sidyma. Moreover, during the first years of the Roman Empire, a temple and stoa were constructed in dedication to Emperor Claudius - An indication that it was a major city at the time.

If you are driving to Dodurga Asarı, the open area that you will find suitable for parking will also be the center of the ancient city. Although new houses and garden walls make it harder to locate some of the ruins of ancient buildings, there are still some ruins that you can easily pinpoint: The gate of the Agora with its frame bearing inscriptions, the stoa with some of its column bases still standing in-situ and, to the north of these, outside the garden of the religious school the architrave blocks and pieces of inscriptions of the temple dedicated to Emperor Claudius, Artemis and some other gods. North of the city square and adjacent to the religious school, you can see a bath. Two of its arches and the sidewalls are still standing to the level of the vaults. We identify these ruins as that of a bath based on our knowledge of other baths in many Lycian cities, such as Tlos, Arykanda, Pınara, Patara, etc. The arrangements of the sections and the direction of the building give us all the clues we need.

Looking west or southwest from the city square, you will see the acropolis of Sidyma on a conical hill. The city walls surrounding the acropolis were fortified with watchtowers at certain points and the walls were made of mortar. The acropolis is reminiscent of late antiquity rather than the oldest settlement in the area. Inside the city walls, there seems to be no major buildings other than a number of cisterns and the ruins of a few tiny buildings.

Walking west of the agora, you will arrive at the outer city walls running northward along the slope of a small hill. The walls are rectagonal, embossed and of skilled masonry. If you follow the city walls, which exceed three meters in height around the gate, or walk past the houses to the west of this neighbourhood, you will find the ruins of 3 or 4 tiers of seats of the theater. The upper structure of the cavea was discovered by pure coincidence.

The most interesting and easily accessible ruins in Sidyma are the mausoleums that you will find scattered on the plain north of the ruins, on the slopes of the hills

Strabon and Stephanos of Byzantion mention Pınara as a great city.

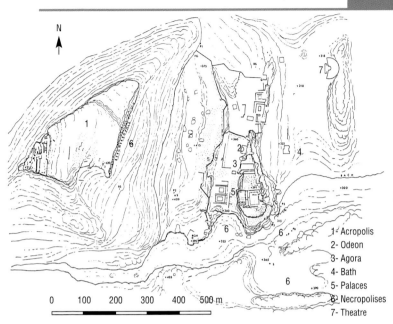

1- Acropolis
2- Odeon
3- Agora
4- Bath
5- Palaces
6- Necropolises
7- Theatre

0   100   200   300   400   500 m

Plan of Pınara, (*Wolfgang Wurster*)

bordering the plain in the north. The heroons that you can find close to the neighbourhood are among the most noteworthy ruins here. Built side by side, the have survived in good condition almost to the level of the roofs. If you follow the street and path to the west of the neighbourhood, you will arrive at a sarcophagus-type mausoleum. The lid is monolith and under the lid, one can find coffered decorative work. In the center of each of these coffers is the depiction of a different person. A similar mausoleum close to the northern end of the necropolis is notable for the monolith body of its sarcophagus divided into two floors. The dead were buried on these two surfaces as if lying on a bunk bed. Where the plain narrows into a pass, there is another grave but this one is a rare example in Lycia: Its body is in the form of a prism.

Pınara (Mİnare)

Off the road between Kaş and Fethiye, the asphalt road leading west from the junction for Eşen will take you to the village of Minare in 5 kilometers. You can either trek to the ruins from the village or, according to the latest news, you

Lycia

Pınara, rock tombs

can also drive there.

The name of the city in the Lycian language was Pinale, which was the word for "round". We believe that the name may have derived from the rocks rising like a minaret behind the city. The rocky structure is indeed round and dotted with pigeonhole style rectangular rock graves. We also learn from Menekrates of Xanthos that the city was founded by colonists from Xanthos. Our knowledge about Pınara is rather limited but Arrianos quotes that this was one of the cities that opened its doors to Alexander, the Great without resistance. Strabon and Stephanos of Byzantion mention Pınara as a great city - one of the six major cities of the Lycian League represented by three votes. The abbreviation that Pınara stamped on the coins of the League was "ΛΥΚΙΩΝ ΠΙ". Following the demise of Alexander, the city remained independent but within the borders of the Kingdom of Pergamon. The city would sooner or later become a Roman city when the Kingdom of Pergamon was annexed to the Roman Empire by inheritance. By the 1st century BC, 4 of the 6 major cities of the Lycian League had managed to survive while Olympos, which turned into a den of pirates, was burnt to ashes by Servilius Isauricus and expelled from the League and Pınara lost its importance because of its isolated location. Although the city somehow came back to life

The east slope of the acropolis forms a terrace with the rocks in front of it

under Roman rule and a number of new buildings were raised, it never truly resumed its prominence and active life as it had in the 1st century BC. The earthquake in 141 that devastated the whole Lycian region was surprisingly enough not a major threat for Pınara as the city was founded on a rocky hill: information we gather from the fact that the rich Opramoas of Rhodiapolis donated only 5,000 denarii to the city to repair earthquake damage. In the wake of the earthquake on August 5th, 240, Pınara was for a short time granted the right to mint coins by exclusive permission of Gordianus, III, like many other Lycian cities.. Mentioned in the ecclesiastical records as Pınara or Pinale, the city was a diocese, continued to exist until the 9th century and then gradually disappeared.

Pınara, a rock tomb with city depiction

The agora stood on a plain between two rocky surfaces. The columns of the stoa that bounded the agora in the west can still be seen in summer.

The crest of the rocky hill that is honeycombed with many pigeonhole rock graves is where you will find the acropolis of Pınara. You can reach the acropolis up a rock-cut stairway the remains of which are to be found in the south of the acropolis. Surrounded by the city walls, the acropolis must have been the place where the first ever inhabitants of the city settled. However, we have no proof of that. East of the acropolis was inhabited during the Byzantine era and this part is also surrounded by city walls.

The east slope of the acropolis forms a terrace with the rocks in front of it. And this terrace was the exact place where Pınara's public and private buildings once stood. Fortified in the north by the city walls and secured in the east by terrace walls where the slope was too shallow on the face of the rock, this terraced land needed only very slight fortification in the south, if any. So, there was built the second acropolis of the city. You must start visiting the second acropolis either at the ramp starting close to the

Pınara, mausoleum and the terrace

northeast corner or the staircase that is south of the temple-type mausoleum with a podium. If you enter the acropolis from the ramp, you will come to a temple on the terrace created on the slope of the first acropolis by a holding wall. This temple has 6x8 columns. The plan and elements of architectural decoration around the building indicate that the temple was built during the Roman times. South of the temple you will find a mausoleum with a podium, crowning the rocks. A temenos wall surrounds the mausoleum. Since the plan of the grave considerably resembles that of a Roman temple, the first impression you get is that it is indeed a temple. However, the structure also looks very much like the mausoleum close to the granarium in Patara. The entrance to the crypt is through a small door, which could be wrongly taken for a window, therefore, there is no doubt that this is a grave. If you walk south of the mausoleum, you will reach the city's Lycian gate that earlier travellers had the chance to see standing in full form but today, only the prismal frames of which are still standing. Opposite the gate was the odeon and you can pretty much locate the tiers of seats but other than that the structure is more like a heap of stones. Entrance to the odeon is through

Pınara, theatre and the valley of Eşençay

the three gates in the east. Or, there is another door near the center of the orchestra and another in the middle of the southern wall. Or indeed you can walk into the agora from the gate opening into the orchestra.

The agora stood on a plain between two rocky surfaces. The columns of the stoa that bounded the agora in the west can still be seen in summer. In this agora, you may find something in common with the one in Tlos - the heart-shaped columns in the corners!

If you walk south from the plain where the agora stands, you will reach the higher south end of the rocks bordering the second acropolis in the east. The west face of this rocky surface is interesting for the remains of a rock grave that somebody started to carve but could not finish. The crest of the rocks is crowned by ruins of palaces, cisterns and other Byzantine buildings. As you walk south of the plain, you will notice many sarcophagi. Climb the terrace wall at the south end of this plain and you will have a wonderful view of the rock graves of the southern necropolis on the face of the rocks and across the valley.

If you leave the plain where the agora stands from the north to south, on the rocks getting sharper in the east, where the rocks take a convex form you will see a bath with three sections in a row. The bath is built to a similar plan to others in Arykanda, Tlos, Kadyanda and so many other

Pınara, theatre

At a junction of the road from Fethiye to Korkuteli and the road from Fethiye to Kaş there is an asphalt road leading south.

Lycian cities. Descending south from this point, you will arrive at the necropolis, known as the "kings' necropolis", and the spring where you can see many water channels cut into the rocks. The most noteworthy of all is the rock grave with a bull's horn in its upper acroter and a scene from a feast in its lintel. You can see a relief of the city of Pınara on the sidewalls of the front room in the grave.

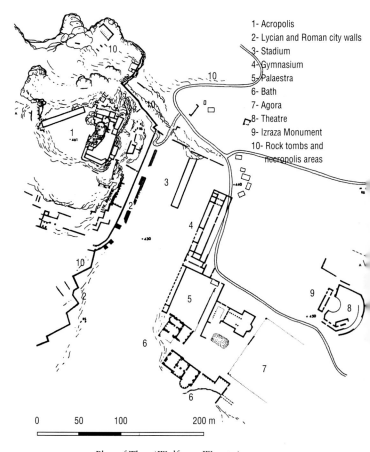

1- Acropolis
2- Lycian and Roman city walls
3- Stadium
4- Gymnasium
5- Palaestra
6- Bath
7- Agora
8- Theatre
9- Izraza Monument
10- Rock tombs and necropolis areas

0   50   100   200 m

Plan of Tlos, (*Wolfgang Wurster*)

> *We know that Tlos was a diocese during the Byzantine Era and was represented in many council meetings.*

On the western slope of a rocky hill opposite and slightly east of the city, you can visit the very well-preserved theater of Pınara. Divided into 9 sections in its theatron, the theater has 27 tiers of seats. It has one thing in common with the theater in Arykanda: Since the theater was constructed on a rocky hill, it was not fatally struck by any earthquakes and this is a major indication that the theater can be dated to antiquity.

TLOS (DÜVER- ASAR CASTLE OR CASTLE ASAR)

At a junction of the road from Fethiye to Korkuteli and the road from Fethiye to Kaş there is an asphalt road leading south. This road will take you to Tlos after some 25 kilometers. I strongly recommend that you pay heed to the road signs; otherwise, you may find yourself driving on the south end of Kınık Plain after turning south from

Tlos, acropolis

Tlos, rock tombs

Güneşli.

The city and in particular, the acropolis of Tlos has a marvellous view overlooking the entire valley of the Eşen Stream (Xanthos). The fertile fields in the environs of the city definitely made the area a haven for settlers throughout time, encouraged by the wealth of water. This must be the reason that Tlos has a place in the literature of archaeology as one of the earliest settlements in Lycia region, as the surface findings have also confirmed. Known as Tlava or Tlave in the Lycian language, the city of Tlos tops the list of excavated cities for the finding of a stone axe that dates back to the 2nd millenium BC. Hittite writings from the 14th century BC refer to the city by the name of Dalawa in the land of Luqqa (Lukka). However, rather unfortunately, we know almost nothing about its history. Nevertheless, we can fill to some extent the gaps in our knowledge about the earliest days of the city, thanks to inscriptions in the Lycian language that were found here, as well as rock graves with reliefs that can be dated to the first half of the 4th century BC based on the style of rock-cutting.

Another document we have found narrates that the city supported Pixodaros - the satrap who ruled after the Hekatomnos dynasty that controlled Karia after the Persian invasion - in his military expedition against Kaunos. One of

Lycia

Tlos, gymnasium

the 6 cities represented by 3 votes in the Lycian League, Tlos was "the liveliest Lycian metropolis" during the days of the Roman Empire. Tlos was devastated by the earthquake in 141 and the greatest helper of the city was Opramoas through the resources both of the Lycian League and of his own accord. Apparently, Tlos was second only to Myra in the amount of donations received. Besides, another rich man of Lycia, namely Licinius Langus, donated 50,000 denarii to Tlos.

We know that Tlos was a diocese during the Byzantine Era and was represented in many council meetings. The most recent ruins in the acropolis are the buildings of Ali Ağa, who ruled in the region in the 19th century. The gravures of the travellers of his times shed light on his palace, stables and barracks in the acropolis.

You will notice the Lycian city walls starting at the rocks on the eastern slope of the acropolis that stands on a steep hill. Lycian rock graves honeycomb the east, northeast and north faces of the acropolis. There are graves - some bearing inscriptions in the Lycian language - in the necropolis that lies partially inside the borders of the Roman city and partially outside the city walls north of the acropolis.

The Roman city walls were built with straight blocks of

> *The Roman city walls were built with straight blocks of stones around the acropolis where the rocky hill was not steep enough for defence purposes.*

stones around the acropolis where the rocky hill was not steep enough for defence purposes. The walls can be best seen on the eastern slope of the hill. On the southeast corner of the city there is a gate providing access to the acropolis. From this point on, the walls were repaired during the Byzantine days and, therefore, lost their original form. Many carved stones and other constructional elements of the Roman city walls were recycled during the repairs.

All the buildings of the city lie outside the Roman city walls that bordered the acropolis in the east in a straight line. The walls doubled up as a protection for the tiers of seats at the stadium. On the side of the field that lies east of the acropolis, you can easily count ten rows of seats from the tribunalis of the stadium, which was probably a standard number for the time. Today, the running track is an agricultural field; however, when there are no crops growing, we can pinpoint with ease the remains of a long rectangular field - most probably, the spina. Still, we will

Tlos, bath

Tlos, theatre

only be sure of the structure after excavating. Right opposite the tribunalis of the stadium, you will notice a building with an arched entrance and an eastern wall which doubled up as an aqueduct. This may well be a basilica like the one which can be seen in Ephesus. The correct function of the structure will only be revealed after the excavations started by Prof. Dr. Havva Iskan Işık.

South of this building, you will find the ruins of, possibly, the gymnasium sharing one wall with the building that we take to be a basilica. The square-like area in the front must be the gymnasium's palaestra. At the south end of the palaestra which has three of its columns still standing in the east, you will find the building that we are sure was the bath, from its plan and heating system. And it is in pretty good condition even today. In my humble opinion, the building with the most magnificent view in Tlos is another bath, south of the one that I have just mentioned. This second bath has a circular terrace in its caldarium to watch the scenery and brings to mind the baths in cities like Arykanda, Pınara and Kadyanda.

There is a large Byzantine basilica that starts from the center of the eastern wall of the palaestra of the gymnasium and points eastward. The crowd of columns and other architectural elements lying around the basilica may well be the signs of a former temple. East of this basilica, you can visit the agora where the heart-shaped columns in the corners are still standing and the remains of a number of columns are traceable.

Northeast of the agora is the theater that had to be repaired after earthquakes hit the city. Now, its theatron has been cleared of rubble and its tiers are visible. The most striking feature of this theater is the large vaulted gallery behind the cavea. I would describe this structure as inspired by the theater in Myra although a slightly different style has been introduced.

The skene building was built as a separate structure from the theatron and the face opposite the theatron is richly decorated with garlands and friezes of Eros.

You can find the ruins of the Izraza Monument under the north analemma wall of the theater. The monument is dated to the 5th century BC and parts of its inscription are still visible today. One relief of a rooster from this monument waits for its visitors at the Fethiye Museum but others were carted off to the British Museum.

There is a huge Roman tower that still stands almost at its full size north of the square in Tlos where the coffeehouses are today.

As I have told you before, the most picturesque and decorative rock graves of Tlos lie north of the acropolis and the most striking of all is the one called the "Grave of Bellerophon" that depicts Bellerophon riding on Pegasos. On the inner walls are the reliefs of sitting leopards or panthers.

ARSADA

The road that runs along the eastern bank in the valley

There is a huge Roman tower that still stands almost at its full size north of the square in Tlos where the coffeehouses are today.

> ## *The name of Araxa in the Lycian language was Araththi.*

of Eşen Stream (Xanthos) leads east close to the south end of the valley and reaches the village of Arsa. An alternative would be the road leading east from Kınık. However, that is a village road and you will never know whether the road is open until you get there. Unless you are driving an off-road vehicle, it would be risky.

Arsada was not even mentioned in any ancient writings but the remains of its city walls are still there on the long hill north of Arsa village. Still, it is hard to estimate the date of the city walls since in Lycia, we cannot reach sound conclusions just by looking at the style of masonry. The uncertainty about the exact date of the city walls is even intensified by the use of chip stones in the wall.

The only ruins you should expect to find in Arsada today, other than the city walls, of course, are a house-type tomb and the relief of a cavalryman that you will find carved into the natural rock just outside Arsa village. The relief resembles the Lycian reliefs of the 4th century BC; however, in my opinion, it cannot be dated any earlier than the Late Roman - Early Byzantine ages.

ARAXA (ÖRENKÖY)

Kemer is some 22 kilometers from Fethiye. Both roads

Araxa, relief on the wall of a house

leading north out of Kemer arrive in Örenköy. If you take the road on the west, which follows the foot of the mountain, you should either take the dirt road leading north from Damlar district or follow the asphalt road until the village of Paşalı and then, take the road leading southeast. After passing a few rock graves you will arrive in Örenköy. There is a second asphalt-covered road that starts in Kemer and reaches Örenköy in a route almost parallel to the first. On this road, you must drive past Karatoplar and Ceylanköy and then, take the road leading west after Eşen (Koca) River. Soon, you will arrive in Örenköy. This road is a continuation of the road coming from Korkuteli and known by the name of Kızılcadağ Road. You can visit these ruins following a visit to Xanthos from where you would first arrive in Fethiye or Kemer, and then take any of the above-mentioned roads. Örenköy also stands on the road to Saklıkent near Fethiye.

The name of Araxa in the Lycian language was Araththi and the city was mentioned in the writings of Alexander Polyhistoriker (1st century BC), Stephanos Byzantios and Ptolemaios (5.3.5). We learn about much of the history of Araxa from an inscription, discovered in the city, that belonged to Athenagoras - one of the foremost individuals who lived in Araxa. According to this inscription, Araxa fought a war with Bubon and later, with Kibyra.

We understand that Araxa can be dated to much earlier times as we find the name of the city on an inscription that belonged to Ptolemaios Philadelphos II and dated to the end of the 2nd century BC. A coin of the Lycian League that Araxa minted around the end of the 2nd century BC provides more evidence that the city was indeed a major settlement.

Today, Araxa is noted for its many rock graves and sarcophagi with Gothic frontals. At the entrance to Örenköy, you will find rock graves on the left side of the road today, they are used for storing fertilizers. North of the village, where you can see the embossed and bevelled city walls

Kemer is some 22 kilometers away from Fethiye. Both roads leading north of Kemer arrive in Örenköy

Lycia

Theatre of Telmessos

standing only in half of their original size, although back in the late 1970's, you could see the same walls preserved up to 3 meters high around the acropolis.

Inside Örenköy, however, you can find a building with its walls still standing. Until recently, the building has been used as a bath but now it is used as a stable as I have heard from the villagers. In fact, this building used to be a Roman bath.

Don't be surprised to find parts of ancient buildings and other structures used as construction materials in the walls of almost each and every house in this village. Lastly, I must add that very recently, the excavations of Prof. Dr. Havva Işkan Işık have revealed a new prismal grave in Araxa.

The well-preserved theater that has recently been discovered by pure chance is a particular must-see with its extraordinary view overlooking the port.

Telmessos, rock tombs with Ionic columns

TELMESSOS (FETHİYE)

Roads from Muğla or Kaş (6 and 30) will take you to Fethiye, or Telmessos by its ancient name. Fethiye is an excellent port and, therefore, has marine connections not only along the Turkish coast but also to the Greek islands. Dalaman Airport was also opened in recent years to connect the area to the rest of the world.

Despite the convenience of transportation it enjoys, Telmessos has always been dependent in terms of administration but thanks to its agricultural wealth, it never ceased to be a major power and, therefore, never stopped struggling against Lycia - despite being Lycian. When, in the mid-2nd century BC, the region was put under the command of Rhodes, Telmessos was again on the opposing side and petitioned the Roman Senate to put an end to the pressure of Rhodes. Apart from these, for me, Fethiye will always remain the one place that I have seen "flying fish", during my first visit to Lycia.

The name of the city was Telebehi in Lycian language.

1- Temple
2- Bath
3- Stadium
4- Agora
5- Gymnasium
6- Theatre
7- City Walls

N

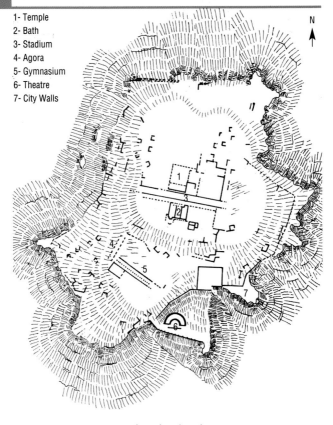

Plan of Kadyanda

As I have told you above, Fethiye or Telmessos is where, in each visit to the area, I have had the privilege to see some of the most breathtaking panoramas of my life. The well-preserved theater that has recently been discovered by pure chance is a particular must-see with its extraordinary view overlooking the port.

I was astonished to find out during my first visit to the city that all the hotels and restaurants were owned by people from the Black Sea region. But today, you will find people from not only all over Turkey but also from many other European countries owning businesses in Fethiye, which has become a centre of both agriculture and tourism.

> *Kadyanda reached its peak during the Roman Empire.*

KADYANDA (ÜZÜMLÜ)

Driving from Korkuteli or Kaş, you should turn right for Üzümlü about 4 kilometers after the first traffic lights on the junction for Fethiye. But if you are driving from Fethiye, you should reach the road 400: First, drive eastward for 5 kilometers and then turn left in the direction of Muğla, which will take you to the same traffic lights as above. Alternatively, you can take a right from Günlükbaşı junction if you proceed northward to Muğla. From this junction, you will reach Üzümlü in 14 kilometers. You must follow the road sign for Kadyanda once you have arrived in Üzümlü. The road will take you right into the parking lot south of the theater. From that point on, you can follow the path that earlier visitors have formed and arrive north into the ruins. If you cannot drive to Kadyanda, you can take a bus or a minibus from Fethiye to Üzümlü, find a guide there and then, climb to Kadyanda in a matter of 45 minutes.

If you are walking to Kadyanda, you will reach the ruins from the north of the city. But if you are driving, you will come in from the south. And this book begins describing the ruins from the south entrance.

Inscriptions carved in Lycian language mention the city by the name of "Kadawanti" - A Luwian name that points to the city being a very ancient settlement. However, the earliest finding to date goes back no earlier than the 5th century BC.

The road sign discovered in Patara (Miliarium Lyciae=Stadios) includes Kadyanda. The city minted coins even before the Lycian League, which is an indication of the wealth created in the city. Kadyanda reached its peak during the Roman Empire. The prosperity of the city, which was reflected in its graves, unfortunately resulted in the destruction and robbery of its northern necropolis as well as some other buildings inside the city. I must briefly recite another memory: In 1968, I visited Kadyanda with the permission of the local gendarmerie. I had taken with me a young boy as my guide from Üzümlü. I thought it was just an exaggeration about the phenomenon of smuggling when he said: "Now, many people are coming to the ruins fully equipped with generators and

Lycia

Kadyanda, theatre

simple engines to start the generators. Anyway, they know that the sound won't make it to Üzümlü." It dawned on me only after seeing the whole of the ruins and being approached in Üzümlü by a man who offered to sell some ancient coins that Kadyanda was an amazingly rich city and was being robbed terribly of all that wealth. The guy asked for 10 times my salary in return for a single golden hemidrahoma from Kadyanda and he did not forget to add that he was asking for 2.5 times less that the normal price and if he would sell it to, say, Von Aulock, he would ask for much more. What could be a better example of the extent of the robbery at Kadyanda?

Let's move on to the ruins or what's left of them: A short walk from the parking lot will take you to the most significant and preserved building: The theater that stands in a recess of the natural structure and the city walls. Recently, the theatron has been cleaned of rubble. With its semi-circular orchestra, the theater is a typical Roman building. Apparently, the skene building was a multi-storey structure and now looks forward to the day that it will be cleaned and restored. I am sure that the skene building was richly decorated with various architectural elements and crowned with many statues. The city walls bordering the theater on the north were built in a rectagonal technique, most probably to match the beauty of this building.

> *A climb northwest from the theater will take you to a stoa and the ruins of an agora adjacent to the stoa.*

A climb northwest from the theater will take you to a stoa and the ruins of an agora adjacent to the stoa. If you walk north from here and look east, you will notice the bath situated almost in the middle of the city. The building is still standing in pretty good shape. Its terrace, or the apsidal end in front of the caldarium, is to the west of the bath. Close to the bath, you may notice the ruins of another building the true function of which remains a mystery but clearly enough, three of its large sections are visible.

North of the agora, you will find an avenue dividing the city east-to-west. Earlier writings would identify the ruins as a stadium. Similar to the avenues of Phaselis and Perge in Pamphylia, there are steps on both sides along the avenue. The east end of the avenue, however, has almost seven steps which must have made many people in the past perceive the structure to be a stadium. After a forest fire, we can now see that the avenue was laid with blocks of stone.

Around halfway along this avenue, there are some steps that were used as a place to rest, look around or simply spend time. Up these steps, there are the ruins of a temple in the Doric order and, probably, in the hexastylos plan. Circling these ruins, you can find a temenos wall. East of the temple, the area protected by the temenos wall and marked with a pile of blocks of stone must have been a part of a bouleuterion. Adjacent to the east of these blocks, you will find the ruins of the bouleuterion in a square-like plan and surrounded by walls. Further east of this building, you will find another square area within walls: Another agora.

The north and west of the city is dotted with graves, mostly in the form of vaulted graves. I would like to warn all visitors to look where they are walking and stay clear of bushes if they cannot see any traces from previous visitors, unless, of course, it is their intention to fall down into the lower floor of any building that may be underneath.

If you trek to the ruins from Üzümlü or if you walk northwest or west of the city, you are sure to notice many Lycian rock graves. There are two striking rock graves bearing inscriptions in Lycian. One of them is still standing

> *Strabon writes that Daedala, a den of pirates, had a steep acropolis fortified with city walls on three sides*

while the other is in ruins. In their vicinity is another rock grave that is an outstanding example of its kind with its relief of a Lycian cavalryman attacking the enemy.

Kadyanda has a marvellous view overlooking both the country side until Fethiye and the valley of Eşençay. If you are independent in terms of accommodation or transport, I strongly recommend you stay and enjoy the landscape during the late hours of the afternoon.

DAEDALA

The city is on the border between Lycia and Karia, according to Strabon. You can reach Daedala along the road between Fethiye and Köyceğiz. A couple of kilometers before arriving in Göcek - a most beautiful seaside city where there is a presidential summer house -, you will be near the Asartepe or Yalnızca neighbourhood of Inlice. Daedala is here on the crest of the rocks that are on the right of the road. If you are staying in Fethiye or Tersane Island, you can take a small boat to Inlice port and climb north to reach Daedala. The moment you see a tiny, black, square hill honeycombed with pigeonhole graves, you will know that you are in Daedala.

Strabon writes that Daedala, a den of pirates, had a steep acropolis fortified with city walls on three sides. The square-like crest of the hill housed a tiny castle. Since the city was a modest-sized settlement, you should not expect to find too many ruins here other than rock-cut stairways, the foundations of a few houses and cisterns.

The west slope of the acropolis especially is dotted with pigeonhole rock-graves and a handful of Lycian sarcophagi.

Although arriving here by land would be a pleasurable and picturesque journey, I would still recommend you visit Tersane Island from Fethiye, first, and then, moor at Inlice or Göcek for a wonderful day witnessing a mix of nature's colors, green and blue. But, here is a warning that you should bear in mind: Unless equipped with a mosquito-net, do not attempt to spend the night at the seaside and especially not in your car with doors open or windows ajar, although it may be awfully hot. If you are a sound sleeper and accustomed to mosquito bite, then there is no problem. But, otherwise, this heaven may just as easily turn to hell for you. Take my word: This is my first-hand experience.

LISSA-LISSE

On Mount Kapı and near a lake, Lissa or Lisse is accessible from the road between Muğla and Fethiye. Some 10 kilometers after Ortaca, you will find a farm named "Zirai Kombinalar Çiftliği". There is a road that leads north of here to the port of Sarsıla. From here, you will have to walk south along the seaside for some kilometers. That is, unless somebody has built a new holiday village there by now. In fact, it would be easier to visit these ruins by taking a boat from Göcek or Fethiye or Tersane Island and arriving at the place locally called "Bath Ruins". You must be prepared for an hour of trekking, in any case.

Mentioned only in the writings of Pliny, Lissa or Lisse gives me the impression that it used to be a pirate base founded to defend Daedala, despite the fact that a counsel decision has been discovered here from the reign of Ptolemaios II (3rd century BC). The acropolis also supports this impression. The city walls were reinforced with towers around the acropolis. The ruins in this city are a few rock graves and sarcophagi in addition to the city walls.

Lydai, tombs

Acropolis: The upper, fortified portion of an ancient Greek city.

Aedicula: An opening framed by columns or pilasters supporting an entablature and pediment, often used decoratively.

Aesculapius: God of Medicine.

Agatarkhides: An author of the fifth century BC.

Agora: The market place. It was the heart of ancient Greek city, the focus of political, commercial, administrative and social activity, the religious and cultural centre, and the seat of justice.

Agrippa: A close friend and ally of Augustus (Octavianus).

Aisle: A passageway of a Christian church or a Roman basilica running parallel to the nave, separated from it by an arcade or colonnade.

Alexander Severus: Roman Emperor (225 - 235 AD).

Altar: A table or flat-topped block, often of stone, on which to make offerings or sacrifices to a deity.

Amazonomachy: A battle between Greeks and Amazons, mythical female warriors said to dwell in Scythia or Asia Minor.

Ambo: A stand for reading the lesson in churches or basilicas; pulpit.

Amphiprostyle: A classical temple or building with a portico at each end.

Amphora: A large vessel, usually with two handles and a narrow neck for transporting wine, olive oil or water.

Analemma: The retaining walls of a theatre.

Anastylosis: The archaeological reassembly of ruined monuments from fallen or decayed fragments.

Anta: A species of pier produced by thickening a wall at its termination, treated architecturally as a pilaster, with capital and base.

Antoninus Pius: Roman Emperor (132 - 164 AD).

Aphrodite=Venus: Goddess of love and beauty.

Apodyterium: The apartment at the entrance of the baths, where one stripped; a dressing room.

Apollo: God of prophesy and fine arts who was twin brother of Artemis.

Apse: A semicircular space, usually at the end of a basilica or church.

Apsidal (building): An oblong building in which one wall is in the form of an apse.

Aquwami: A Lycian dynast of the fifth century BC. Coins were minted in the name of him.

Arcadius: Roman Emperor (395 - 408 AD).

Architrave=Epistyle: In classical architecture, the beam which extends across the top of the columns; it forms the lowest part of the entablature.

Ares: Greek god of war.

Artemis: Greek goddess of hunting and archery who was twin sister of Apollo.

Aqueduct: Roman water channel.

◄ *Myra, rock tomb*

Lycia

Athena: Greek goddess of wisdom and war.

Athenaios: An author of the second century BC.

Atrium: The inner courtyard of a Roman villa.

Attic-Ionic base: A peculiar form of molded base for a column or pilaster.

Attic: The upper part of a triumphal arch.

Attica: The territory of Athens in ancient Greece.

Augustus (Octavianus): The first Roman Emperor (BC 27 - AD 14).

Basilica: In ancient Roman architecture, a large building most often used for the law courts. Rectangular in form with a roofed hall, the building usually contained an interior colonnade, with an apse at one end or at each end. The central aisle tended to be wide and was higher than the flanking aisles. From its original use as a Roman law court, the basilica form was adapted by the Christians for their churches.

Bossage: Rustic work, consisting of stones which seem to advance beyond the level of the building.

Bouleuterion: A building for city council (Boule) meetings.

Brutus: Roman commander of the first century BC who played part in Caesar's murder.

Caldarium: The hot room of a Roman bath.

Caria: An ancient region of southwestern Anatolia surrounded by Ionia, Phrygia and Lycia.

Caryatid: A supporting column carved in the shape of a woman.

Cascade: A waterfall or a series of small waterfalls on watercourses.

Cavea: The seating area of a theatre.

Cella=Naos: Inner shrine of a temple, housing the cult statue.

Cenotaph: An empty grave memorializing a person who was originally buried at some other place.

Centaurs: In classical mythology, a race of creatures with the body and legs of a horse and the torso, head and arms of a man.

Chapel: A small church.

Charles Fellows: An English traveller of the 18th century.

Cilicia: An ancient region on the south coast of Anatolia.

Conglomerate: A clastic sedimentary rock that forms from the cementing of rounded cobble and pebble sized rock fragments.

Consol: An ornamental bracket used to support a cornice, usually in a curved form.

Corinthian Order: The latest of the three Greek orders, similar to the Ionic, but with the capital decorated with carvings of the acanthus leaf.

Crater: A large bowl used for mixing wine with water.

Crepis, crepidoma: The stone base of a building upon which the brick or stone walls are built. In Greek temples this base is stepped.

Crypt: An underground vault or chamber beneath a symbolic grave that is used as a burial place.

Cyclopean wall: Wall built of enormous blocks of stone.

Dedication stele: An upright slab or pillar usually with an inscription or sculpture, dedicated to gods either for the fulfilment of a wish or for thanksgiving after getting a wish fulfilled.

Demeter: Greek goddess of agriculture.

Demos: The people.

Denarius: A Roman silver coin, so called from being worth originally ten of the pieces called "as".

Dentils: An even series of rectangles used as ornament to decorate cornices of classical buildings.

Diazoma: A large walkway which divides the upper story of a Greek theatre from the lower portion.

Diocletian = Diocletianus: Roman Emperor (284 - 286 AD).

Dioscuri: The hero twins who were worshipped in some parts of Anatolia and in Thrace.

Domitian = Domitianus: Roman Emperor (81 - 96 AD).

Doric Order: The simplest and most severe order of Greek architecture. Characteristic features are the columns without base, the column capitals, the so-called Doric frieze of triglyphs and metopes, and the cornice of different section.

Ekklesiasterion: Place of public assembly.

Elagabalus: Roman Emperor (218 - 232 AD)

Epigraphic: Of or pertaining to epigraphy.

Eros: A god of love usually depicted as a winged child.

Ethnos: A body of people having a common national or cultural tradition.

Euthynteria: The upper layer of the foundations of a structure; the levelling course.

Exedra: A walled area for displaying statues.

Façade: Any important face of a building usually the principal front with the main entrance.

Fascia: A flat member of an order or building, like a flat band or broad fillet; especially one of the three bands which make up the architrave.

Fauna: All the animal life in a particular region.

Flora: All the plant life in a particular region.

Forum: Market and meeting place in ancient Roman towns, corresponding to the Greek agora.

Frigidarium: The cold room of a Roman bath.

Galatia: Ancient territory of central Anatolia around modern Ankara.

Granarium: Roman storehouse for grain.

Gordianus III: Roman Emperor (238 - 244 AD).

Gymnasium=Gymnasion: A building complex in which youths trained and exercised.

Hadrian = Hadrianus: Roman Emperor (117 - 138 AD).

Hecate: The moon goddess connected with darkness and magic. She is most often depicted as having three heads.

Helios: The Sun.

Hellenistic Period: The period from the death of Alexander the Great in 323 BC to the conquest of Egypt by Rome in 30 BC.

Hephaistos: God of the forge and master of fire in classical mythology; son of Zeus and Hera.

Hera: Greek Goddess of marriage. She was daughter of Kronos and Rheia and wife of Zeus.

Hercules = Herakles: Most famous and most beloved hero of ancient times. He was worshipped in many temples all over Greece and Rome.

Hermaios: A reputable, wealthy person from Arycanda, also a Lyciarch.

Hermes: The messenger of the gods and guide of dead souls to the Underworld.

Heroon: A building dedicated to the cult of a hero or a heroized dead person.

Homer: Greek (Ionian) epic poet of the 8th century BC; the poet of the *Iliad* and the *Odyssey*.

Honorific: Conferring honour.

Honorius: Roman Emperor (393 - 423 AD).

Hygeia: Goddess of health who was the daughter and assistant of Aesculapius, the god of Medicine.

Hypocaust: The chamber formed under the floors of the Roman baths, through which the hot air from the furnace passed. Roman underground heating.

Hyposorion = Hyposorium: Burial chamber placed over the podium of a mausoleum or a sarcophagus.

In Antis: A form of temple having antas in front attached to the walls which enclosed the cella and in the middle, between the antas, two columns supporting the architrave.

In situ: Latin expression meaning "in its original position".

Ionia: In ancient geography, the name given to a portion of the west coast of Anatolia, adjoining the Aegean Sea and bounded on the east by Lydia.

Ionic column capital: A kind of capital characterized by scroll-like volutes which are linked on lateral sides by cylindrical members.

Ionic Order: Second of the three Greek orders. Its capital is decorated with spiral scrolls (volutes).

Julius Caesar: Roman consul and dictator (59 - 44 BC) who was murdered by his closest associates.

Kakasbos: A local god who was worshipped in western Anatolia and Thrace.
Kerkides, kerkis: The wedged shaped seating section in cavea.
Kibyratis: Northwestern district of Lycia.
Kline: A couch made of stone for sitting or placing a sarchopagus on it.
Kupprili: A Lycian dynast of the fifth century BC. Coins were minted in the name of him.

Laconicum: Hot room (dry heat) in a Roman bath-suite.
Lapiths: A legendary Greek nation inhabiting the north of ancient Greece. The principal myth associated with them concerns their war with the Centaurs.
Latrine: Public lavatory.
Leto: A goddess who was one of the consorts of Zeus and the mother of Apollo and Artemis.
Lintel: Wooden beam or stone slab lying horizontally above a doorway (or window).
Luwi: People who lived in southwestern Anatolia in the second millenium BC.
Lycia: An ancient region in southwestern Anatolia stretched from Fethiye to Antalya; modern Teke peninsula.
Lycian League: The union of Lycian cities under a federation which was formed during an assembly meeting each year with the votes of the member cities. The cities had different numbers of votes in this assembly, according to their political and financal strenght. Xanthos (the capital), Pınara, Tlos, Patara, Myra and Olympos were the important cities with three votes against the others with only one or two votes for governing the federation.
Lyciarch: Lycian governor.

Mausolus: Satrap (Persian governor) of Caria who lived in Halicarnassus (Bodrum) in the fourth century BC.
Maximianus: Roman Emperor (235 - 238 AD).
Medusa: One of the Gorgons with hair of living snakes. She turned into stone all who looked into her eyes.
Meleager: A Greek hero.
Men: Moon God.
Milliaria: Roman mile-stones.
Mithras: A local god who was worshipped in Anatolia, particularly in Phrygia.
Monogram: Two or more letters, especially a person's initials.
Monolith: A single block of stone.
Mystery: A secret, hidden or inexplicable matter.

Naos: See cella.

Narthex: The transverse entrance hall of a church.

Necropolis: An ancient cemetery or burial place.

Nemesis: Goddess of divine retribution who punished excessive pride, undeserved happiness, and the absence of moderation.

Niche: A shallow recess in a wall; blind window.

Nike = Victory: Goddess of victory in Greek and Roman pantheon.

Numismatics: The study of coins.

Nymphaeum: A monumental fountain.

Nymphs: Minor female deities who were the protectors of springs, mountains, and rivers. They are represented as young, pretty girls.

Octavianus: See Augustus.

Odeon: A concert hall.

Opisthodomos: Back room of a temple, often used as a treasury, normally on the west.

Opramoas: A reputable, wealthy Lyciarch from Rhodiapolis.

Orchestra: The flat, semicircular space in front of the stage of a Roman or Greek theatre.

Orthostates: Blocks of cella walls, originally of sun-baked clay then replaced by stone.

Paganism: Polytheism.

Palaestra: An open area used for athletic exercise.

Palaeobotany: The study of fossil plants.

Pantheon: A group of deities that belong to one specific culture and/or time period.

Parados: A broad passage on each side of a theatre between the projecting wings of the stage and the seats of the spectators, through which the chorus entered the orchestra.

Pax Romana: Roman peace; state of comparative tranquility throughout the Mediterranean world from the reign of Augustus (27 BC - AD 14) to that of Marcus Aurelius (AD 161 - 180).

Pediment: The triangular, gabled end of a ridged roof.

Pericles: Early 4th century BC dynast of Limyra (east Lycia).

Peristyle: The rectangular courtyard surrounded by porticoes.

Persian: A native or inhabitant of ancient Persia or modern Iran.

Phrygian: A native of Phrygia.

Piscina: A cold water tank or a pool used also for swimming in Roman baths.

Pliny: Roman historian and author (AD 23/4 - 79), best known as the author of Naturalis Historiae.

Podium: Raised platform (especially used of temples).

Pompeius: Roman general and statesman of the first century BC.

Pontus = Pontos: An ancient region of northern Anatolia on the Black Sea.

Portico: 1. A roof supported by columns usually attached as a porch to a building. 2. A colonnaded and roofed walk.

Postament: Pedestal; frame.

Praefurnium: The furnace room of a Roman bath.

Prohedria: In ancient theatres the seats of honour reserved for distinguished persons.

Pronaos: The front section of the ancient Greek temple, with a door leading into the naos.

Propylon: A monumental gateway.

Proscenium: The part of the stage in front of scene building.

Prostyle: A building with columns only at the front.

Protom: Upper part of human or animal body.

Prytan: A distinguished citizen.

Prytaneion: The administrative building used as the city officials' working place and also for official receptions. The eternal flame which was the symbol of the city burned there.

Pteron: The colonnades surrounding all four sides of a building, usually a temple.

Ptolemies: Macedonian rulers of Egypt. The dynasty founded by Ptolemy, who took charge of Egypt after Alexander's death.

Ptolemy Philadelphus: A king of Ptolemy dynasty who lived in 2nd century BC.

Rectangular: Having the shape of a rectangle.

Sabina: Wife of Emperor Hadrian.

Sarcophagus: A coffin for inhumation made of wood, lead, stone or terracotta.

Satrap: The Persian title for the governor of a formal territorial subdivision known as a satrapy.

Scene: The stage of a theatre or odeon.

Sebasteion: A shrine to the emperors.

Seleucus: One of the generals of Alexander the Great, who took charge of Syria after his death.

Septimius Severius: Roman Emperor (198 - 208 AD).

Sluiceway: An artificial channel, especially one for carrying off excess water.

Sozon: A local god of Anatolia, probably equivalent of Greek sun god Helios.

Stadium = Stadion: 1.A measure of length about 600 feet. 2. A course for a foot-race. 3. An athletic or sports ground.

Stele: A stone pillar, often decorated.

Stoa: An oblong, one or two storeyed building with one long side open and fronted by a colonnade.

Stucco: A textured exterior plaster finish consisting of cement, lime, sand and water.

Stylobate: A continuous base supporting a temple or a colonnade.

Synthronon: The row of built seats, frequently stepped, on which the clergy sat in the sanctuary conch of a church or basilica.

Tabula Ansata: A table bearing an inscription on a column or sarchopagus.

Temenos: An area surrounded by walls in which sacred buildings are located and deities are worshipped. A sanctuary in general.

Tepidarium: The warm room of a Roman bath.

Terminus: Determined time.

Territory: The extend of the land under the jurisdiction of a ruler, state or city.

Tessera: A small square bit or cube of stone, glass or terracotta for mosaic work.

Tetrastyle: A building with four columns in front.

The Forum of Trajan: One of the most important monuments of Imperial Rome built for Emperor Trajan.

Topos: A place.

Torso: A statue of the human body with the head and limbs omitted or removed.

Tragalassos: An ancient city which signed a nonaggression pact with Arykanda. The location of the city is unknown.

Traianeum: A building complex dedicated to Emperor Trajan.

Trajan = Traianus: Roman Emperor (98 - 117 AD).

Tribunal: 1. A raised area for seats in a stadium. 2. A seat for a judge in a basilica.

Tubuli: Wall heating elements in the form of terra cotta pipes through which hot air was channeled in Roman baths.

Tumulus: An ancient burial mound or barrow.

Tyche: A Greek goddess of fortune and chance.

Unguentarium: A small vessel used to hold perfume and scented oils.

Vault: An arched structure of masonry forming a ceiling or canopy.

Vespasian = Vespasianus: Roman Emperor (69-79 AD).

Vitruvius: A Roman architect of the first century BC best known by his book De Architectura.

Zeus: Supreme god of the Greek pantheon.